KIERKEGAARD IN CONTEXT

A Festschrift for Jon Stewart

MERCER UNIVERSITY

MERCER UNIVERSITY PRESS

Endowed by

TOM WATSON BROWN

and

THE WATSON-BROWN FOUNDATION, INC.

KIERKEGAARD IN CONTEXT

A Festschrift for Jon Stewart

Edited by

LEE C. BARRETT AND PETER ŠAJDA

MERCER UNIVERSITY PRESS
Macon, Georgia
1979–2019
40 Years of Publishing Excellence

MUP/ H981

Published by Mercer University Press
1501 Mercer University Drive
Macon, Georgia 31207

9 8 7 6 5 4 3 2 1

Books published by Mercer University Press are printed on acid-free paper that meets the requirements of the American National Standard for Information Sciences—Permanence of Paper for Printed Library Materials.

Printed and bound in the United States.

This book is set in Adobe Caslon Pro

Book jacket design by Burt&Burt.

ISBN 978-0-88146-723-9
Cataloging-in-Publication Data is available from the Library of Congress

This volume is dedicated to Jon Stewart, for his tireless labors on the monumental *Kierkegaard Research: Sources, Reception, and Resources* series, and for his numerous contributions to the study of Kierkegaard, Hegel, Golden Age Denmark, and modern Continental philosophy.

Contents

Contributors

Lee C. Barrett, Lancaster Theological Seminary

María J. Binetti, CONICET (National Council for Scientific and Technical Research), Argentina.

István Czakó, Pázmány Péter Catholic University, Hungary.

Roe Fremstedal, Department of Philosophy, University of Tromsø, Norway.

Darío González, Department of Media, Cognition and Communication, University of Copenhagen, Denmark.

Finn Gredal Jensen, Society for Danish Language and Literature, Denmark.

Nathaniel Kramer, Department of Comparative Arts and Letters, Brigham Young University

Peter Šajda, Institute of Philosophy, Slovak Academy of Sciences, Slovakia.

Gerhard Schreiber, Institute for Theology and Social Ethics, Technical University of Darmstadt, Germany.

Heiko Schulz, Institute for Systematic Theolgoy, Goethe University, Frankfurt am Main, Germany.

K. Brian Söderquist, Denmark's International Study Program, University of Copenhagen.

Curtis L. Thompson, Department of Religion, Thiel College

Abbreviations

Danish Abbreviations

Pap. *Søren Kierkegaards Papirer*, vols. I to XI–3, ed. by Peter Andreas Heiberg, Victor Kuhr, and Einer Torsting (Copenhagen: Gyldendalske Boghandel, Nordisk Forlag, 1909–48); second, expanded ed., vols. I to XI–3, ed. by Niels Thulstrup, vols. XII to XIII supplementary volumes, ed. by Niels Thulstrup, vols. XIV to XVI index by Niels Jørgen Cappelørn (Copenhagen: Gyldendal, 1968-78).

SKS *Søren Kierkegaards Skrifter*, vols. 1-28, vols. K1-K28, ed. by Niels Jørgen Cappelørn, Joakim Garff, Jette Knudsen, Johnny Kondrup, Alastair McKinnon and Finn Hauberg Mortensen (Copenhagen: Gads Forlag, 1997-2013).

English Abbreviations

BA *The Book on Adler*, trans. by Howard V. Hong and Edna H. Hong (Princeton: Princeton University Press, 1998).

CA *The Concept of Anxiety*, trans. by Reidar Thomte in collaboration with Albert B. Anderson (Princeton: Princeton University Press, 1980).

CD *Christian Discourses*, trans. by Howard V. Hong and Edna H. Hong (Princeton: Princeton University Press, 1997).

CI *The Concept of Irony*, trans. by Howard V. Hong and Edna H. Hong (Princeton: Princeton University Press, 1989).

COR *The Corsair Affair; Articles Related to the Writings*, trans. by Howard V. Hong and Edna H. Hong (Princeton: Princeton University Press, 1982).

CUP1 *Concluding Unscientific Postscript*, vol. 1, trans. by Howard V. Hong and Edna H. Hong (Princeton: Princeton University Press, 1982).

CUP2 *Concluding Unscientific Postscript*, vol. 2, trans. by Howard V. Hong and Edna H. Hong (Princeton: Princeton University Press, 1982).

EO1 *Either/Or*, Part I, trans. by Howard V. Hong and Edna H. Hong (Princeton: Princeton University Press, 1987).

EO2 *Either/Or*, Part II, trans. by Howard V. Hong and Edna H. Hong (Princeton: Princeton University Press, 1987).

EPW *Early Polemical Writings*, including among others: *From the Papers of One Still Living*; *Articles from Student Days*; *The Battle Between the Old and the New Soap-Cellars*, trans. by Julia Watkin (Princeton: Princeton University Press, 1990).

EUD *Eighteen Upbuilding Discourses*, trans. by Howard V. Hong and Edna H. Hong (Princeton: Princeton University Press, 1990).

FSE *For Self-Examination*, trans. by Howard V. Hong and Edna H. Hong (Princeton: Princeton University Press, 1990).

FT *Fear and Trembling*, trans. by Howard V. Hong and Edna H. Hong (Princeton: Princeton University Press, 1983).

JFY *Judge for Yourself!*, trans. by Howard V. Hong and Edna H. Hong (Princeton: Princeton University Press, 1990).

JP *Søren Kierkegaard's Journals and Papers*, vols. 1–6, ed. and trans. by Howard V. Hong and Edna H. Hong, assisted by Gregor Malantschuk (vol. 7, Index and Composite Collation) (Bloomington and London: Indiana University Press, 1967-78).

KJN *Kierkegaard's Journals and Notebooks*, vols. 1–11, ed. by Niels Jørgen Cappelørn, Alastair Hannay, David Kangas, Bruce H. Kirmmse, George Pattison, Vanessa Rumble, and K. Brian Söderquist (Princeton and Oxford: Princeton University Press, 2007ff).

M *The Moment and Late Writings*, trans. by Howard V. Hong and Edna H. Hong (Princeton: Princeton University Press, 1998).

PC *Practice in Christianity*, trans. by Howard V. Hong and Edna H. Hong (Princeton: Princeton University Press, 1991).

PF *Philosophical Fragments*, trans. by Howard V. Hong and Edna H. Hong (Princeton: Princeton University Press, 1985).

PV *The Point of View* including *On My Work as an Author*, *The Point of View for My Work as an Author*, and *Armed Neutrality*, trans. by Howard V. Hong and Edna H. Hong (Princeton: Princeton University Press, 1998).

R *Repetition*, trans. by Howard V. Hong and Edna H. Hong (Princeton: Princeton University Press, 1983).

SLW *Stages on Life's Way*, trans. by Howard V. Hong and Edna H. Hong (Princeton: Princeton University Press, 1988).

SUD *The Sickness unto Death*, trans. by Howard V. Hong and Edna H. Hong (Princeton: Princeton University Press, 1980).

SUDP *The Sickness unto Death*, trans. by Alastair Hannay (London and New York: Penguin Books, 1989).

TA *Two Ages: The Age of Revolution and the Present Age. A Literary Review*, trans. by Howard V. Hong and Edna H. Hong (Princeton: Princeton University Press, 1978).

UD *Upbuilding Discourses in Various Spirits*, trans. by Howard V. Hong and Edna H. Hong (Princeton: Princeton University Press, 1993).

WA *Without Authority* including *The Lily in the Field and the Bird of the Air, Two Ethical-Religious Essays, Three Discourses at the Communion on Fridays, An Upbuilding Discourse, Two Discourses at the Communion on Fridays*, trans. by Howard V. Hong and Edna H. Hong (Princeton: Princeton University Press, 1997).

WL *Works of Love*, trans. by Howard V. Hong and Edna H. Hong (Princeton: Princeton University Press, 1995).

Preface

In an essay in this volume María Binetti divides recent Kierkegaard studies into a "before Stewart" era and an "after Stewart" era.[1] While the intensifying methodological diversification of Kierkegaard studies may resist any simple categorization, there is much to recommend Binetti's periodization. The impact of Jon Stewart has been incalculable on both the rising generation of scholars and on seasoned researchers. In many ways, Stewart's work has provided a salutary corrective to the extreme rhetorical and deconstructive readings that tend to treat Kierkegaard's texts in abstraction from their historical particularity. Throughout his career Stewart has emphasized the need to situate the writings of Kierkegaard, Hegel, and other nineteenth-century thinkers in their specific historical contexts, that is, in very particular conversations, disputes, and trends.[2] Even more importantly, he has modeled that strategy with exemplary skill. His own writings on Kierkegaard, Hegel, German idealism, phenomenology, and existentialism have all expanded our understanding of the concrete intellectual and cultural issues to which these authors and movements responded. Most particularly, his interdisciplinary work on the philosophy and culture of Golden Age Denmark has fostered a significant reexamination of Kierkegaard, Heiberg, and the Danish Hegelians, and their complex relations to one another. In regard to disseminating familiarity with the nineteenth-century context, perhaps Stewart's influence has been even more widely felt through his editorial and translation work, as well as through his administration of various research projects and programs.

Stewart's attention to the historical situatedness of philosophical, theological, and literary writers has been evident throughout his career. His initial scholarly focus was on Hegel's authorship and legacy. His research on Hegel exhibited the international character that has typified his work, taking him from the University of California, San Diego, to the Westfälische Wilhelms-Universität in Münster. After that he also did research as a post-doctoral

---

[1] María J. Binetti, "Kierkegaard's Relations to Idealism Demystified," in the present volume, p. 98.

[2] See, for example, Jon Stewart, "Kierkegaard's Relation to Hegel and *Quellenforschung*: Some Methodological Considerations," *Filozofia*, vol. 68, no. 1, 2013, 17–26.

scholar at the Université Libre in Brussels, the Katholieke Universiteit in Leuven, and the Humboldt-Universität in Berlin. Much of his early work argued for the unity and coherence of Hegel's project, particularly his *Phenomenology of Spirit*.[3]

Even in his earliest projects Stewart demonstrated his passion for treating texts in their historical contexts, something that would become a hallmark of all his work. Stewart's approach often could bear controversial fruit that challenged prevailing interpretive orthodoxies. In *Kierkegaard's Relations to Hegel Reconsidered* he raised serious objections to the influential view of Niels Thulstrup that Kierkegaard was the absolute antithesis to Hegel in all significant respects.[4] Against this generally held interpretation, Stewart's detailed attention to Kierkegaard's actual appropriation of Hegel (and various Hegelianisms) reveals a much more complex story. Stewart unearths a multidimensional relationship that evolved over time, in which Kierkegaard was sometimes inspired by Hegel, sometimes sought to revise Hegel, and sometimes was sharply critical of Hegel. In 2003 Stewart was awarded the degree of Dr. habil. theol. for this work by the Faculty of Theology at the University of Copenhagen. In 2004 there was a special session of the American Academy of Religion Conference, Nineteenth-Century Theology Group, dedicated to this book.

When he came to Copenhagen in 1995, he immersed himself in the academic culture of nineteenth-century Denmark in particular and of northern Europe in general. Stewart has been concerned to understand how thinkers like Kierkegaard, Heiberg, and Martensen would have been understood in their own era, given the scholarly debates and cultural crises that raged around them. His monumental *A History of Hegelianism in Golden Age Denmark*, in two tomes, is a masterpiece of meticulous source-work research.[5] For Tome 1 of this work he was awarded the degree of Dr. habil. phil. from the University of Copenhagen.

---

[3] See, Jon Stewart, *The Unity of Hegel's Phenomenology of Spirit: A Systematic Interpretation* (Evanston, Illinois: Northwestern University Press, 2000).

[4] Jon Stewart, *Kierkegaard's Relations to Hegel Reconsidered* (New York: Cambridge University Press, 2003).

[5] Jon Stewart, *A History of Hegelianism in Golden Age Denmark*, Tome I, *The Heiberg Period: 1824–1836* (Copenhagen: C. A. Reitzel, 2007) (*Danish Golden Age Studies*, vol. 3) and *A History of Hegelianism in Golden Age Denmark*, Tome II, *The Martensen Period: 1837–1842* (Copenhagen: C. A. Reitzel, 2007) (*Danish Golden Age Studies*, vol. 3). See Helmut Schneider's review in *Hegel-Studien*, vol. 46, 2011, 275–279.

In many of his other writings Stewart has extrapolated from his detailed research to draw broader conclusions about the continuities linking nineteenth- and twentieth-century Continental philosophy. In *Idealism and Existentialism: Hegel and Nineteenth and Twentieth-Century European Philosophy* Stewart has argued that, contrary to what is often assumed, no radical rupture divided existentialism from idealism.[6] *The Cultural Crisis of the Danish Golden Age: Heiberg, Martensen, and Kierkegaard* contends that this era was enormously creative and has bequeathed to the contemporary world the constellation of issues associated with relativism, nihilism, and subjectivism.[7]

Taking an even broader view of the history of philosophy in *The Unity of Content and Form in Philosophical Writing*, Stewart has explored the correlation of different genres and styles of philosophical writing to the intellectual concerns of specific cultural periods.[8] In 2015 and 2016 there were two conferences entitled "The Registers of Philosophy" that were dedicated to this work. Both conferences took place in Budapest and were organized by the Institute of Philosophy of the Hungarian Academy of Science.

Stewart's *Hegel's Interpretation of the Religions of the World* evidences years of study of Hegel's philosophy of religion.[9] This book addresses a neglected aspect of Hegel's thought with its focus on his treatment of religions other than Christianity. Consistent with his earlier works, Stewart presents a picture of Hegel in dialogue with the numerous contemporary sources of information about the religions of China, India, Persia, Egypt, etc. He likewise shows that Hegel's engagement with this material has relevance for our current discussions about multiculturalism and religious pluralism today.

Stewart's most recent work, *Faust, Romantic Irony, and System: German Culture in the Thought of Søren Kierkegaard*, provides a series of meticulous studies of Kierkegaard's numerous Germanophone sources.[10] With chapters

---

[6] Jon Stewart, *Idealism and Existentialism: Hegel and Nineteenth- and Twentieth-Century European Philosophy* (New York and London: Continuum International Publishing, 2010) (*Continuum Studies in Philosophy*).

[7] Jon Stewart, *The Cultural Crisis of the Danish Golden Age: Heiberg, Martensen and Kierkegaard* (Copenhagen: Museum Tusculanum Press, 2015) (*Danish Golden Age Studies*, vol. 9).

[8] Jon Stewart, *The Unity of Content and Form in Philosophical Writing: The Perils of Conformity* (London, New Delhi, New York and Sydney: Bloomsbury, 2013) (*Bloomsbury Studies in Philosophy*).

[9] Jon Stewart, *Hegel's Interpretation of the Religions of the World: The Logic of the Gods* (Oxford: Oxford University Press, 2018). Also published in Chinese, trans. by Tianwang Jinjian, Beijing: Huaxia Press, 2018.

[10] Jon Stewart, *Faust, Romantic Irony, and System: German Culture in the Thought of Søren Kierkegaard* (Copenhagen: Museum Tusculanum Press 2019) (*Danish Golden Age Studies*, vol. 11).

on a gallery of figures such as Goethe, Schleiermacher, Schelling, Solger and Hegel, this work traces the complex network of ideas and connections between Kierkegaard and these thinkers. This new work thus gives the reader a glimpse of Kierkegaard's huge debt to German philosophy, theology and literature.

Stewart's influence has by no means been restricted to his research monographs. His approach has been disseminated through his work at the Søren Kierkegaard Research Center in Copenhagen with which he was affiliated in various capacities from 1996 to 2016. His presence there attracted numerous guest researchers to the institute. There in addition to his usual teaching duties, he helped educate blossoming scholars from around the globe, and made familiarity with Kierkegaard more available to diverse audiences. He has served as a mentor for many young Kierkegaard scholars at the beginning of their careers and has always been keen to involve them in whatever projects he happened to be working on.

He has always been appreciated as a team player, inviting his colleagues and others to participate in his projects. These different projects thus involved a large number of people from both Denmark and around the world, and served to raise the international profile of the Søren Kierkegaard Research Centre immeasurably. His different publication series represented a huge enrichment of the research activities of the Centre. Everyone who has worked with him in these different contexts has appreciated his work ethic and professionalism. As is attested to by his extensive editorial work, his organization of numerous conferences and seminars, and his engaged student supervision, he has always been happy to set aside his own research in order to create opportunities for others.

A project worthy of special mention is the enormously successful MOOC that he created for the University of Copenhagen in 2013, entitled *Søren Kierkegaard: Subjectivity, Irony, and the Crisis of Modernity*. This course, which is still running on the Coursera platform, functions as an introduction to Kierkegaard's thought and cultural era and has attracted thousands of online students. These video lectures opened up the thought of Kierkegaard to numerous students around the world who did not have the means to come to

Copenhagen. Its popularity spawned a book with the same title.[11] This work has recently appeared in Spanish, Portuguese and Chinese translations.[12]

Perhaps Stewart's most important legacy has been the series of volumes that he has translated and edited. Stewart has been in charge of two collective publication projects, which have contributed greatly to the popularization of the culture of the Danish Golden Age in the English-speaking world. In 2005 he initiated the translation series *Texts from Golden Age Denmark*, each volume of which contains comprehensive historical introductions and detailed explanatory notes. The classic texts that he has selected to publish by Mynster, Martensen, Heiberg, Sibbern and others constitute the immediate intellectual context in which Kierkegaard's thought evolved and exemplify the intellectual dynamics of emergent modernity. The parallel monograph series, *Danish Golden Age Studies* was launched in 2007 and has been an important forum for the publication of works on the key figures of Danish culture during Kierkegaard's time. Both of these series have done much to promote historical source-work research, and have enabled the international intellectual community to gain insight into the lives and work of key contemporaries of Kierkegaard in an unprecedented way.

From 2000 to 2004, and again since 2010 Jon Stewart has been co-editor of the *Kierkegaard Studies Yearbook* and *Kierkegaard Studies Monograph Series*. He helped to establish these series as important organs for the publication of international Kierkegaard research and always actively encouraged young scholars to contribute to them.

Stewart's most ambitious project to date has been *Kierkegaard Research: Sources, Reception and Resources*. From 2007 to 2017 he served as the editor-in-chief of this 58-volume series that included articles by more than 200 Kierkegaard scholars from some 50 countries around the world. It thus represents the largest research project in the history of Kierkegaard studies. The territory covered by the series is expansive, including Kierkegaard's appropriation of classical Greco-Roman thought, Christian theologians from the Patristic period through the post-Reformation era, literary authors from various periods,

---

[11] Jon Stewart, *Søren Kierkegaard: Subjectivity, Irony and the Crisis of Modernity* (Oxford: Oxford University Press, 2015).

[12] Jon Stewart, *Søren Kierkegaard: subjetividad, ironía y la crisis de la Modernidad*, trans. by Azucena Palavicini Sánchez (Mexico City: Universidad Iberoamericana, 2017). *Søren Kierkegaard: Subjetividade, Ironia e a Crise da Modernidade*, trans. by Humberto Quaglio (Petrópolis, RJ: Vozes, 2017). *Søren Kierkegaard: Subjectivity, Irony, and the Crisis of Modernity*, trans. by Tianwang Jinjian (Beijing: Huaxia Press, 2018).

and contemporary Danish and German philosophers. Other volumes are devoted to Kierkegaard's influence upon social scientists, philosophers, theologians, literary critics, and writers of more imaginative literature. Still other volumes provided introductions to Kierkegaard's concepts, his use of literary figures, and his employment of various pseudonyms. The series has been widely used throughout the globe, is cited in almost every new book and essay about Kierkegaard, and has become a primary orienting resource for a new generation of scholars. There can be no doubt that it has had a great impact on the contemporary global discourse on Kierkegaard and continues to inspire new research.

Stewart has also long been active at disseminating interest in Kierkegaard studies internationally. Over the past few decades, he has organized more than 30 conferences, seminars, and workshops in numerous countries. He has taught or held positions as guest researcher at universities in Belgium, Denmark, Germany, Iceland, Chile, Mexico, Sweden, and Slovakia. He has delivered more than 200 invited lectures at universities in dozens of countries around the world. His work has been translated into various foreign languages: Chinese, German, Hungarian, Italian, Norwegian, Polish, Russian, Slovak, and Spanish. From 2011–2014 he was the project leader for "The Nordic Network for Kierkegaard Research" that was funded by Nordforsk. Most recently, in 2017 Stewart was offered a research position at the Institute of Philosophy of the Slovak Academy of Sciences in Bratislava, Slovakia. With his cosmopolitan view, Stewart has helped to shape Kierkegaard studies by incorporating different, previously isolated traditions of research into the mainstream of the field. He has been a keen promoter of Kierkegaard studies in Central and Eastern Europe as well as Latin America.

Stewart's contributions to Continental philosophy and specifically Kierkegaard studies have been recognized by many academic honors. His research has been supported by the Alexander von Humboldt-Stiftung, the Belgian-American Educational Foundation, the Heinrich Hertz-Stiftung, the National Academy of Education, the Collegium Budapest, Institute for Advanced Study, the Danish National Research Foundation, the Danish Research Council for the Humanities, and the German Academic Exchange Service Grant (DAAD). In 2000 he received the Inger Sjöberg Translation Prize from the American-Scandinavian Foundation for his translation of Johan Ludvig Heiberg. In 2007 he was elected as a foreign member of the Royal Danish Academy of Science. He is also a member of various academic boards and committees. Recently, he has held appointments at the Radcliffe Institute for Advanced Study and the Center for European Studies, both at Harvard University.

It does not diminish Stewart's accomplishments to mention that in his many endeavors, he was always aided by his wife and informal colleague Dr. Katalin Nun Stewart, to whom Kierkegaard studies also owes a great debt of gratitude. In her capacity as board member of *Kierkegaard Research: Sources, Reception and Resources*, *Texts from Golden Age Denmark*, and *Danish Golden Age Studies*, she has done extensive editorial work, collaborating closely with authors throughout the world. She has also made great contributions in disseminating the work of these series with her beautiful homepages and cover designs. She is also well known to *many* scholars for her work in organizing numerous Kierkegaard conferences and seminars. She is an accomplished scholar in her own right, and her highly readable book on Danish Golden Age women shed light on a largely neglected dimension of the period.[13]

The essays in this volume represent the sweep of Stewart's interests and influence. Some continue his historical investigations by exploring the contexts of the specific issues with which Kierkegaard and his contemporaries wrestled. Some explore the overt or more surreptitious influence of Kierkegaard upon later thinkers. Other essays take a broader look at the history of modern philosophy, searching for the type of continuities that Stewart has discerned. Still others use Kierkegaard as a springboard and a resource to launch their own creative philosophical and theological reflections. In all instances the influence of Jon Stewart is evident, and the variety of essays is a testimony to the multi-faceted nature of his work.

—Lee C. Barrett
Peter Šajda

---

[13] Katalin Nun, *Women of the Danish Golden Age: Literature, Theater and the Emancipation of Women* (Copenhagen: Museum Tusculanum Press, 2013) (*Danish Golden Age Studies*, vol. 8).

Introduction

The essays presented here are indebted in very diverse ways to different aspects of the research, writing, and teaching of Jon Stewart. Most of the essays combine multiple dimensions of Stewart's interests. Some of them continue his efforts to situate Kierkegaard's writings in the context of specific cultural tensions and academic dynamics in Golden Age Denmark. Others shed light on important thinkers of mid-nineteenth century Denmark who were important to Kierkegaard, such has his brother Peter. Other essays locate Kierkegaard's authorship in the broader development of continental thought, tracing continuities and divergences between his work and trends that both preceded and succeeded it. Some of the contributions concentrate on Kierkegaard's reception by particular thinkers in the twentieth century. One essay even shifts the focus to Nietzsche, reflecting Stewart's interest in the relation of existentialism to continental thought in general. Finally, some of the authors use Kierkegaard as a springboard for their own constructive philosophical and theological reflections.

The essays by Schreiber, Barrett, and Kramer continue the project of clarifying Kierkegaard's work by locating it in particular aspects of his cultural and intellectual context. Schreiber's contribution sheds light on the ostensible shift in Kierkegaard's understanding of faith as a positive relation to the world to his valorization of the renunciation of the world by interpreting the change in the light of his personal life as expressed in his journals and notebooks. Kierkegaard's evolving engagement with late medieval mysticism, Pietism, Lutheranism, and Hegel's critique of classical logic reveals both continuities and discontinuities in his authorship. Schreiber also considers the importance of the more visceral factors of Kierkegaard's increasingly tense financial situation and his conflict with the *Corsair.* Throughout the essay changes in Kierkegaard's theology are linked to changes in his interpretation of his own lived reality. While the author notes that Kierkegaard's focus on inwardness, subjectivity, and individuating decisions continues throughout his authorship, Schreiber does detect a change away from faith as a "double movement" that includes the possibility of earthly happiness by virtue of the absurd to the necessity of expressing religious inwardness outwardly through suffering in the world.

Barrett discusses Kierkegaard's elaboration of Trinitarian motifs in relation to the theological controversies of his day. Although Kierkegaard never dealt with the doctrine in a sustained way, Trinitarian themes pervade his authorship. Trinitarian doctrine had been critiqued by Enlightenment thinkers and downplayed by Pietists, but a new interest in the Trinity arose in Denmark, partly due to Hegel's contention that the concept "Trinity" expressed the triadic movement of Spirit from undifferentiated unity, through self-othering, to reconciliation. Martensen modified this Hegelian schema by insisting that the triadic movement was not merely a dynamic immanent element in human consciousness, but typified the life of God as a free, self-conscious, transcendent agent. Kierkegaard inherited the Enlightenment and Pietist suspicion of metaphysics, but implicitly accepted Martensen's characterization of God *in se* as the joyful life of loving relationality. Rather than metaphysically describing God's inner life, Kierkegaard sought to exhibit in his writing three forms of pathos that corresponded to the Creator, Redeemer, and Consummator, including dependence, contrition, and the humble ascription of growth in faith to God.

Kramer situates Kierkegaard's reflections on memory and repetition in the context of the cultural crisis of northern Europe in the nineteenth century. The rise of political liberalism, industrialization, proto-capitalism, and mass communication disrupted traditional life, and therefore undermined the channels of memory that were tied to place and domicile. In burgeoning modernity, memory was increasingly recognized to be an active process rather than a passive storehouse of reified objects. Kramer argues that Kierkegaard's *Repetition* is an exposé of this crisis of memory. Because remembering is crucial for maintaining a sense of personal continuity, individual identity was jeopardized when access to memory became problematic. For the pseudonym Constantin Constantius the past is experienced as something constructed, and therefore as an unmanageable and potentially traumatic source of chaos. Constantin's compulsion to control the past by repeating it is a doomed project. Kramer points out that this issue of problematized memory was bequeathed to Deleuze, Adorno, Heidegger, and Derrida.

In order to illumine the context of Golden Age Denmark, Jensen turns his attention from Søren Kierkegaard to his brother Peter Christian, who was a significant theologian in his own right. Jensen investigates Peter's diaries that provide a rich case study of the maturation and vicissitudes of a Danish Christian intellectual. Jensen describes Peter's youthful travels through Germany, and his impressions of such luminaries as Neander, Hegel, and Schleiermacher. The diaries reveal how Peter's ambitions for an academic career were compromised by his attachment to Grundtvig, and how a university appointment became increasingly unlikely. After becoming a priest in a rural area, Peter's refusal to comply with the policy of compulsory baptism further complicated his relationship to the ecclesial authorities. Nevertheless, Peter enjoyed a brief political career, serving for a short period as minister of ecclesiastical affairs, and also became bishop of Aalborg. His diaries end with his escalating consciousness of sin and his debilitating melancholy.

Binetti and Fremstedal situate Kierkegaard in the history of continental philosophy. Binetti builds upon Stewart's work on the continuity of German Idealism and contemporary thought in order to challenge the historiographic myth structured around the conflict between idealism and anti-idealism, with Kierkegaard as a protagonist of the anti-metaphysical camp. Following Stewart, Binetti argues that Kierkegaard's work was never dominated by the monolithic polemic against Hegel that has been ascribed to him. A more nuanced reading reveals the influence of idealism on Kierkegaard's existentialism. According to Binetti, idealism did not exhibit the forgetfulness of the individual that many interpreters of Kierkegaard have decried. She identifies idealism with a focus on the immanence of the dynamic absolute in human self-consciousness rather than on divine transcendence, on the free subject rather than on substance, and on the potency of the negative moment rather than on the power of the perfect act. She adds that Kierkegaard and idealism shared an appreciation of the triadic structure of spiritual becoming, and a conviction that the movement of self-consciousness results in action. In Kierkegaard's work the negative force of contradiction is mediated by faith and love that reunite the ideal and the actual, and the eternal and the temporal. Binetti concludes that for Kierkegaard the individual is a synthesis of opposites in love, and that Kierkegaard's repetition resembles Hegelian mediation.

Fremstedal's contribution to this volume explores the continuity of Kierkegaard's writings with earlier philosophy, particularly that of Kant. While not arguing that Kierkegaard consciously based his reflections on subjectivity on Kant, he argues that the Dane's treatment of hidden inwardness and the truth of subjectivity echoes the Kantian contention that maxims ground actions. Kant's "highest maxim" is a long-term disposition, a second-order volition, that is expressed in a person's character and motivational core (which for Kant was respect for the law). While expressed in actions, this character is not directly available to observation. No individual action or set of actions is a sufficient condition for asserting that an individual possesses a certain type of motivational character. Similarly, Kierkegaard insists that love is visible in its fruits, but then cautions that no act is proof of the presence of love. Fremstedal concludes that Kierkegaard's later assertion of the necessity to perform acts of suffering love in imitation of Christ is simply a change of emphasis. He also suggests that the theme "subjectivity is truth," far from being irrational, provides a pragmatic defense of faith, for it answers a natural need to overcome despair.

Darío González also reflects Stewart's interest in the genealogy of continental thought, but shifts the focus from Kierkegaard to Nietzsche. He traces the path from Kant's relegation of God to the noumenal realm, through Nietzsche's theme of "the death of God," to Deleuze's and Foucault's critiques of moral objectivism. Nietzsche, González argues, construed moral systems as regimes of valuation, and as modes of sensitivity to life in general. Therefore, for Nietzsche Christianity is not to be argued against, but should be treated as a disease of valuation in which life in the world is hopelessly devalued. Rather than engage in a rational refutation of theism, Nietzsche sought to expose the history of the Christian moral ideal. According to González, Nietzsche's work should be read not as a critique of pure reason, but as a critique of moral prejudice. By exposing the roots of historically conditioned ideals, Nietzsche pioneered the genealogical approach to moral and ideological regimes that would proliferate in the twentieth century.

The essays by Czakó, Šajda, and Söderquist explore the reception of Kierkegaard by later thinkers. Czakó focuses on the appropriation of Kierkegaard's writings by Karl Jaspers. Jaspers' use of Kierkegaard was by no means an uncritical assimilation, although, as Czakó notes, he did laud Kierkegaard's honesty. According to Jaspers, Kierkegaard totally negated the value of the world in order to relate directly to transcendence. Moreover, Kierkegaard's category of "the absurd" was a negation of reason. Jaspers arrived at this increasingly critical interpretation by reading Kierkegaard's entire *corpus* in the light of his later attack upon Christendom. Czakó objects that such a construal of the authorship is reductionist, and that it ignores the earlier pseudonyms' more dialectical relation to finitude. Czakó concludes that although Jaspers' acosmic reading of Kierkegaard is one-dimensional, it nevertheless draws attention to a dynamic that really is present in his later work.

Peter Šajda explores the reception of Kierkegaard in Carl Schmitt's political theology, which was an important episode in the Kierkegaard renaissance in the German-speaking world during the early decades of the twentieth century. Schmitt's use of Kierkegaard was a productive reception, including not only explicit borrowings, but also many implicit ones. As Šajda points out, Schmitt's reading of Kierkegaard was strongly influenced by the Catholic convert Theodor Haecker, who insisted that Kierkegaard's project presupposed dogmatic Christianity. Schmitt elaborated what he took to be the political implications of Kierkegaard's theologically inspired critique of modernity. Relying upon *A Literary Review*, Schmitt castigated bourgeois liberalism, particularly its understanding of the nature of the state and law. In the modern world paralyzing reflection generates ambiguity, evasion, indecision, and the leveling of the qualitative distinctions that make decisiveness possible. Schmitt concluded that the loss of an appreciation for authority led to the glorification of general principles that admit no exceptions. As a corrective Schmitt proposed that the sovereign should be able to suspend legal order when the situation demands such action.

Söderquist, inspired by Stewart's interest in Kierkegaard's appropriation by phenomenologists and existentialists, focuses on the significance of Anti-Climacus' emphasis of the factical placement of the self (actuality) and the self's establishment by something other than itself. His source work research reveals that this focus on actuality is a continuation of Kierkegaard's critique of the German Romantics. Anti-Climacus' discussion of defiant despair suggests that the self is not self-grounded or autonomous. Rather, the self is dependent on the self's facticity and groundedness in its given context of social concretion and embodiment. By no means was Kierkegaard an advocate of self-enclosed subjectivity or of acosmic transcendence. According to Söderquist the theme that the self is grounded in God's gift of situatedness resembles Sartre's discussion of the dialectical relation of facticity and transcendence, but goes beyond Sartre by seeing facticity as if it were a gift grounded in divine infinitude.

Curtis Thompson and Heiko Schulz use Kierkegaard as a resource for their own constructive projects. Thompson's essay exhibits a novel productive reception of Kierkegaard by putting the Dane in conversation with authors like Michael Tomasello who investigate the social dimension of the evolution of human thinking and morality, as well as with theologians who emphasize "incarnational entanglements" like Catherine Keller and Niels Henrik Gregersen. Thompson concludes that collaborative activity, embedded in cultural formations, has occasioned momentous developments in thinking and morality. He then argues that although Kierkegaard valorized individuality and personal moral decisiveness, his creativity was actually empowered by his rich interdependency on the cultural milieu of Golden Age Denmark. Kierkegaard's own worldly entanglements, including affective experiences and social practices, influenced his understanding of the individual's cognitive and moral regeneration. Just as Jesus, the Incarnate Word, was enmeshed in the cosmos, so also Kierkegaard was enmeshed in his inheritance from the past, and in his own nexus of relationships. As a specific instance of this, Thompson considers Kierkegaard's contention that the prospect of death lifts individuals out of ordinary routines and makes possible the individual's recognition of being nothing before God. Thompson shows that here Kierkegaard was "entangled" with the apophatic tradition of mysticism and the spirituality of Pietism.

Heiko Schulz uses Kierkegaard as a springboard for his own theological proposals concerning divine revelation. Schulz identifies revelation as a communicative act of God that discloses God's ability and willingness to provide for God's creatures. According to Schulz, in order for a communication to count as a genuine revelation, that which is revealed must be co-extensive with that which was hidden. The revelation must also be a self-authenticating event. Moreover, a divine revelation in the strictest sense must itself constitute the condition for understanding and receiving it. Schulz opines that only the understanding of revelation in Christianity, but not in Islam or Judaism, possesses this last characteristic. In these reflections the echo of the voice of Johannes Climacus in *Philosophical Fragments* can be clearly heard.

This selection manifests how variegated Jon Stewart's legacy actually is. The authors hail from a variety of countries, employ different methods, represent a plurality of disciplines, and write with different cultural issues in mind. Moreover, the authors often do not agree with one another. Some see Kierkegaard as continuing the grand tradition of speculative German Idealism, and some regard him as vehemently rejecting that heritage. Some assume that Kierkegaard was an orthodox theist, and some propose that he identified the divine with the dynamics of the human spirit. Some discern an element of world affirmation in his work, while others detect a severe negation of earthly life. But however much they may differ, all the authors manifest significant traces of the work of Jon Stewart.

On the (Dis)Continuity in Kierkegaard's Understanding of Faith

Gerhard Schreiber

Faith was not only the theme of Kierkegaard's life but also the systematic center of his thought. The theory of faith held by the mature Kierkegaard, whom we will here call "Kierkegaard the author," has important aspects and elements that are already prefigured in the journal entries and writings of his "*vita ante acta*"[1]—that is, of his earlier life "from childhood until I became an author"[2]—and which can be fully understood only against the backdrop of those early reflections.[3] Yet despite important moments of continuity between Kierkegaard the student and Kierkegaard the author, one major difference stands out. Whereas up through the *Concluding Unscientific Postscript*, Kierkegaard understands and describes the relation between faith and reality as a positive one, in his later works a negative assessment of the relation of faith to reality grows more and more important, ultimately culminating in the demand for a world-renouncing imitation Christianity, i.e., a Christianity focused on the imitation [*Efterfølgelse*] of Christ.

In what follows, I would like to point out at least a few moments of continuity between the young Kierkegaard and the later Kierkegaard, in order to examine this fundamental change in terms of its background, along with the factors and circumstances conditioning it—and to highlight the role of Luther in this context.

---

[1] *SKS* 16, 58 / *PV*, 79.

[2] Ibid.

[3] See Gerhard Schreiber, *Apriorische Gewissheit. Das Glaubensverständnis des jungen Kierkegaard und seine philosophisch-theologischen Voraussetzungen* (Berlin and Boston: De Gruyter, 2014) (*Kierkegaard Studies Monograph Series*, vol. 30).

I. MOMENTS OF CONTINUITY

Kierkegaard's development as a thinker is marked by a wide array of educational and discursive contexts. Both close involvement in his youth with other thinkers—some of whom were quite different in outlook—and engagement with certain contemporary philosophical-theological debates in his immediate environment had lasting influence on the development of his theory of faith. Kierkegaard's early journals and notebooks—to which he repeatedly returned, when preparing his later writings, in order to make the thoughts and considerations formulated there bear literary fruit—reveal multiple relations of reception, both on the level of terminology and/or on the level of thematic content.

That Kierkegaard engaged in the literary reception and reworking of earlier notes on faith in his work as an author up to the "turning point"[4] of the *Concluding Unscientific Postscript* (1846) is particularly evident in the Climacus writings. Thus, for example, in the drafts of his treatment of "the absolute paradox" in the third chapter of *Philosophical Fragments* (1844) and its subsequent Appendix,[5] Kierkegaard makes explicit reference to his 1836 journal entries on Johann Georg Hamann (1730-1788)[6] and his 1838 sketches for a piece on "Telegraph message from an effervescent to a clairvoyant about the relation between Christianity and philosophy."[7] Similarly, his critique of N. F. S. Grundtvig (1783-1872) in the *Postscript* is in broad and partly literal agreement with his 1835 notes on the latter's "church theory."[8] Even though the immediate occasion for the project undertaken in Kierkegaard's Climacus writings was his reading of the *Christian Doctrine* [*Glaubenslehre*] of David Friedrich Strauss (1808-1874), including the account of the religious and historical philosophy of Gotthold Ephraim Lessing (1729-1781) conveyed in that text,[9] the project's foundation had already been laid during Kierkegaard's years as a student.

Among the essential moments of continuity between the understanding of faith of Kierkegaard the student and that of Kierkegaard the author are,

---

[4] *SKS* 16, 11 / *PV*, 63.

[5] See Ms. 2 in *SKS* K4, 175, [1r] (KA, B pk. 14 læg 2; *Pap.* V B 6:1) as well as Ms. 4 in *SKS* K4, 175, [16r] (KA, B pk. 14 læg 2; not in *Pap.*).

[6] See, e.g., *SKS* 27, 149f., Papir 185 / *JP* 2, 1540.

[7] *SKS* 27, 213, Papir 259:1 / *JP* 3, 3266.

[8] *SKS* 27, 101–105, Papir 69 / *JP* 5, 5088.

[9] See Gerhard Schreiber, "On the Origins of Kierkegaard's Climacus Writings and Paradox Christology," *Kierkegaard Studies Yearbook*, 2017, 313–341.

to mention the most important ones: his interpretation of faith as neither a mediated (sublated) nor a reflexively mediable (sublatable), and hence special, form of immediacy;[10] his emphasis on the inwardness of faith, and on the indifference of this inwardness to its manifestation in external things; his characterization of faith as an *a priori* form of certainty; his development of the concept of faith along simultaneously apologetic and anti-speculative lines; and his accentuation of the subjective-personal aspect of the faith.[11] The last of these is already evident in the distinction that Kierkegaard draws—responding to an 1833 sermon by Grundtvig—between "immediate, spontaneous faith" and "an intensified faith"[12] that presupposes the individuating moment of personal decision; as well as in Kierkegaard's presentation of an essential subjectivity that is indispensable for the individual's faith, an account that derives from a critical encounter with Grundtvig's so-called "ecclesiastical view" (1835),[13] and which is in keeping with the "theory of subjectivity"[14] that would later emerge in the *Postscript*.[15]

Moreover, key elements of Kierkegaard the author's theory of faith are already contained *in nuce*, or are applied implicitly, in the writings and journal entries of Kierkegaard the student. An example is the idea of the "leap" into faith that appears in notebook entry Not5:23 (1840),[16] when describing the transition from the consciousness of sin to the certainty of the forgiveness of sins, in the course of which a new quality is set.[17] This "free act,"[18] which is linked to the historical fact of the appearance of Christ, and

---

[10] See Heiko Schulz, "Second Immediacy. A Kierkegaardian Account of Faith," in *Immediacy and Reflection in Kierkegaard's Thought*, ed. by Paul Cruysberghs et al. (Leuven: Leuven University Press, 2003), 71–86; Gerhard Schreiber, "Kierkegaard's Account of Faith as 'The New Immediacy,'" *Filozofia*, vol. 68, 2013, 27–37.

[11] See Schreiber, *Apriorische Gewissheit*, 28–31, 46–53, 58–61, 97–102, 144–161, 216–220, 234–236, 320–335, 340–351.

[12] *SKS* 27, 34, Papir 5:1 / *JP* 5, 5056.

[13] For an account of the development of Grundtvig's "ecclesiastical view" with regard to his idea of "the living word," which underwent several modifications or enhancements, see the commentaries (to Kierkegaard's journal entries NB15:53 and NB26:109) written by Niels Jørgen Cappelørn in *SKS* K23, 80f., and *SKS* K25, 118–120.

[14] *SKS* 7, 50 / *CUP1*, 45; see also *SKS* 7, 57 f. / *CUP1*, 53–54.

[15] See, e.g., *SKS* 27, 105, Papir 70 / *JP* 5, 5090 and *SKS* 27, 112, Papir 91 / *JP* 1, 578.

[16] *SKS* 19, 185f., Not5:23 / *KJN* 3, 181f.

[17] On Kierkegaard's concept of the leap see Gerhard Schreiber, "Leap," in *Kierkegaard's Concepts*, ed. by Steven M. Emmanuel, William McDonald and Jon Stewart, Tome IV (Farnham and Burlington: Ashgate, 2014) (*Kierkegaard Research: Sources, Reception and Resources*, vol. 15), 71–78.

[18] *SKS* 19, 186, Not5:23 / *KJN* 3, 182.

which appears "impossible" and "incomprehensible" to human wisdom and understanding, confronts human beings in the ethical-religious demand "Thou shalt," as it is described in entry HH:25 (1840–41),[19] and which acquired decisive importance for Kierkegaard's understanding of faith in his later works.[20] Furthermore, the peculiar perception that is ascribed to faith in Kierkegaard's first book *From the Papers of One Still Living* (1838) can be interpreted as a prefiguration of the notion of the "autopsy of faith," which designates a specific perception of faith that is paradoxically transformative.[21] Finally, the notebook entry Not7:22 (1840)[22] contains an early hint of the *pistological* paradox;[23] whereas traces are entirely lacking of the *Christological* paradox of incarnation in the young Kierkegaard, as is evident in the juxtaposition of Socrates and Christ in the first part of Kierkegaard's dissertation *On the Concept of Irony* (1841).[24]

Conversely, important aspects of Kierkegaard the author's theory of faith can only be fully understood as responses to his own early reflections. For example, the key to Kierkegaard's criticisms of the understanding of faith as "the immediate," which Kierkegaard uses as a negative foil for his own position in many of his pseudonymous writings without identifying the objects of his critique, is to see them as emerging from his early clashes with J. L. Heiberg (1791–1860) and H. L. Martensen (1808–1884).[25] Another example is the controversy about Hegel's critique of classical logic that took place in Kierkegaard's milieu in the late 1830s.[26] The central contributions to that controversy served as the backdrop not only to Kierkegaard's refer-

---

[19] *SKS* 18, 138f., HH:25 / *KJN* 2, 129f.

[20] See Schreiber, *Apriorische Gewissheit*, 306–319.

[21] See ibid., 225–233 and 243–248.

[22] *SKS* 19, 211, Not7:22 / *KJN* 3, 207.

[23] See Schreiber, *Apriorische Gewissheit*, 335–349.

[24] See Schreiber, "On the Origins," 315–322.

[25] See Gerhard Schreiber, "The Real Targets of Kierkegaard's Critique of Characterizing Faith as 'the Immediate,'" in *Kierkegaard: East and West*, ed. by Roman Králik et al. (Toronto: Kierkegaard Circle, University of Toronto 2011) (*Acta Kierkegaardiana*, vol. 5), 137–167.

[26] See Jon Stewart, "Introduction: The Debate Surrounding Hegel's Criticism of the Laws of Classical Logic in Golden Age Denmark," in *Mynster's "Rationalism, Supernaturalism" and the Debate about Mediation*, trans. and ed. by Jon Stewart (Copenhagen: Museum Tusculanum Press, 2009) (*Texts from Golden Age Denmark*, vol. 5), 3–45; István Czakó, "Das Problem des Glaubens und der Geschichte in der Philosophie Kierkegaards und Karl Jaspers," *Kierkegaard Studies Yearbook*, 2000, 373–382; István Czakó, "Das Unbekannte. Die Aufhebung der klassischen theologia naturalis in der negativen Theologie des Johannes Climacus," *Kierkegaard Studies Yearbook*, 2004, 235–249.

ences to and criticism of "mediation," but also and especially to his contrasting of (the idea of) "mediation" and the (absolute) paradox of faith in *Fear and Trembling* and the Climacus writings.[27]

It is only when the young Kierkegaard's intellectual development is taken into account that both Kierkegaard's critique of the understanding of faith as "the immediate" and his protest against applying the "idea of mediation" to Christological dogma can be understood in their true intention and thrust. When this is done, it becomes clear that Kierkegaard's position in both contexts is a reaction to certain philosophical-theological discussions in his local environment. In other words, the targets of his critique are not to be found in far-off Germany, but in Copenhagen. Accordingly, the fact that Kierkegaard is commonly stylized as Hegel's "polar opposite" is at the very least questionable, particularly since Kierkegaard's own reception of Hegel during his student years was fundamentally productive; although before he took his theological examination, his acquaintance with Hegelian philosophy was mainly secondhand.[28] In any case, the fact that investigating Kierkegaard the student can contribute to a better understanding of Kierkegaard the author is further illustrated by Kierkegaard's condemnation of the philosophical "volatilization" of central Christian concepts. The background and origin of this condemnation—which Kierkegaard directed above all against Philipp K. Marheineke (1780–1846),[29] but also, particularly in his *Book on Adler* (ca. June 1846–November 1847), against Hegelian philosophy in general[30]—was Kierkegaard's critical encounter in 1837 with the younger Fichte (Immanuel Hermann Fichte [1796–1879]).[31] In that context, the "volatilization" of the concept of faith means its improper use in a philosophical context—improper because the concept is here given only an everyday or ordi-

---

[27] See Schreiber, *Apriorische Gewissheit*, 270–297.

[28] See Jon Stewart, *Kierkegaard's Relations to Hegel Reconsidered* (New York: Cambridge University Press, 2003), 90–131; Jon Stewart, "Hegel: Kierkegaard's Reading and Use of Hegel's Primary Texts," in *Kierkegaard and His German Contemporaries*, Tome I, *Philosophy*, ed. by Jon Stewart (Aldershot and Burlington: Ashgate, 2007) (*Kierkegaard Research: Sources, Reception and Resources*, vol. 6), 97–165 as well as Schreiber, *Apriorische Gewissheit*, 106–130.

[29] See Heiko Schulz, "Marheineke: The Volatilization of Christian Doctrine," in *Kierkegaard and His German Contemporaries*, Tome II, Theology, ed. by Jon Stewart (Aldershot and Burlington: Ashgate, 2007) (*Kierkegaard Research: Sources, Reception and Resources*, vol. 6), 117–142.

[30] See, e.g., *SKS* 15, 258f. / *BA*, 103; *SKS* 15, 276f. / *BA*, 118.

[31] See Gerhard Schreiber, "Die philosophische Verflüchtigung des Glaubensbegriffs. Kierkegaards Auseinandersetzung mit Immanuel Hermann Fichte," *Kierkegaard Studies Yearbook*, 2013, 345–376.

nary meaning, emptied of its specific Christian content, so that its Christian *proprium* is no longer recognizable.

In psychological terms, what is unique about Christian faith is its *a priori* mode of certainty. *A priori* certainty is the nexus at which the young Kierkegaard's various statements about faith converge, though it should be noted that these early statements center on faith as an *act* (*fides qua*), rather than on its propositional *content* (*fides quae*). Rather, as an expression for the "transubstantiation of experience"[32] in/of pre-eschatic reality, this certainty of communion with Christ—which can no longer be shaken by happiness, guilt, and/or suffering—is radically different from the self-certainty of reason, or other empirical certainties. This communion with Christ, of which the believer is certain, *is* a reality on the part of God, and *will become* reality on part of individuals in faith. It is (only) already present in and with the act of faith, even though, in this world, it is also always conceived as still in the process of becoming. For this reason, faith is "victory over the world, and yet it is a struggle."[33] The *a priori* certainty of faith—a certainty that faith does not create or possess, but itself *is*—is neither an objectless state and thus a groundless one, nor is it a certainty founded solely on subjective experience, and so ultimately an unfounded one. Rather, the *a priori* certainty of faith is certainty about the reality of the reconciliation that, *in principle*, has already been accomplished in Christ, and which is now to be attained by the believer by reenactment. As such, the *a priori* certainty of faith is in fact also an expression for the human being's own "ec-centric existence,"[34] which is neither the ground for his own self nor the ground of this certainty.

Faith is directed toward a reality that cannot be experienced as an object of natural experience, but only in faith's peculiar mode of perception. This is why the experience of faith is an experience of *another* kind: "a deeper experience" [*en dybere Empirie*].[35] Nonetheless, *a priori* faith and life experience do not necessarily exclude one another, since belief that is not based on experience is *itself* the ground of experience. After Kierkegaard had made this realization himself—coming to grasp the relation between *a priori* faith and life experience, which he had initially regarded as an opposed relation, as a constructive one instead—he proceeded to conclude that the certainty of

---

[32] *SKS* 1, 32 / *EPW*, 76.

[33] *SKS* 1, 349 / *CI*, 319.

[34] Eberhard Jüngel, *Das Evangelium von der Rechtfertigung des Gottlosen als Zentrum des christlichen Glaubens* (6th ed., Tübingen: Mohr Siebeck, 2011 [1998]), 206.

[35] *SKS* 1, 32 / *EPW*, 76.

faith that is *unconditioned* by experience is, precisely thereby, a certainty that *conditions* experience; as in his 1841 trial sermon,[36] in which he characterized the certainty of faith as the precondition for the active shaping of the world and the positive impetus for a Christian's action in the world as "God's coworker."[37] Here, in the practical consequences for life that he is able to draw from faith's certainty, the robustness of Kierkegaard's understanding of faith is evident. Although the *a priori* certainty of faith has its ground beyond the human self, it does not lead to an abandonment of the world, but rather makes possible man's positive freedom in relation to the given reality. Still, the Yes that faith speaks to the world is not an absolute and unreserved Yes, but a Yes that has passed through the cathartic No of resignation: it is a *differentiated* Yes.

II. FROM A POSITIVE TO A NEGATIVE RELATION OF FAITH TO REALITY

This positive relationship between the believer and this-worldly reality—as it is explicated in Kierkegaard's *From the Papers of One Still Living*,[38] as well as in *The Concept of Irony*,[39] as the result of a certain interrelationship with reality that contains negation as a suspended moment—was essential for Kierkegaard's understanding of faith until the publication of *Fear and Trembling*, which appeared in Copenhagen bookshops on October 16, 1843, together with *Repetition* and the *Three Upbuilding Discourses* (1843), and which was mainly prepared, according to the editors of *SKS*, in June 1843.[40] In what Johannes *de silentio* describes as the "double-movement"[41] of faith, the movement of infinite resignation—understood as the renunciation of some irreplaceable finite thing by one's own power—is followed by the movement of faith in the narrower sense, in or through which the believer regains that same finite thing "by virtue of the absurd."[42] This double

[36] *SKS* 27, 245–257, Papir 270 / *JP* 4, 3915.

[37] *SKS* 27, 254, Papir 270 / *JP* 4, 3915, 53; see also Schreiber, *Apriorische Gewissheit*, 340–352.

[38] See *SKS* 1, 21–25 / *EPW*, 65–69 together with Schreiber, *Apriorische Gewissheit*, 225–236.

[39] See *SKS* 1, 135 / *CI*, 76; *SKS* 1, 296 / *CI*, 257f.; *SKS* 1, 310 / *CI*, 274; *SKS* 1, 316 / *CI*, 279; *SKS* 1, 349 / *CI*, 318f. and *SKS* 1, 357 / *CI*, 328f. together with Schreiber, *Apriorische Gewissheit*, 392–398.

[40] See the *SKS* editors' critical account of *Fear and Trembling* in *SKS* K4, 97.

[41] *SKS* 4, 131 / *FT*, 36.

[42] Ibid.

movement of faith thus consists, in general terms, first of losing "everything finite,"[43] "and then to win the very same finitude again by virtue of the absurd."[44] The Knight of Faith "finds pleasure in everything, takes part in everything,"[45] and yet at every moment he makes the movement of infinity, accomplishing even the very least thing "by virtue of the absurd:"

> He drains the deep sadness of life in infinite resignation, he knows the blessedness of infinity, he has felt the pain of renouncing everything, the most precious thing in the world, and yet the finite tastes just as good to him as to one who never knew anything higher, because his remaining in finitude would have no trace of a timorous, anxious routine, and yet he has this security that makes him delight in it as if finitude were the surest thing of all. And yet, yet the whole earthly figure he presents is a new creation by virtue of the absurd. He resigned everything infinitely, and then he grasped everything again by virtue of the absurd. He is continually making the movement of infinity, but he does it with such precision and assurance that he continually gets finitude out of it.[46]

A paradigm of such faith is Abraham. His faith was not merely directed toward a future, otherworldly life, but he "had faith specifically for this life."[47] Inasmuch as Abraham is willing to sacrifice Isaac, he seems to give up hope of a happy earthly life. But by believing in and holding fast, with unbroken trust, to the promise for *this* life that he was given by God, he receives Isaac and his earthly happiness again "by virtue of the absurd" (i.e., "that God, who required it of him, should in the next moment rescind the requirement"[48]): "[I]t is great to lay hold of the eternal, but it is greater to hold fast to the temporal after having given it up."[49]

The "life-renewing meaning"[50] of this "faith directed at something temporal"[51] also appears in several journal entries from the early summer of

---

[43] Ibid.

[44] *SKS* 4, 132 / *FT*, 36.

[45] *SKS* 4, 134 / *FT*, 39.

[46] *SKS* 4, 135 / *FT*, 40f.

[47] *SKS* 4, 116 / *FT*, 20.

[48] *SKS* 4, 131 / *FT*, 35f.

[49] *SKS* 4, 115 / *FT*, 18.

[50] Kristoffer Olesen Larsen, "Über den Paradoxbegriff. 2. Seine Entstehung nach den 'Papieren,'" in his *Søren Kierkegaard. Ausgewählte Aufsätze* (Gütersloh: Mohn, 1973), 15–33, 27.

[51] According to Emanuel Hirsch in *Søren Kierkegaard. Furcht und Zittern* (Düsseldorf and Cologne: Diederichs, 1950) (vol. 3 of *Søren Kierkegaard. Gesammelte Werke*, vols. 1–27, trans. and ed. by Emanuel Hirsch, Hayo Gerdes and Hans Martin Junghans (Düsseldorf and Cologne: Diederichs, 1950–69)), 145 (note 18).

1843. Journal entry JJ:116, which was written in Berlin in mid-May, contains the following passage: "Faith therefore has hopes for this life, but, be it noted, on the strength of the absurd, not on the strength of hum[an] understanding, otherwise it is only good sense, not faith."[52] Therefore, as Kierkegaard concludes in the next entry, faith is also "what the Greeks called div.[ine] madness,"[53] a faith whose hope defies human understanding and calculation while also having man's everyday reality as its point of reference.[54] Remarkably, Kierkegaard applies this "basically 'optimistic' faith that man is given back anew as a gift that which he has voluntarily given up,"[55] a faith sometimes referred to as "Abrahamic faith,"[56] to his own relationship with his former fiancée Regine Olsen (1822-1904). At the start of journal entry JJ:115, which was also written in Berlin in mid-May, and which was later overwritten in the manuscript with dense bows of ink by Kierkegaard's hand, it is stated frankly: "Had I faith I would have stayed with Regine. Praise and thanks be to God, I have now understood it."[57] His sin was, as Kierkegaard writes elsewhere, that he had no faith—"faith that for God all things are possible,"[58] and that "at this very instant[, God] could make everything good."[59]

Journal entry JJ:146, which may have been written in August 1843, but was certainly written after July 1843, provides the first indication that Kierkegaard had begun to distance himself from this belief:

> That is what is difficult about having both the O.[ld] and the N.[ew] Testaments, because the O. has entirely different categories. For what would the NT say about a faith that believes that things should go very well for it in the world, in the temporal sphere, instead of giving this up to grasp the eternal? This is the source of the erratic nature of ecclesiasti-

---

[52] *SKS* 18, 179, JJ:116 / *KJN* 2, 166.

[53] *SKS* 18, 179, JJ:117 / *KJN* 2, 166.

[54] See *SKS* 18, 181, JJ:124 / *KJN* 2, 168.

[55] Ulrich Klenke, *Denken und Glaube beim jungen Kierkegaard. Kritische Strukturanalyse seiner Grundlegung der dialektischen Wahrheitsbestimmungen humaner und christlicher Existenz* (Dissertation, University of Münster, 1969), 64.

[56] See, for example, Hayo Gerdes, *Das Christusverständnis des jungen Kierkegaard. Ein Beitrag zur Erläuterung des Paradox-Gedankens* (Itzehoe: Die Spur, 1962), 29; Klenke, *Denken und Glaube beim jungen Kierkegaard*, 27, 31f. and 40; and Emanuel Hirsch, *Kierkegaard-Studien* (Gütersloh: Bertelsmann, 1933), 650 (continuous pagination).

[57] *SKS* 18, 177, JJ:115 / *KJN* 2, 164.

[58] *SKS* 19, 231, Not8:20 / *KJN* 3, 226.

[59] *SKS* 18, 184, JJ:138 / *KJN* 2, 170.

> cal discourse, all according to whether the O. or the NT is transparent within it.[60]

Here, for the first time in his authorship, Kierkegaard takes the view that the Old and New Testaments are in a relationship of mutual antagonism, such that Old Testament faith is oriented toward this world, while an orientation toward the next world is characteristic of New Testament faith.[61] This view is the first articulation of an insight that would become ever more definitive for Kierkegaard, to the effect that Christian faith is *not* the hope of a happy earthly life, but rather fundamentally presupposes the renunciation of temporal life as preparation for eternal life. "For Kierkegaard, the path of 'Christian faith' still leads through resignation's 'Bridge of Sighs'; but this path does not lead back to the joy of life, but rather into 'religious' suffering."[62]

III. ON THE BACKGROUND TO THE REVOCATION OF "ABRAHAMIC FAITH"

As background for this change in Kierkegaard's understanding of faith, which occurred in the summer of 1843, various Kierkegaard researchers[63] refer to Regine Olsen's engagement to another man—an event that, as Hayo Gerdes (1928-1981) put it, "with its staggering effect on Kierkegaard, helped him to reach the insight...that true Christian faith [consists of] hope of the eternal, and thereby renunciation of the world."[64] Although Gerdes locates the earliest "documentary evidence"[65] for Kierkegaard's revocation of "Abrahamic faith" in "the 'retraction' of the Abraham story"[66] found in journal entry NB28:41 from about mid-1853,[67] entitled "New '*Fear and Trem-*

---

[60] *SKS* 18, 188, JJ:146 / *KJN* 2, 174.

[61] On Kierkegaard's (religiously grounded) criticism of the Old Testament and Old Testament faith, see Gerdes, *Das Christusverständnis des jungen Kierkegaard*, 29–36; Emanuel Hirsch, "Das Alte Testament und die Predigt des Evangeliums" (1936), in his *Das Alte Testament und die Predigt des Evangeliums. Mit anderen Arbeiten Emanuel Hirschs zum Alten Testament*, ed. by Hans Martin Müller (Tübingen: Katzmann and Goslar: Thuhoff, 1986), 33–126.

[62] Klenke, *Denken und Glaube beim jungen Kierkegaard*, 32.

[63] See, e.g., Hirsch, *Kierkegaard-Studien*, 642; Gerdes, *Das Christusverständnis des jungen Kierkegaard*, 30 and 32, Klenke, *Denken und Glaube beim jungen Kierkegaard*, 31f. and 64f.

[64] According to Gerdes in *Søren Kierkegaard. Die Tagebücher*, vols. 1–5, selected, trans. and ed. by Hayo Gerdes (Düsseldorf and Cologne: Diederichs, 1962–74), vol. 1, 409 (note 862).

[65] Gerdes, *Das Christusverständnis des jungen Kierkegaard*, 29.

[66] Ibid.

[67] See *SKS* 25, 248f., NB28:41 / *KJN* 9, 250f.

bling,'" which contains a tale in which Abraham actually carries out the sacrifice of Isaac—he holds that Kierkegaard's "break"[68] with such faith took place some ten years earlier, when Kierkegaard—"probably in July 1843"[69]—learned of Regine's new engagement:

> While in the midst of working on the pair of books *Fear and Trembling* and *Repetition*, Kierkegaard learned of the second engagement of his former bride. In the final months of their engagement, Regine had made Kierkegaard swear to remain with her, both by appealing to his father's memory and by threatening that she would not survive the dissolution of the engagement. And after the break, all of Kierkegaard's actions and feelings were under the influence of these oaths and the hope of regaining Regine "by virtue of the absurd." Now, however, he surely perceived the implacable reality of Regine's engagement as an irony annihilating the whole holy sincerity of his concern for her—and the understanding of faith bound up in this.[70]

Because and *in light* of Regine's new engagement, respectively, Kierkegaard not only came to see "Abrahamic faith" as "a false belief...based on a selfish hope for the earthly, unmasked by reality itself,"[71] but also—as was first and foremost claimed by Emanuel Hirsch (1888-1972)—reworked the books *Fear and Trembling* and *Repetition* accordingly, and only then composed his *Three Upbuilding Discourses* (1843) as a "true and decisive correction of both works."[72]

This cannot be the place to examine the correctness of this assumption in detail. It should be noted, however, that Regine Olsen and Johan Frederik Schlegel (1817-1896) did not actually become engaged until August 28, 1843 (!)[73]—a fact that militates not only against the above assumption, but also against the account of the genesis of *Fear and Trembling* and *Repetition* in the *SKS* edition.[74] It is thus not at all certain that journal entry JJ:146, as the first indication of Kierkegaard's distancing from "Abrahamic faith," presupposes knowledge of Regine's second engagement, nor that Kierkegaard

[68] Gerdes, *Das Christusverständnis des jungen Kierkegaard*, 29.

[69] Ibid., 81 (note 7).

[70] Ibid., 30.

[71] Ibid., 31.

[72] According to Hirsch in his introduction to *Furcht und Zittern* (see note 51 above), VII–XIII, X; see also his *Kierkegaard-Studien*, 649ff.

[73] See Kirsten Boas, "Regines ring," *Kristeligt Dagblad*, May 2, 2003; Ejnar Hauberg, "Regines anden ring," *Kristeligt Dagblad*, May 26, 2003.

[74] See *SKS* K4, 83–97 (*Tilblivelseshistorie*).

rewrote the double-work *Fear and Trembling* and *Repetition* for this reason. The latter assumption can no longer be supported, at least not on the basis of the account of the genesis of these two books that has been generally accepted.

Whatever may have brought about this change in Kierkegaard's understanding of faith, it is a matter of importance that, until the publication of the *Postscript*, it is faith as "the inner certainty that anticipates infinity"[75] (as it is described in *The Concept of Anxiety* (1844) with reference to G. W. F. Hegel) and "the religious suffering," respectively, that are established as "the expression for the relationship with God" and "the sign of the relationship with God," respectively,[76] in the (or, more accurately, in such an) inwardness of the human being, but bearing no outward marks. Even within the *Postscript*, the suffering of inwardness—the "dying to immediacy,"[77] as is essential to immanent religiosity (A)—is primarily understood as παθειν, in the sense of "*letting* oneself be overcome,"[78] i.e., the transformation of one's own existence, as is evident not least in Kierkegaard's criticism of the "monastic movement of the Middle Ages."[79] This relation of incommensurability between (religious) inwardness and outwardness manifests itself above all in *Fear and Trembling*, where the Knight of Faith, who performs the "double-movement" of faith at every moment, is outwardly absorbed completely in reality. No outward mark betrays him, which is why he can easily deceive by his appearance, and resemble a man of the petty bourgeoisie, his gait like that of a postman.[80] The point, then, is "[t]o exist [*existere*] in such a way that my contrast to existence constantly expresses itself as the most beautiful and secure harmony with it."[81]

It is precisely on this point, the question of the *outward expression* of religious inwardness, that the *Postscript* emerges as a turning point. In *Fear and Trembling*, the inwardness of faith is characterized as an incommensurate "new interiority"[82] for which there can be no adequate outward expres-

[75] *SKS* 4, 456 / *CA*, 157.

[76] *SKS* 7, 412 / *CUP1*, 453.

[77] *SKS* 7, 392 / *CUP1*, 431 et passim.

[78] Dorothea Glöckner, *Kierkegaards Begriff der Wiederholung. Eine Studie zu seinem Freiheitsverständnis* (Berlin and New York: De Gruyter, 1998) (*Kierkegaard Studies Monograph Series*, vol. 3), 71.

[79] *SKS* 7, 352 / *CUP1*, 387 (emphasis removed).

[80] See *SKS* 4, 133f. / *FT*, 38f.

[81] *SKS* 4, 144 / *FT*, 50.

[82] *SKS* 4, 161 / *FT*, 69.

sion, but merely a "paradoxical expression"[83] *sub contrario specie*. By contrast, in his late works—beginning with his Easter entries from 1848—Kierkegaard wished to interpret just such a "religiousness of hidden inwardness"[84] marked by invisibility (as was first mentioned in the trial sermon of 1841, and which represents the climax[85] of Religiousness A in the *Postscript*) as characteristic of Christendom's volatilization of the truth of Christianity. Between the early and late works stands the "effort" that emerges in the *Postscript* "to keep the hidden inwardness separate from the external," but at the same time to reinforce the inwardness in the paradoxical religiousness of Religiousness B, "to strengthen it to the point where it can no longer remain in the medium in which it is to be held captive."[86] This "paradoxical inwardness," which marks the breach with "the hidden immanence of the eternal"[87] by its relation to the "absolute paradox" of the God-man, which it encounters as a historical fact, "is the greatest possible"[88] form of inwardness and *differentia specifica* of what is Christian by contrast to "all other inwardness;"[89] but it is ultimately not viable without a (corresponding) external outward-expression.

Whereas faith is still defined in the Climacus writings as the passion in which "the understanding and the paradoxical happily encounter each other in the moment,"[90] in Kierkegaard's late works this passion of faith, as "an infinite interest in one's own eternal happiness,"[91] crystallizes ever more clearly as a passion that generates suffering, and at that not merely "suffering…in their inner beings," i.e., in the inner world [*i det Indvortes*],[92] but suffering in the outer world, in the imitation of Christ. "The Christianity of

---

[83] *SKS* 4, 162 / *FT*, 70.

[84] *SKS* 7, 486 / *CUP1*, 510.

[85] See Wolfgang Struve, "Die neuzeitliche Philosophie als Metaphysik der Subjektivität. Interpretationen zu Kierkegaard und Nietzsche," *Symposion. Jahrbuch für Philosophie*, vol. 1, 1948, 207–335, 271.

[86] Hermann Deuser, "Bekenntnis und Handlung—nach Søren Kierkegaard," in his *Was ist Wahrheit anderes als ein Leben für eine Idee? Kierkegaards Existenzdenken und die Inspiration des Pragmatismus. Gesammelte Aufsätze zur Theologie und Religionsphilosophie*, ed. by Niels Jørgen Cappelørn and Markus Kleinert (Berlin and New York: De Gruyter, 2011), 25–39, 35.

[87] *SKS* 7, 520 / *CUP1*, 571.

[88] *SKS* 7, 520 / *CUP1*, 572.

[89] *SKS* 7, 554 / *CUP1*, 610.

[90] *SKS* 4, 261 / *PF*, 59.

[91] *SKS* 7, 31 / *CUP1*, 24.

[92] *SKS* 7, 399 / *CUP1*, 439.

hidden inwardness is replaced by the Christianity of imitating the Lord."[93] This is especially evident in the section entitled "Christ as the Prototype" of the manuscript of *Judge for Yourselves! For Self-Examination, Recommended to the Present Age*, which was mainly written between the autumn of 1851 and the middle of 1852:

> Christ is the prototype, to which corresponds *imitation*. There is really only one true way to be a Christian—to be a disciple. The disciple has among other marks also this: to suffer for the doctrine. Anyone who has not suffered for the doctrine has in one way or another incurred the guilt of using his sagacity to spare himself in a secular way.[94]

Up through the *Postscript*, Kierkegaard had understood the "martyrdom of faith"[95] primarily as an *intellectual* martyrdom, i.e., "faith's crucifixion of the understanding"[96] in the encounter with the "absolute paradox." Now, in the writings and journal entries of his late period, Kierkegaard—who referred to his own involvement with the *Corsair* as a "martyrdom of laughter"[97]—occupied himself more and more with the question of martyrdom in the imitation of Christ. An impressive example of Kierkegaard's struggle with this question and its consequences, not least for himself personally, is found in journal entry NB24:103, from early August 1851:

> My most profound doubt, which has now been removed. Oh, when I have heard these millions upon millions speak of the leniency of Xnty: to me it was inconceivable.
>
> This is how it has been with me. Deep down (however much I have in fact been humbled before my Lord and Savior) I have believed that I would have come out of it better if only I had to deal solely with God the Father—that it was precisely "the Mediator" who makes the situation so difficult. For if I have only to deal with God the Father, then no "imitation" [*Efterfølgelse*] is required. And so the situation was like this: If I, a sufferer and as wretched as the most wretched, turn to Xt—and he helps me: What then? Then he says: But then you must imitate me [*følge mig efter*], die away, suffer for the teaching, be hated by all peop[le]—in short,

---

[93] According to Gerdes in his introduction to *Søren Kierkegaard. Der Liebe Tun* (Düsseldorf and Cologne: Diederichs, 1966) (vol. 14 in *Søren Kierkegaard. Gesammelte Werke*, vols. 1–27, trans. and ed. by Emanuel Hirsch, Hayo Gerdes and Hans Martin Junghans (Düsseldorf and Cologne: Diederichs, 1950–69)), ix–xii, x.

[94] *SKS* 16, 252 / *JFY*, 207.

[95] *SKS* 7, 508 / *CUP1*, 559.

[96] *SKS* 7, 513 / *CUP1*, 564.

[97] *SKS* 21, 279, NB10:42 / *KJN* 5, 289.

> agony on a scale such as has never been suffered by any hum. being other than a Xn. But good Lord, to be helped in that way!
>
> Now I understand that imitation is not in fact to be brought to bear in that way, that it is there to keep order, to teach humility and the need for grace, to put a stop to doubt.
>
> Then there is reassurance and blessedness—and then it would not be impossible that a hum. being could be so moved at all this love and feel himself so blessed that for him dying away would become love's joy.
>
> If that moment does not come for a hum. being: well, then there is grace, and as Luther says so excellently, "imitation" must hurl him neither into despair nor into presumptuousness. If the moment does come, then despite all its pain, imitation is a matter of love, and thus is indeed blessed.[98]

Kierkegaard's effort to show state-bourgeois Christendom its gnawing distance from the Christianity of imitating Christ—an endeavor expressed in ever more drastic terms—could not fail to exert an influence on his understanding of faith. In his final years of life, in which Kierkegaard preached "virtually the denial of life,"[99] the inseparable unity of faith and suffering came to the fore in such a way that, in the ninth issue of his journal *The Moment* (1855), which appeared shortly before his death, he regarded "one's willingness to suffer for one's faith"[100] as the only proof of one's faith.

If one does not wish to assume that this breakthrough of religious inwardness *into the outer world*, in the readiness to imitate Christ, that emerges in the period following the *Postscript* is not based *purely* on Kierkegaard's working out the intrinsic consequences of his thinking, then one must ask what else could have given Kierkegaard occasion for this breakthrough—and for his concomitant reevaluation of reality as a reference-point for faith.

IV. FACTORS AND CIRCUMSTANCES

If I understand the matter correctly, then temporal coincidence alone indicates two external and two internal factors that may help explain this change. Let us start with the two external factors: Kierkegaard's increasingly tense financial situation; and the *Corsair* affair.

---

[98] *SKS* 24, 383f., NB24:103 / *KJN* 8, 388f.

[99] Walter Ruttenbeck, *Sören Kierkegaard. Der christliche Denker und sein Werk* (Berlin and Frankfurt/Oder: Trowitzsch & Sohn, 1929) (*Neue Studien zur Geschiche der Theologie und der Kirche*, vol. 25), 256 (emphasis removed).

[100] *SKS* 13, 386 / *M*, 324.

The first mention of Kierkegaard's critical economic situation[101] can be found in journal entry NB:2 from the spring of 1846, which was inscribed on a loose sheet that was glued into the *Journal NB* on the verso side of the flyleaf: "It was only after the publication of the last big book, *Concluding Postscript*, that I dared give myself the time to look around and concern myself with my ext[e]rn[a]l existence. My finances no longer permit me to be an author."[102] During the same time, Kierkegaard had the idea of giving up his writing career in order "to become a country priest"[103]—but soon qualified this plan, and finally shelved it at the end of January 1847. Subsequently, Kierkegaard's financial situation worsened to such a degree that in late 1847, he had to sell his parents' home at Nytorv in Copenhagen. This financial insecurity and the question it prompted, as to whether and how his activity as a writer could continue, had profound implications for Kierkegaard's self-image as an author: "I needed economic independence [earlier], but those fortunate circumstances concealed from me, perhaps, the truth: that I am essen.[tially] a poet. Now I've understood it. Now patience."[104]

A second external factor, however, should be regarded as much more important in explaining the shift in Kierkegaard's late work from a world-facing to a world-shunning position, namely, the conflict he himself initiated with the political-satirical weekly *The Corsair*. At the end of Kierkegaard's newspaper article "The Activity of a Traveling Esthetician and How He Still Happened to Pay for the Dinner,"[105] which was published under the pseudonym Frater Taciturnus on December 27, 1845, Kierkegaard requested that he himself soon appear in *The Corsair*, as it was "really hard for a poor author to be so singled out in Danish literature that he … is the only one who is not abused there."[106] Soon thereafter, and mainly during the first half of 1846, *The Corsair* published a number of satirical articles and cartoons about Kierkegaard. From a current-day perspective, *The Corsair*'s treatments seem not truly witty, but also not malicious, but rather inane (among other things, Kierkegaard was depicted in a ridiculous outfit with trousers of different lengths, much too big boots, and an isabelline flower

---

[101] See Frithiof Brandt and Else Thorkelin, *Søren Kierkegaard og pengene*, 2nd ed. (Copenhagen: Spektrum, 1993 [1935]), 86–90.

[102] *SKS* 20, 10, NB:2 / *KJN* 4, 6.

[103] *SKS* 20, 52, NB:57 / *KJN* 4, 50.

[104] *SKS* 21, 359, NB10:192 / *KJN* 6, 371.

[105] See *SKS* 14, 79–84 / *COR*, 38–46.

[106] *SKS* 14, 84 / *COR*, 46.

with two unequal stems presented as "Beauty of Kierkegaard"[107]). For Kierkegaard himself, however, the ridicule with which his contemporaries treated him came to be increasingly unbearable.

This feud with *The Corsair*, which Kierkegaard carried on almost exclusively within the privacy of his journals and notebooks,[108] left him with a deep aversion to "the daily press"[109] as "the evil principle in the modern world,"[110] as well as to the mob behavior[111] of "the crowd,"[112] as his journals from that period eloquently attest. Added to this was the weariness he felt at being a misunderstood genius "in a country as small as Denmark;"[113] even worse, at having to eke out a marginal existence as a "half-crazy oddball"[114] in such a "provincial town"[115] as Copenhagen. In the course of this debate, Kierkegaard withdrew more and more from the public into his existence as a "single individual," and so into a position opposed to society as an expression of the universal. This problematic and conflict-laden relationship with his contemporaries, including his church superiors, also left a lasting mark on Kierkegaard's further intellectual development, and did not fail to influence his account of the relationship between Christianity and the world in general[116] and that of faith and reality in particular.

Aggravating these two external factors was the fact that, during the period following 1846, Kierkegaard either rediscovered afresh, or discovered for the first time, a number of other thinkers, such as Abraham a Sancta Clara (1644–1709)[117] and Arthur Schopenhauer (1788–1860),[118] respective-

---

[107] "Catalog over et rigt og betydeligt Udvalg af de nyeste og smukkeste Pragt-Georginer, (Dadalisser) disponible i Aaret 1846, bestemte til at udstilles Tid efter anden i 'Corsarens' Blomsterhave," *Corsaren*, 1846, no. 289 (April 3), column 13.

[108] For Kierkegaard's reasons, see *SKS* 20, 154, NB2:34 / *KJN* 4, 152.

[109] See *SKS* 20, 128, NB:215 / *KJN* 4, 127 et passim.

[110] *SKS* 20, 152, NB2:29 / *KJN* 4, 150.

[111] See *SKS* 20, 16, NB:7 / *KJN* 4, 12 et passim.

[112] *SKS* 20, 128, NB:215 / *KJN* 4, 126 et passim.

[113] *SKS* 20, 17, NB:7 / *KJN* 4, 14.

[114] *SKS* 20, 401, NB5:69 / *KJN* 4, 402.

[115] See, e.g., *SKS* 20, 117, NB:194 / *KJN* 4, 117.

[116] See *SKS* 22, 221, NB12:131 / *KJN* 6, 222.

[117] See Peter Šajda, "Abraham a Sancta Clara: An Aphoristic Encyclopedia of Christian Wisdom," in *Kierkegaard and the Renaissance and Modern Traditions*, Tome II, *Theology*, ed. by Jon Stewart (Farnham and Burlington: Ashgate, 2009) (*Kierkegaard Research: Sources, Reception and Resources*, vol. 5), 1–20.

[118] See Niels Jørgen Cappelørn, "Historical Introduction: When and Why Did Kierkegaard Begin Reading Schopenhauer," in *Schopenhauer-Kierkegaard. Von der Metaphysik des Willens zur Philosophie der Existenz*, ed. by Niels Jørgen Cappelørn, Lore Hühn, Søren K. Fauth,

ly—and was also occupied intensely with works of Christian edification, as well as with Martin Luther (1483–1546). These interests should be regarded as *internal* factors for the shift described above.

Much as Pietism (chiefly in the form of the Moravian Brethren in Copenhagen) bore an importance for the Kierkegaard family that is scarcely to be underestimated,[119] for Kierkegaard himself, as Christopher Barnett has shown,[120] the study of the edifying literature of late medieval mysticism and its Pietistic recipients gave him a powerful impetus to reconsider anew the relation between Christianity and secular society.[121] According to Barnett,[122] this is already evident in the contrast between Kierkegaard's critique of the monastic movement in the *Postscript* and his critique of the "present age" in the third section of *A Literary Review* (1846): "Whereas the *Postscript* argues that authentic religious existence is primarily a matter of 'hidden inwardness' …*A Literary Review* shows Kierkegaard reworking this conclusion in light of the ills of modern secularity."[123] To Barnett, the view expressed in *A Literary Review* that the present age needs no religiosity of "hidden inwardness," but rather "a religiousness of suffering servanthood,"[124] is a crucial precursor to the reception of the thought of *imitatio Christi* in Kierkegaard's late work. The latter represents not merely the "key aspect"[125] of Christian edification literature, but also Kierkegaard's "most significant debt to the Pietist tradition."[126]

However, it should be noted that in his published writings, it is not until *Upbuilding Discourses in Various Spirits* (1847) that Kierkegaard speaks of Christ as the "paradigm," or of "the imitation of Christ" (and its theological consequences); and apart from a few earlier passages,[127] it is not until 1849 that both motifs regularly recur in his journals and notebooks. If it is true

and Philipp Schwab (Berlin and Boston: De Gruyter, 2012) (*Kierkegaard Studies Monograph Series*, vol. 26), 19–32.

[119] See Bruce H. Kirmmse, *Kierkegaard in Golden Age Denmark* (Bloomington und Indianapolis: Indiana University Press, 1990), 28–35.

[120] Christopher B. Barnett, *Kierkegaard, Pietism and Holiness* (Farnham and Burlington: Ashgate, 2011); see my review in *Theologische Literaturzeitung*, vol. 137, 2012, columns 451f.

[121] See Barnett, *Kierkegaard, Pietism and Holiness*, 111–168.

[122] See *SKS* 8, 66–73 / *TA*, 68–76.

[123] Barnett, *Kierkegaard, Pietism and Holiness*, 141.

[124] Ibid.

[125] Ibid., 171.

[126] Ibid., 68.

[127] For what may be the earliest such reference, see the marginal note *SKS* 20, 227, NB2:227a / *KJN* 4, 227 (1847).

that—as Barnett concludes on the basis of vanishingly few documents, compared to what is available from after 1847—Kierkegaard was "obviously intimate with the *Erbauungsliteratur* tradition"[128] from his *youth*, why, then, do we first find his reception of the thought of *imitatio Christi* only during this later period? On the other hand, if, as Kierkegaard's journals and notebooks indicate, an intensified devotion to the Christian edification literature did not really begin until *after* 1846, then it may be considered probable that it is Kierkegaard's experiences with the *Corsair* that serve as background not only to this later occupation with the edification literature, but also to his reception of the thought of *imitatio Christi* in his literary works focusing on the requirement of Christianity. In the words of Hermann Deuser:

> That he, as a single individual, attracted vicarious mockery and scorn, and the crowd enjoyed what the good citizens and the clergy simultaneously took the dark pleasure of *Schadenfreude* in—a theme found irrevocably, in infinite variations, throughout the entire corpus of diary entries produced with his late works!—this increasingly assumes Christological significance, forcing him to draw the conclusion: "But there is one thing I have learned: the authentic Christian collision. This collision was not originally part of my stock and it is only thanks to the conflict with the masses that I have it. My collision is the genuinely Christian one: I am persecuted—because of having been well-intentioned."[129]

The *Corsair* affair led Kierkegaard to the conclusion that a true Christian does not blend in invisibly, in "hidden inwardness," into the reality of the established order, nor does he distinguish himself from the established order merely externally; but rather, "*contrary* to the nature of the established order, [he] gives ethical expression to the *antithesis* of Christian and world in [his] perceptible form of life."[130] Once his earlier basic conviction that "hidden inwardness" was the place of true faith foundered, it became clear to Kierkegaard "that true faith, purely as such, is in collision with the established order and with the imitation of the Lord."[131] In the writings, journal

---

[128] Barnett, *Kierkegaard, Pietism and Holiness*, 78 (note 99).

[129] Hermann Deuser, "Kierkegaards Spätwerk als dialektische Theologie," in his *Was ist Wahrheit anderes als ein Leben für eine Idee?* (see note 86 above), 3–24, 11f. The Kierkegaard quotation originates from *SKS* 21, 346, NB10:177 / *KJN* 4, 358.

[130] Emanuel Hirsch, *Geschichte der neuern evangelischen Theologie im Zusammenhang mit den allgemeinen Bewegungen des europäischen Denkens*, vols. 1–5 (Gütersloh: Mohn, 1949–54); vol. 5, 441 (emphases mine).

[131] According to Gerdes in his introduction to *Søren Kierkegaard. Das Buch über Adler* (Düsseldorf and Cologne: Diederichs, 1962) (vol. 26 of *Søren Kierkegaard. Gesammelte Werke,*

entries, and notes of his late period, Kierkegaard is anxiously preoccupied with "the ideal of the martyrdom of Christian imitation"[132]—without, however, "arguing for an undialectical [form of] martyrdom,"[133] despite certain appearances; for "even if Kierkegaard claims ever so strongly that the inward mind cannot shy away from outward suffering, and even if he makes such suffering the very condition of true inwardness, he is nonetheless still bringing the self-sacrifice of martyrdom *into* his theory of inwardness."[134]

V. THE SIGNIFICANCE OF LUTHER

It must therefore be regarded as probable that Kierkegaard's engagement with Christian edification literature was motivated by his painful experiences with the *Corsair*, and that this led to his reception of the idea of *imitatio Christi* in his later works. However, another internal factor must also be taken into account, one that did not remain without influence on Kierkegaard's "Proclamation of the strict imitation Christianity,"[135] and which, interestingly enough, *accompanied* his reading of the edification literature: namely, Kierkegaard's intensive study of Luther.[136]

Kierkegaard drew his knowledge of Luther "essentially"[137] from Luther's sermons, as translated into Danish by Jørgen Overgaard Thisted (1795–1855) in his edition of Luther's church and house postils,[138] though it

---

vols. 1–27, trans. and ed. by Emanuel Hirsch, Hayo Gerdes and Hans Martin Junghans [Düsseldorf and Cologne: Diederichs, 1950–69]), ix–xxiv, xix.

[132] Deuser, "Kierkegaards Spätwerk als dialektische Theologie," 11.

[133] Friedrich Hauschildt, *Die Ethik Søren Kierkegaards* (Gütersloh: Mohn, 1982) (*Studien zur evangelischen Ethik*, vol. 15), 215.

[134] Ibid.

[135] Hermann Deuser, "*Die Taten der Liebe*: Kierkegaards *wirkliche* Ethik," in his *Was ist Wahrheit anderes als ein Leben für eine Idee?* (see note 86 above), 106–126, 119.

[136] See Gerhard Schreiber, "Sieg über die Welt? Glaube und Wirklichkeit bei Kierkegaard und die Bedeutung Luthers für sein Verständnis der *imitatio Christi*," in *Christliche Existenz heute. Zur Gegenwartsbedeutung der Theologie Søren Kierkegaards*, ed. by Christine Axt-Piscalar und Mareile Lasogga (Leipzig: Evangelische Verlagsanstalt, 2015), 119–183.

[137] According to Gerdes in *Søren Kierkegaard. Die Tagebücher* (see note 64 above), vol. 2, 262 (note 186). On this see Hermann Diem, *Die Existenzdialektik von Sören Kierkegaard* (Zollikon-Zürich: Evangelischer Verlag, 1950), 156.

[138] Martin Luther, *En christelig Postille, sammendragen af Dr. Morten Luthers Kirke– og Huuspostiller*, trans. by Jørgen Thisted, vols. 1–2 (Christiania: Selskabets Forlag, 1828). Thisted's translation is based on the selection edited by Benjamin Lindner, *Kraft- und Saftvoller Kern der evangelischen Wahrheiten aus der Kirchen- und denen beyden Haus-Postillen des seligen Herrn D. Martini Lutheri sorgfältig heraus gesuchet, Mit nöthigen und nützlichen Registern*

was not until the spring of 1848 that Kierkegaard read the sermons regularly, and indeed "in regular rotation,"[139] for his own edification. When considering the influence of Luther on Kierkegaard's reception of the idea of *imitatio Christi*, what is of more importance than Luther's *sermons* themselves is his "Preface" to the Church Postil of 1522,[140] with which Thisted begins his edition—the text in which Luther first expressly distinguishes between Christ as *gift* and as *example*. In his journals during the period from March 1849 to January 1852 alone, Kierkegaard refers a full eight times to this preface.[141] And in the course of analyzing the distinction drawn there, Kierkegaard arrives not only at a deeper understanding of the idea of *imitatio Christi*, but also at a clarification of his own position.

While his initial reaction to Luther's preface was critical and hostile,[142] Kierkegaard would soon qualify his criticism, and focus more on the context of Luther's position as a polemic against "the error of the Middle Ages, meritoriousness."[143] He writes,

> What Luther says in the preface to the *Postil* about the difference betw.[een] Christ as example and as gift is quite correct. I am also well aware that I have tended in the direction of Christ as example. But in this connection something must be borne in mind. Luther was confronted by the exaggerated misuse of Christ as example, and he therefore emphasizes the opposite. But nowadays Luther has long since triumphed in Protestantism and has caused Christ to be entirely forgotten as an exemplar, and the whole business has r[ea]lly become a pretense about hidden inwardness. Furthermore, I have also been of the opinion that as example Christ must be used in a different manner than that act[ua]lly contemplated by Luther or the Middle Ages. As example Christ must in fact jack up the price so frightfully that the prototype is the very thing that teaches hum.[an] beings to take refuge in grace. The error of the Middle Ages consisted in imagining that it was possible to resemble Christ.

---

versehen, vols. 1–3, 2nd edition (S[a]alfeld and Leipzig: Zu Commision bey Joh. Michael Teubner, 1754).

139 *SKS* 20, 349, NB4:126 / *KJN* 4, 349.

140 See "Dr. Morten Luther's Fortale," in *En christelig Postille*, vol. 1, XII–XIV (" 11–14" according to the table of contents).

141 See *SKS* 21, 296f., NB10:76 / *KJN* 5, 307; *SKS* 21, 337, NB10:165 / *KJN* 5, 165; *SKS* 22, 241, NB12:162 / *KJN* 6, 243; *SKS* 22, 366–368, NB14:41 / *KJN* 6, 371f.; *SKS* 23, 26, NB15:32 / *KJN* 7, 23; *SKS* 23, 469f., NB20:148 / *KJN* 7, 477f.; *SKS* 24, 82, NB21:132 / *KJN* 8, 78f.; *SKS* 24, 460, NB25:35 / *KJN* 8, 466.

142 See *SKS* 21, 296f., NB10:76 / *KJN* 5, 307.

143 *SKS* 13, 46 / *FSE*, 17.

> Then came sanctification by works and the like. Then, just so, Luther came and emphasized Christ as gift, making the same distinction betw.[een] Christ as gift and as example as that between faith and works. But I wonder if Luther could have dreamed of the pretense about hidden inwardness that this has engendered. And further, I wonder whether Luther, when he married, could have dreamed that this would finally be carried so far that a priest would come to believe more or less that if only he got married, he would have done everything that God required of him. I can very well see how someone could mount an attack on me precisely from Luther's standpoint; but truly, I too have understood Luther quite well—and I have also been careful not to blunder about in the fog, as if everything were still as it was in Luther's day.[144]

Kierkegaard finds in Luther a necessary "corrective,"[145] albeit one that was subsequently "made into the normative" until it produced the opposite of its original purpose: "the most refined child of secularism and paganism."[146] Inasmuch as, in contemporary Christendom, one has failed to think the thought of discipleship and has taken grace in vain, one "has removed the dialectical element from Luther's doctrine of faith" and forgotten completely that "Luther emphasized faith in order to counter a fantastically exaggerated asceticism."[147] Such decay must be counteracted: "It is of course quite clear that it is Christ as example that must now be brought forward dialectically, precisely because the dialectical (Christ as gift) that Luther brought forward has been taken utterly in vain, so that 'the imitator' resembles the example in no way whatever but is absolutely heterogeneous and then simply slips in grace."[148]

Consequently, Kierkegaard understood his own position as a necessary modification of the Lutheran position: "but if Luther's definition [i.e., Christ as gift] is to come again, it must be modified."[149]

In journal entry NB25:35, from January 1852, Kierkegaard sketches what this modification of the Lutheran position may look like: "Luther rightly puts it as follows: Xt is a gift—to which faith corresponds. Furthermore, he is the Exemplar [*Forbilledet*]—to which imitation corresponds. But with greater accuracy it might be said: 1) imitation, tending toward decisive

---

[144] *SKS* 22, 241, NB12:162 / *KJN* 6, 243 (translation slightly modified).
[145] *SKS* 25, 279, NB28:82 / *KJN* 9, 281.
[146] Ibid.
[147] *SKS* 21, 323, NB10:132 / *KJN* 5, 334 (translation slightly modified).
[148] *SKS* 23, 26, NB15:32 / *KJN* 7, 23 (translation slightly modified).
[149] *SKS* 24, 82, NB21:132 / *KJN* 8, 78.

action, through which the situation for becoming a Xn comes into existence; 2) Xt as gift—faith; 3) imitation as the fruit of faith."[150] It is thus a matter of, in the first place, coming "into the situation in which I can become a Xn"[151]—a situation of existential exertion that Kierkegaard elsewhere identifies with the "anguished conscience."[152] The person who has "involuntarily" become unhappy thus has "less difficulty" becoming Christian than the happy person does. "But—as one might act[ua]lly pose the hum [an] objection to Xnty—if I am among the fortunate, am I permitted voluntarily to make myself unhappy like this so that I might get a proper taste for Xnty? This is the question of the voluntary, of the imitation of Xt [*Christi Efterfølgelse*]."[153] Nevertheless, Kierkegaard did not draw the consequences for himself that he found necessary in his argument with Luther: "Kierkegaard never wanted to take responsibility himself for the full imitation [of Christ]."[154] Rather, Kierkegaard remained a mere "'corrective' to the established order of Christendom"[155] until his early death.

The factors outlined above are to be regarded as decisive in motivating the demand for an imitation Christianity that is set forth in Kierkegaard's late authorship. Here we encounter the ultimate fruition of the negative determination of the relation of faith to reality that was already present *in nuce* in the transition from Kierkegaard's early works to his late works. For Kierkegaard's revaluation of reality as a reference object for belief went hand in hand with his revaluation of his own lived reality. Given this theological processing of his own life story, it must have now seemed paradoxical to the late Kierkegaard—who no longer had any expectation of coming to terms with (t)his world—to regard faith as the basis for man's positive freedom in relation to the given reality, as he had still done in his student days let alone to find "the true reconciliation"[156] with it in the religious sphere. For the late Kierkegaard, any such "victory over the world"[157] achieved in faith by virtue of an inner movement of "resignation" toward reality would ultimately

[150] *SKS* 24, 459, NB25:35 / *KJN* 8, 466.

[151] Ibid.

[152] See *SKS* 20, 69, NB:79 / *KJN* 4, 68 et passim.

[153] *SKS* 24, 459, NB25:35 / *KJN* 8, 466.

[154] Deuser, "Kierkegaards Spätwerk als dialektische Theologie," 12.

[155] Hermann Diem, *Theologie als kirchliche Wissenschaft. Handreichung zur Einübung ihrer Probleme*, vol. 2, *Dogmatik. Ihr Weg zwischen Historismus und Existentialismus* (Munich: Chr. Kaiser, 1955), 23.

[156] *SKS* 1, 330 / *CI*, 297.

[157] *SKS* 1, 349 / *CI*, 319.

prove—if this *a priori* certainty in faith has no *outward* consequences, and does not lead to the ultimate consequence in the imitation of Christ—to be a Pyrrhic victory.

Kierkegaard on the Trinity: The Challenge and Solace of Triune Pathos

Lee C. Barrett

References to Kierkegaard's writings do not usually appear in contemporary theological discussions of the doctrine of the Trinity. The absence of Kierkegaard's voice in the current lively trinitarian conversation is perfectly understandable. After all, Kierkegaard did not write a monograph to deal with this doctrine in the way that *The Concept of Anxiety* sheds light on the concept of sin, and *Works of Love* probes the love commandment. Furthermore, the Trinity is not the explicit theme of any of his overtly Christian discourses. In none of his writings, published or unpublished, is the word "Trinity" common. Accordingly, most commentators, including those who read Kierkegaard as an author with deep-rooted theological interests and purposes, seldom pay much heed to trinitarian motifs in his authorship.

Nevertheless, trinitarian motifs do pervade Kierkegaard's writings. His engagement with Christianity was significantly informed by the doctrine, and much of his authorship was implicitly an effort to show what faith in God as Creator, Redeemer, and Consummator involves. In fact, his use of trinitarian discourse pointed to a novel way to render language about this seemingly abstruse and possibly irrelevant mystery more meaningful. Kierkegaard did so by pursuing a strategy he employed in his treatment of all theological topics. Throughout his literature he sought to clarify the meanings of doctrines by exhibiting the forms of pathos appropriate to them rather than by discursively defining or describing them. Consequently, Kierkegaard's presentation of trinitarian themes is often indirect and even somewhat covert. Because his theological discourse always seeks to elicit the particular passions and dispositions that must accompany a specific Christian concept, his trinitarian convictions are communicated through his efforts to encourage three forms of Christian pathos.

I. THE DOCTRINE OF THE TRINITY IN KIERKEGAARD'S HISTORICAL CONTEXT

In order to appreciate the significance of Kierkegaard's approach to the concept of the Trinity, we must first situate his writings in the context of the theological culture of eighteenth- and nineteenth-century northern Europe. That milieu conditioned the way in which he engaged the doctrine. His intellectual and religious environment accounts for his polemic against older scholastic and newer speculative understandings of the Trinity, as well as his unique and critical appropriation of the theological turn to subjectivity that characterized many of his contemporaries. Ironically, the speculative approach that he so vehemently railed against also helps account for the prominence of the theme of reconciling love in his discussions of God.

The doctrine of the Trinity had not been a central topic in orthodox Protestant circles in the eighteenth century, except when it seemed necessary to defend it against the critiques of skeptics and free-thinkers. Of course, coteries of confessionalists continued to proclaim the doctrine, but they usually just repeated traditional creedal language without much explication, or modified it slightly with the help of Leibniz.[1] Several different intellectual movements contributed to this benign negligence and outright hostility to the doctrine of the Trinity. Each one would have an impact, positive or negative, upon Kierkegaard.

One trajectory that promoted an overtly critical attitude toward the Trinity emerged from the many forms of Enlightenment Rationalism. For most English Deists and German Neologians, the Trinity was a relic of "positive" religion based exclusively on the claims of a dubious revelation. The lack of corroborating logical arguments or empirical evidence rendered its claim to truth very questionable. Besides doubting the doctrine's epistemic basis, Deists also often denounced the doctrine as a prime example of ecclesial mystification. Not only was it not grounded in the dictates of reason, but, even worse, it seemed to contradict fundamental rational principles, for an entity cannot simultaneously be one and also be three. According to the Deists, past attempts to justify and explicate the doctrine had quickly dissolved into unintelligibility; the church's efforts to explain the Trinity and make it sound reasonable were mere exercises in sophistry in-

---

[1] See Ulrich Lehner, "The Trinity in the Early Modern Era," in *The Oxford Handbook of the Trinity*, ed. by Giles Emery, O. P., and Matthew Levering (Oxford: Oxford University Press, 2011), 240–53.

tended to prop up ecclesial power.[2] In many ways, the work of Immanuel Kant was a culmination of this type of critique, for his restrictions on the legitimate range of pure reason prohibited speculation about all transcendent matters, including God *in se*. Moreover, many of the moralistic proponents of the Enlightenment had frequently claimed that the doctrine plays no useful role in the living of the religious life; it serves no practical purpose. Giving voice to this sentiment, Kant dismissed the doctrine as unnecessary for the pursuit of moral rectitude. Far from being comprehensible in terms of pure reason, it could not even be defended as a postulate of practical reason.

Another critical impulse concerning the Trinity emerged from a very different source—Pietism. Although most Pietists nominally affirmed the Trinity, they focused their theological attention more intensively on doctrines that could be extrapolated directly from the experiences of sin and redemption. At most they contented themselves with alluding to the experience of the trinitarian mystery. By this they usually meant the three ways of experiencing God as Creator, Redeemer, and Sanctifier, the activities historically associated with the "economic" Trinity, the view which interpreted the Trinity in terms of God's three-fold actions toward the created order. This more experiential approach to the Trinity was exemplified by Count Zinzindorf, whose legacy informed the Moravian community in Copenhagen that influenced the young Kierkegaard.[3]

The principle of *sola scriptura* and the consequent biblicism unleashed by Luther's Reformation also eroded confidence in the traditional doctrine, in spite of the conservatively orthodox intentions of the Lutheran and Reformed theologians of the sixteenth and seventeenth centuries. Because of the valorization of the primacy of Scripture, inherited doctrines had to be evaluated in terms of their fidelity to the biblical texts. This generated a problem, for apart from a confessional hermeneutic, it was not clear that the Bible did actually teach the Nicene doctrine. Consequently, theological parties like the Socinians could plausibly claim that the Trinity lacked Scriptural support. In the eighteenth century the emergence of even more daring forms of historical criticism of the sacred texts further undermined confidence in Trinitarian doctrine, as was glaringly evident in the writings of H. S. Reimarus.

---

[2] See for example Anthony Collins, *Priestcraft in Perfection* (London: B. Bragg, 1710).

[3] See Peter Zimmerling, *Gott in Gemeinschaft. Zinzindorfs Trinitätslehre* (Hildesheim: Olms, 2002).

The influence of all of these trajectories that discouraged interest in the Trinity continued to be felt by Kierkegaard's generation. For example, the mildly rationalistic Karl Bretschneider, whose textbook on doctrine Kierkegaard often consulted, did not ascribe enduring authority to the traditional trinitarian language.[4] The influential German biblical scholar and theologian Wilhelm Martin Leberecht de Wette, whose biblical expositions Kierkegaard studied, continued the mildly rationalistic critique of the traditional doctrine of the Trinity.[5] He cautioned that all the speculation about the divine nature of Christ in the Formula of Concord, a major Lutheran confessional document, is not biblically supported. Moreover, he warned that inquiries into the inner workings of the Godhead generate nothing but vacuous concepts and irrational propositions. Theologians influenced by Schleiermacher's revised and chastened Pietism, like Henrik Nicolai Clausen, persisted in downplaying the doctrine.[6] Even more dramatically, the Biblical investigations of scholars like David Friedrich Strauss undermined confidence in the pre-existent Logos as a component of the self-understanding of the historical Jesus.[7]

In spite of these continuing trends that discouraged attention to the Trinity, by the first decade of the nineteenth century new theological sensibilities were becoming evident. As a result, the doctrine of the Trinity attracted much more attention and became a more widely discussed issue in Kierkegaard's Copenhagen. Among the educated classes of Denmark's Golden Age, well-publicized and sometimes vitriolic controversies put the Trinity back into the limelight.[8] In these debates a few different trajectories became important features of the context of Kierkegaard's work.

One trajectory was indebted to speculative Idealism, particularly to the thought of G. W. F. Hegel. The prominence of trinitarian language in He-

---

[4] Karl Bretschneider, *Handbuch der Dogmatik der evangelisch-lutherischen Kirke*, vols. 1–2, 3rd edition (Leipzig: Johann Ambrosius Barth, 1828).

[5] Wilhelm Martin Leberecht de Wette, *Dogmatik der protestantischen Kirche*, vols. 1–2 (Berlin: Reimer, 1840).

[6] Henrik Nicolai Clausen, *Catholicismens og Protestantismens Kirkeforfatning* (Copenhagen: Andreas Seidelin, 1825).

[7] David Friedrich Strauss, *The Life of Jesus Critically Examined*, trans. by George Eliot (Ramsey: Sigler, 1994).

[8] See Jon Stewart, *A History of Hegelianism in Golden Age Denmark, Tome II: The Martensen Period: 1837–1842* (Copenhagen: C. A. Reitzel, 2007), 71, 81, 110, 223–5, 294, 331–2, 385, 390–1, 651–2. Jon Stewart, *Kierkegaard's Relations to Hegel Reconsidered* (New York: Cambridge University Press, 2003), 351, 475, 483, 636.

gel's work was unmistakable.[9] Hegel famously argued that a triadic movement informs the "Spirit" that animates all reality and all thought. This movement begins with undifferentiated identity, proceeds through differentiation and alienation, and culminates in the synthesis of identity and difference, actualized in the concrete individual. According to Hegel this triadic dynamic is the implicit meaning of the doctrine of the Trinity, for it is the articulation in a proper conceptual form of the more pictorial language of Father, Son, and Holy Spirit. In his view the Trinitarian persons correspond to the basic moments of the evolution of Spirit. Hegel associated the Father with the undifferentiated (and not actualized) origin, and the Son with the self-othering of this source in creation. Because creation is typified by individuated finite existence, it necessarily involves the pain of separation and alienation. The traditional language about the Holy Spirit then points to the reconciliation of the universal and the particular in human self-consciousness.

The fidelity of Hegel's reconceptualization of trinitarian language to the traditional doctrine became a controversial issue. In Hegel's writings the exact relation of this immanent triadic historical movement to a transcendent source was notoriously elusive.[10] According to some of his disciples, Hegel was suggesting that this dynamic is rooted in God's inner being, logically prior to and apart from its enactment in the world. If so, then Hegel might have been proposing that his functional equivalent of an "immanent" Trinity, God's life *in se*, is the source of the trinitarian economy evident in human history. But even if this was his meaning, Hegel could still be suspected of heterodoxy, for he seemed to be claiming that God was not fully real in abstraction, apart from the historical evolution of Spirit. For Hegel, many suspected, God becomes actual only through the drama of creation and redemption; put in traditional language, the immanent Trinity requires the economic Trinity in order to become fully real. Accordingly, traditional teachings about God's eternal perfection, self-sufficiency, and aseity must be jettisoned. Moreover, even if Hegel did assume the existence of some sort of immanent Trinity, he was clearly not suggesting that the Trinity is a transcendent fellowship of three in-dwelling persons.

---

[9] See Peter C. Hodgson, *Hegel and Christian Theology: A Reading of the Lectures on the Philosophy of Religion* (Oxford: Oxford University Press, 2005).

[10] Cyril O'Regan, "The Trinity in Kant, Hegel, and Schelling," in *The Oxford Handbook of the Trinity*, ed. by Giles Emery, O. P., and Matthew Levering (Oxford: Oxford University Press, 2011), 254–66.

Awareness of Hegel's speculative interpretation of the doctrine of the Trinity was mediated to Kierkegaard in a variety of ways. In 1837 Johan Ludvig Heiberg, the influential Danish poet, playwright, and philosopher, started a new journal titled *Perseus*, which featured a review of the Danish pastor Valdemar Henrik Rothe's *Doctrine of the Trinity and Reconciliation.*[11] In that review Heiberg lauded Hegel for correctly perceiving that the traditional doctrine of the Trinity should be translated into a metaphysical principle. According to Heiberg, Hegel was entirely correct that the doctrine of the Trinity suggests the fundamental conceptual truth that all thought and reality are the movement of three elements: universality, particularity, and their synthesis in individuality.

Kierkegaard heard similar Hegelian motifs expressed by Philip Marheineke, whose lectures he attended in Berlin in 1841–1842. Kierkegaard also encountered this view of the Trinity in Marheineke's textbook on Christian doctrine, a work that Kierkegaard cites in his journals.[12] Both in the lectures and in the more detailed book Marheineke utilized the doctrine of the Trinity as the structural organizing principle of his theological system. Kierkegaard was well aware of this structure, for he notes that N. Clausen's lectures on theology, which he either heard or transcribed, drew attention to the fact that Marheineke's theological method was trichotomistic.[13]

Kierkegaard's detailed notes on Marheineke's Berlin lectures reveal a basically Hegelian understanding of the Trinitarian dialectic articulated in a way that suggested at least some sort of divine transcendence.[14] According to Marheineke, speculation cannot be content with an economic Trinity, but must grasp the inner relations that characterize the life of God *in se*. The immanent three-in-oneness is due to the fact that God becomes an other to God's own self, through the act of relating to God's self. The Trinity is the dynamic of God's self-knowledge and self-delight. In true Hegelian fashion God's life is the reconciliation of identity (the Father) and difference (the

---

[11] Johan Ludvig Heiberg, "Recension over Hr. Dr. Rothes *Treenigheds – og Forsoningslære*," *Perseus*, no. 1, 1837, 1–89. This work is translated as Johan Ludvig Heiberg, "Review of Dr. Rothe's *Doctrine of the Trinity and Reconciliation*," in *Heiberg's Perseus Other Works*, ed. and trans. by Jon Stewart (Copenhagen: Museum Tusculanum Press, 2011) (*Texts from Golden Age Denmark*, vol. 6), 81–149. See also Jon Stewart, *A History of Hegelianism in Golden Age Denmark, Tome II*, 223–5.

[12] Philipp K. Marheineke, *Lehrbuch des christlichen Glaubens und Lebens für denkende Christen*, 2nd edition (Berlin: Nicolai, 1836).

[13] *SKS* 19, 16 NB1:4 / *KJN* 3, 12.

[14] *SKS* 19, 293–6, Not 10:8 / *KJN* 3, 291–4.

Son), for the Holy Spirit is the synthesis of identity and difference through love. By asserting this Marheineke was elaborating the Augustinian "psychological" model of the Trinity, with the Spirit functioning as the bond of love between God and God's self-objectification. As it was for Hegel, so also for Marheineke the creation and continuing existence of the world is an element in God's self-actualization, for the Son is God's positing of Himself outside of Himself, and the Spirit becomes fully actual as humans come to comprehend this divine dynamic.

In contrast to the Hegelians, Friedrich Schelling provided a seemingly more orthodox speculative understanding of the Trinity. Kierkegaard attended Schelling's much anticipated Berlin lectures delivered from November 1841 to March 1842. Although Kierkegaard's initial enthusiasm waned to the point that he did not stay for the conclusion of the lecture series, he did take notes on Schelling's trinitarian speculations.[15] By the time of this lecture series, later published as *The Philosophy of Revelation*, Schelling was stressing the gratuity of God's actions in a way that the Hegelians did not.[16] He contended that both human history and the cosmos as a whole are the products of an originating free act that transcends both the being of the world and also rationality itself. God is not to be located in the realm of necessity and is not to be identified pantheistically with nature. Therefore, only God's self-revelation can provide epistemic access to this originating act. Schelling insists that speculation should proceed from the concrete self-revelation of God to a general understanding of the world, articulating the implications of revelation in a systematic manner. These methodological convictions led Schelling to begin speculation with the economy of God's free actions, which then grounds his approach to comprehending God *in se*. God is revealed as three potencies: the Ground, the Logos, and the Spirit, which are identified with the three persons of the Trinity. At times Schelling differentiates these three potencies or persons so sharply that his language sounds almost tritheistic. Indebted to Joachim of Fiori, Schelling proceeded to identify the actualization of the divine potencies with the three ages of Christian history: the Petrine (order), the Pauline (freedom), and the Johannine (love).

Another trajectory of reflection about the Trinity was more eclectic. Some speculative theologians borrowed themes from both Hegel and Schel-

---

[15] *SKS* 19, 333–59, Not 11:22–36 / *KJN* 3, 333–58.

[16] Friedrich Schelling, *Philosophie der Offenbarung*, ed. by Manfred Frank (Frankfurt: Suhrkamp Taschenbuch Verlag, 1977).

ling and developed them in seemingly orthodox directions. In Denmark Hans Lassen Martensen did more than anyone to modify Hegel's ruminations about the Trinity and recast them in a more traditional guise. As early as 1833 Martensen was critiquing Schleiermacher's claim that knowledge of God's inner life was impossible and began to speculate about the nature of the Trinity.[17] Martensen was enormously important for Kierkegaard's development, for he served as Kierkegaard's theology tutor and later became the target of many of Kierkegaard's polemics. Kierkegaard heard Martensen's lectures on speculative theology, observed his rise to theological and ecclesiastical prominence, and reacted negatively to his influential tome on Christian doctrine published in 1849.[18]

Although he was deeply indebted to Hegel, throughout his career Martensen sought to articulate a speculative understanding of God's being apart from the world. Martensen feared that Hegel's trinitarian language could be construed as a sophisticated way of pointing to an allegedly necessary and impersonal dialectical movement that animates all of life. In *De Autonomia* of 1837, Martensen appropriated many Hegelian elements, but cautioned that Hegel's problem was his tendency to subordinate religious truth to conceptual speculation.[19] He protested that the Trinity is not just the unity of universality, particularity, and individuality; it is not just the necessary moments in God's life in which difference returns to unity. Paralleling the German theologian Isaac Dorner, Martensen asserted that God is free and self-conscious in the acts of creation and redemption. God does not just exist as the history of the universe or as the unfolding evolution of human self-consciousness. Hegel was wrong to regard negativity as a necessary moment in God's life in which the infinite transitions to the differentiations of finitude. Moreover, for Martensen God is emphatically not a power that only achieves self-consciousness in humans.

Martensen continued to develop the themes of God's transcendence and freedom throughout his career. In his lectures of 1838 Martensen described God as the timeless ground of the drama of the Incarnation in time,

---

[17] Robert Leslie Horn, *Positivity and Dialectic: A Study of the Theological Method of Hans Lassen Martensen* (Copenhagen: C. A. Reitzel, 2007) (*Danish Golden Age Studies*, vol. 2), 44–55.

[18] Hans Lassen Martensen, *Den christelige Dogmatik* (Copenhagen: C. A. Reitzel, 1849).

[19] Hans Lassen Martensen, *De autonomia conscientiæ sui humanæ in theologiam dogmaticum nostri temporis introducta* (Copenhagen: I. D. Quist, 1837). This work appears in English as *The Autonomy of Human Self-Consciousness in Modern Dogmatic Theology* in *Between Hegel and Kierkegaard: Hans L. Martensen's Philosophy of Religion*, translations by Curtis L. Thompson and David J. Kangas (Atlanta: Scholars Press, 1997), 73–147.

an event that actualizes in history God's eternally reconciling love.[20] He reiterated that God is prior to the world as an infinite free self-conscious subject, for the Incarnation shows God to be a personal agent, not an impersonal dialectical movement. The doctrine of the Trinity, therefore, is the foundation of the Christian faith. Creation, redemption, and consummation are the outworkings of God's inner life; the economic Trinity must be seen as the expression of the immanent Trinity. By 1839 in the celebrated essay "Rationalism, Supernaturalism" Martensen was self-consciously and explicitly employing the trans-temporal Trinity as the key to the systematic understanding of everything. [21]

Later, in *Christian Dogmatics*, Martensen further expounded the inner dynamics of the immanent Trinity.[22] The Trinity is prominently positioned at the beginning of the book, and the volume as a whole has a trinitarian structure. Martensen boldly asserted that theology in essence is the activity of making explicit the knowledge of God implicit in God's self-revelation as triune. His trinitarian orientation was a function of his conviction that the Incarnation is the pivotal revelation of God, and that this divine act of self-revelation shows God's very essence to be reconciling love. Martensen emphasized the claim that God is not only capable of loving, but is love-in-itself. The metaphysical perfections of God, like omnipotence and omnipresence, must be understood in the context of the actively loving nature of God, for God exists in Himself as God acts in His manifestation in the Incarnation.

God could not have been revealed in the Incarnation as love if God had not eternally differentiated Himself as an "I" and a "Thou," and then understood Himself as the Spirit of love. Accordingly, Martensen polemicized against what he took to be Schleiermacher's and mysticism's view that God is the changeless and unknowable ground of all things. Against this apophaticism he insisted that the Trinitarian God is living and dynamic. Contrary to Hegel's view, God is not completed through the drama of creation and redemption, for God eternally enjoys blessedness perfectly within

[20] *SKS* 18, 374–86, KK:11 / *KJN* 2, 342–52.

[21] Hans Lassen Martensen, "Rationalisme, Supranaturalisme, og *principium exclusi medii*, in *Tidsskrift for Litteratur og Kritik*, vol. 1, 1839, 456–73. This works appears in English as "Rationalism, Supernaturalism and the *principium exclusi medii*," in *Mynster's "Rationalism, Supernaturalism" and the Debate about Mediation*, ed. and trans. by Jon Stewart (Copenhagen: Museum Tusculanum Press, 2009) (*Texts from Golden Age Denmark*, vol. 5), 127–143.

[22] See Martensen, *Den christelige Dogmatik*.

Himself. For Martensen God's perfect life as love is antecedent to creation; the Trinity is not just the drama of the divine self-actualization in history. Rather, God's economy is grounded in the inner relations of the divine being.[23] To explicate this, Martensen adopts Augustine's metaphor of human self-consciousness, claiming that God differentiates Godself as a subject (an "I") from Godself as an object (a "Thou"), and then affirms Godself as the reconciliation of subject and object in love. This triunity that is constitutive of God's inner life is then manifested outward as a universe of finite creatures with which God can be reunited in love. God's inner dynamic of love is the basis for the projection of that otherness into that which is not God, so that God and God's other can be reunited in love.

Yet another theological trajectory present in Kierkegaard's theological culture remained suspicious of speculation about God's trinitarian life *in se* and continued the trinitarian reservations of Pietism and the Enlightenment. Friedrich Schleiermacher was the most influential of these anti-speculative theologians. Schleiermacher famously relegated the Trinity to an appendix at the end of his classic *Christian Faith*.[24] For Schleiermacher, theology can only be the articulation of the lived experience of redemption. Traditional trinitarian doctrine claims to know too much about God, for it is not directly an exposition of the believer's spiritual dependence upon Jesus Christ. The language about three eternally distinct persons inter-relating to one another in exceedingly complex ways is nothing more than speculation divorced from the experience of faith. Schleiermacher's location of the discussion of the Trinity at the conclusion of his *magnum opus* did not imply that he rejected all trinitarian language.[25] Rather, he was suggesting that the doctrine could only be understood as a second-order codification of the twin experiences of redemption through Jesus Christ and the church's empowerment by the Holy Spirit, coupled with the basal experience of absolute dependence upon God for existence itself. By so saying, Schleiermacher was continuing Pietism's insistence that only the economic Trinity might be a

---

[23] See George Pattison, "Martensen, Speculation, and the Task of Modern Theology," in *Hans Lassen Martensen: Theologian, Philosopher and Social Critic*, ed. by Jon Stewart (Copenhagen: Museum Tusculanum Press, 2012) (*Danish Golden Age Studies*, vol. 6), 23; see also Lee C. Barrett, "Martensen as Systematic Theologian: The Architectonics of Incarnation," in ibid., 73–98.

[24] Friedrich Schleiermacher, *The Christian Faith*, trans. by H. R. Macintosh and J. S. Stewart (Edinburgh: T. & T. Clark, 1999).

[25] Samuel M. Powell, *The Trinity in German Thought* (Cambridge: Cambridge University Press, 2001), 87–103.

useful way of thematizing Christian experience, while the immanent Trinity was a capitulation to empty speculation.

Henrik Nicolai Clausen, a leading professor of theology at the University of Copenhagen under whom Kierkegaard studied, combined Schleiermacher's reservations about the traditional formulation of the doctrine with Kantian objections to its metaphysical pretensions. Kierkegaard's notes from Clausen's lectures from 1839–1840 contain no mention of the Trinity in the sections concerning God's nature.[26] In those lectures Clausen asserted that talk about the preexistence of the Logos is not necessary for understanding Christ's salvific work. Speculation about the Second Person incarnate in Christ only led to "various kinds of ideas that occasioned intense conflicts, and, in time, a series of dogmatic definitions that could not promote real insight into the nature of the mystery and so the character of the mystery was often distorted and new difficulties thereby generated."[27] In a later work from 1853 Clausen preferred to use the language of self-consciousness rather than substance to conceptualize God, but resisted the speculative tendency to posit a triadic dynamic of self-objectification and reconciliation in God's self-knowledge.[28]

A final trajectory in Kierkegaard's academic ethos objected to the apparent doctrinal implications of speculative Idealism in order to argue for a more orthodox view. Frederik Christian Sibbern, a professor of philosophy at the University of Copenhagen, provoked heated debate about the Trinity during Kierkegaard's young adulthood. In 1838 he published a widely discussed critique of Hegel's doctrine of the Trinity interpreted as the dialectical development of universality, particularity, and singularity.[29] Sibbern argued that if the moments of the triadic movement represent the being of God *in se*, the creation of the world, and the reconciliation of the two in the Spirit, then there is no real redemptive work for the Son, for that function is accomplished by the Spirit. Moreover, the Holy Spirit is reduced to nothing more than the evolving and then consummated spirit of humanity, through

---

[26] *SKS* 19, 42, Not 1:7 / *KJN* 3, 36–37.

[27] *SKS* 19, 42, Not 1:7 / *KJN* 3, 37.

[28] Henrik Nikolai Clausen, *Christelig Troeslære* (Copenhagen: C. A. Reitzel, 1853).

[29] Frederik Christian Sibbern, *Bemærkninger og Undersøgelser fornemmlig betreffende Hegels Philosophie* (Copenhagen: Reitzel, 1838). This work appears in English as *Remarks and Investigations Primarily Concerning Hegel's Philosophy* in *Sibbern's Remarks and Investigations Primarily Concerning Hegel's Philosophy*, ed. and trans. by Jon Stewart (Copenhagen: Museum Tusculanum Press, 2018) (*Texts from Golden Age Denmark*, vol. 7), 55–194. See Stewart, *A History of Hegelianism in Golden Age Denmark, Tome II*, 223–5.

which God returns to God's self. In Hegel's pages, Sibbern feared, the Trinity was nothing more than a pictorial way of suggesting that God achieves self-consciousness only through the consciousness of human beings. Consequently, Hegel cannot affirm that any divinity exists beyond human subjectivity, which implied that the divine is actual only as being immanent in the world. Later in Kierkegaard's lifetime, in 1849, the Icelandic theologian Magnús Eiríksson (who later became a free-thinker launched a similar attack against Martensen's view of the Trinity, protesting that he implies that the Father is not a self-conscious, free personal agent without the Son.[30]

II. KIERKEGAARD'S ALTERNATIVE APPROACH TO TRINITARIAN DISCOURSE

Although Kierkegaard was very cognizant of these controversies concerning the Trinity, he did not directly contribute to the speculative and anti-speculative arguments that were advanced to defend or critique the various positions. However, he did sometimes ridicule the speculative impulse in regard to the Trinity. For example, his pseudonym Haufniensis criticized Schelling's effort to comprehend the secret passional dynamics of God's inner life.[31] Haufniensis protests that "the creative birth pangs of the deity" are not a fit subject for human curiosity. In this sense Kierkegaard had something in common with those authors like Clausen who rejected the attempt to engage in metaphysical speculation about the Trinity. To an extent, Kierkegaard was the heir of the Kantian suspicion of metaphysics that had deep roots in the Enlightenment. However, Kierkegaard's resistance to trinitarian speculation did not lead him to discount trinitarian language, as Clausen tended to do.

Kierkegaard's disdain for the speculative approach to the Trinity was intense and was grounded in his basic understanding of the way that Christian language works. Kierkegaard did not believe that the meaning of the doctrine of the Trinity could be articulated in a mood of academic neutrality, as if the Trinity were the conclusion of a syllogism or the resolution of a metaphysical puzzle. For Kierkegaard the wedding of metaphysics and orthodox language is a sterile union that undermines the very mood of self-

---

[30] Magnús Eiríksson, *Speculativ Rettroenhed, fremstillet efter Dr. Martensens 'christelige Dogmatik'* (Copenhagen: J. G. Salomon, 1849). See the useful collection *Magnús Eiríksson: A Forgotten Contemporary of Kierkegaard*, ed. by Gerhard Schreiber and Jon Stewart (Copenhagen: Museum Tusculanum, 2017) (*Danish Golden Age Studies*, vol. 10).

[31] *SKS* 4, 363–4 / *CA*, 59.

involvement that any discussion of God requires. In fact, the mood of cool objectivity typical of the speculative impulse is all wrong. The Trinity is not some sort of curious object that could be described in the way that one might describe a cat or a building. Kierkegaard writes, "The Christian God is not like something one buys in a shop, or like a piece of property."[32] Consequently Kierkegaard does not attempt to clarify the concept "Trinity" by situating it in a metaphysical schema, no matter how sophisticated or how revised to accommodate Christian doctrines that schema might be. Such an impersonal and abstract strategy must be avoided. Instead, Kierkegaard seeks to clarify the passions which are constitutive of the meaningful use of trinitarian discourse. The failure of the metaphysical approach to the Trinity does not imply that trinitarian language is utterly vacuous or pointless. Although the Trinity cannot be described or analyzed directly, the emotions, passions, and dispositions that constitute a life lived in the light of the Trinity can be imaginatively depicted. The Trinity *in se* cannot be conceptually grasped, but the passion-laden activities of being thankful for creation, trusting in redemption, and hoping for fulfillment can be sketched and rendered intelligible. For Kierkegaard, the meaningfulness of trinitarian discourse is dependent upon the ability to imagine the hopes, fears, and loves that accompany its use. The meaning of "the Trinity" can only be elucidated by clarifying the way that the doctrine functions to inform the passions and actions of the faithful individual.

Many of Kierkegaard's treatments of various features of the Christian faith can be read as dramatizations of the three forms of pathos that correlate to each of the trinitarian persons. He implicitly presents the reader with a functional equivalent of an economic view of the Trinity. For example, many of Kierkegaard's edifying and Christian discourses serve as acts of praise for God's activities of creation, redemption, and sanctification, respectively. Ever since Augustine articulated his theory of appropriation, each of these activities has been associated with a particular person of the Trinity. As such, Kierkegaard's authorial enactments of three forms of praise function as clarifications of the three operations of the economic Trinity. This economic trinitarian dynamic is clearly manifested in the structure of the opening prayer of *Works of Love*. The initial clause invokes the "source of all love in heaven and on earth," while the second one addresses "our Savior and Redeemer" who revealed what love is, and the last one praises the "Spirit of

---

[32] *SKS* 10, 96 / *CD*, 88.

love" who must "remind us of that love-sacrifice" and enjoins "the believer to love as he is loved and his neighbor as himself."[33] Together, the source, the redeemer/savior, and the reminding Spirit constitute "Eternal love." An economy of trinitarian action is also explicit in a journal entry in which Kierkegaard writes, "...it is the Father who points to the Son, the Son who points to the Spirit, and only then is it the Spirit who leads to the Son, and the Son who leads to the Father."[34]

III. KIERKEGAARD AND THE PATHOS APPROPRIATE FOR THE FIRST PERSON OF THE TRINITY

Themes classically associated with the First Person of the Trinity fill Kierkegaard's authorship. He often employs traditional language in these contexts, referring to the "Creator of heaven and earth," and to the one who "creates out of nothing."[35] He also generously uses the vocabulary of God as "Father," particularly as the "Almighty Father."[36] Such references are always embedded in passion-laden devotional acts which involve distinctive passions and dispositions. These "First Person of the Trinity" passions and dispositions can be grouped together in a few different categories.

Kierkegaard often uses "Creator" and "Father" language to express absolute dependence upon God for the gracious gift of one's own life, and for the ongoing existence of all things.[37] The Father is the source of every good and perfect gift, from whose hand we should willingly receive all things.[38] In diverse ways, much of his authorship fosters the awareness that we humans are not the creators, sustainers, or masters of our own lives. Kierkegaard frequently intones, "Without God, we could do nothing." Recognition of our own contingency and fragility is a foundational virtue that should be carefully cultivated and cherished. In light of our ontological insecurity, we should nurture the habit of relying upon God for every aspect of our existence. Talk of God as Creator refers to the undefinable object of our reliance. In this vein Kierkegaard exhorts his readers "to be contented with being a human being, with being the humble one, the created being who can no

---

[33] *SKS* 9, 12 / *WL*, 3–4.

[34] *SKS* 25, 142, NB27:23 / *KJN* 9, 141.

[35] *SKS* 10, 138 / *CD*, 127.

[36] *SKS* 5, 45 / *EUD*, 37.

[37] *SKS* 5, 39–56 / *EUD*, 32–48.

[38] *SKS* 22, 100, NB11:169 / *KJN* 6, 96.

more support himself than create himself."[39] An individual must avoid trying "to entrench himself, so to speak, in a little or large area where he will not be the object of God's providence and the supporting care of the heavenly Father."[40] Often when Kierkegaard admonishes his readers to become "nothing before God" (as he does with regularity), he cites instances of abandoning any project to secure one's own earthly security or spiritual felicity through one's own ingenuity and industry.

For Kierkegaard, this dependence upon the Creator entails other closely related virtues and dispositions, all of which should be construed as gifts from God. One is a profound and all-encompassing humility, for we cannot be proud of any of our alleged achievements. The heart of all edification is rapt delight in God's beneficence and is emphatically not the celebration of our own abilities. Focusing on her own alleged prowess actually leaves an individual feeling insecure and disappointed. Kierkegaard lyrically accentuates this point by exclaiming that "to need God is man's highest perfection."[41] Our most profound joy is the recognition of the limitless extent of our need for God. Given his conviction that the pathos of a religious communication must be commensurate with its content, Kierkegaard is careful to exhibit a celebratory mood as he shifts attention away from the individual's paltry ostensible accomplishments in order to encourage a disposition of joyful humility.

Kierkegaard further clarifies what it is to believe in God the Creator by associating the themes of dependence and humility with the motif of gratitude for sheer existence. Kierkegaard urges his readers to "give thanks that it was granted…to us to be human beings."[42] The individual's life and all that sustains it are expressions of the gracious beneficence of God the Creator. An over-arching attitude of receptivity, not possessiveness or self-assertion, should characterize the Christian's life. Of course, he cautions, God's bounty cannot be directly perceived, for nature often appears to be a violent and tragic struggle for survival and our lives seem to be riddled with woes. But nevertheless a disposition to construe all events as gifts can and should be cultivated. Kierkegaard encourages the reader to be thankful to God at all times, not only in moments of flourishing, but also in moments of tribulation. Gratitude should not be restricted to physical well-being or social ful-

---

[39] *SKS* 8, 276 / *UD*, 177.

[40] *SKS* 8, 276 / *UD*, 178.

[41] *SKS* 5, 297 / *EUD*, 303.

[42] *SKS* 5, 186 / *EUD*, 182.

fillment, but should encompass ills and misfortunes. For example, the individual should be grateful for the opportunities to grow spiritually by being weaned away from reliance upon earthly sources of happiness.

Belief in God the Creator also involves profound trust in God's continuing solicitude throughout the course of a lifetime. Individuals vexed by life's vicissitudes should rest in the Creator's divinely gentle love.[43] Kierkegaard exhorted his readers to learn from the lilies of the field and the birds of the air the lesson of freedom from debilitating worldly concerns.[44] Kierkegaard did not advocate a prosperity gospel according to which earthly blessings will always be showered upon the faithful; he was convinced that suffering, doubts about God's providential care, inappropriate and unfulfilled wishes, and fear of the world are unavoidable aspects of the Christian life.[45] Nor did he offer a theodicy to show how all events, no matter how calamitous, work for the best. Rather, Kierkegaard used his authorial strategies to display for the reader the intrinsic satisfactions of a life of trust, a trust so resilient and indomitable that it could flourish even in the face of tragedies. With profuse expressions of thankfulness, Kierkegaard affirms that both "prosperity and adversity serve for strengthening in the inner being."[46]

IV. KIERKEGAARD ON THE PATHOS APPROPRIATE TO THE SECOND PERSON OF THE TRINITY

Kierkegaard's various discussions of the forms of pathos associated with the Second Person of the Trinity, the Redeemer, revolve around his exposition of the significance of Jesus Christ. The offensiveness of Christianity, the "sign of contradiction," is the claim that "an individual human being, just like others, a lowly unimpressive human being" is God.[47] Lutherans had traditionally identified Jesus' "person," his principle of self-subsistence, with the Second Person of the Trinity. All of Jesus' actions and passions, including those appropriate to his human nature, must be ascribed to the divine person. Jesus did possess two natures, but only one person, and that person was divine. Kierkegaard himself exhibited this tendency, describing Jesus as "he who was equal with God," "he who could command legions of angels,

[43] *SKS* 16, 227 / *JFY*, 180.
[44] *SKS* 8, 255–308 / *UD*, 155–212.
[45] *SKS* 18, 140, HH:28 / *KJN* 2, 130.
[46] *SKS* 5, 104 / *EUD*, 98.
[47] *SKS* 12, 130 / *PC*, 126.

indeed, could command the world's creation and its destruction," and "he who was lord of creation."[48] For Kierkegaard, the life, death, and resurrection of Jesus must be seen as God's graciously redemptive act.

Because Kierkegaard resisted the temptation to speculate about metaphysics, he did not attempt to solve the cognitive puzzle of the union of infinite divinity and finite humanity. For him, the assertion that eternity had entered time was not a philosophical obscurity to be illumined by a more brilliant and sophisticated speculative system. The apparent incompatibility of the metaphysical perfections of divinity and the creaturely imperfections of humanity was not a conceptual conundrum to be settled by dispassionate reflection. The presence of God in Christ cannot be discerned by peering through the lens of a set of propositions explaining how the properties of divinity and humanity could be exchanged. Kierkegaard avoided the intricate Lutheran debates about the supernatural mechanics of "*anhypostasia*," the conceptual mystery that Jesus did not possess a human "person" that could function as the subject of his human predicates, but only a divine person to which the human predicates adhered. Instead, Kierkegaard sought to promote clarity about the Incarnation by ensuring that the pathos of discourse about Christ was appropriate to the theme of redemption. Comprehension occurs not through strenuous reflection, but only through the ability to imagine a new way of life laden with new dispositions and passions. In a journal entry Kierkegaard articulated this theme, succinctly advising, "Have faith that Christ is God — then call upon him, pray to him, and the rest will work itself out for you."[49]

Kierkegaard was convinced that a sense of contrition and a profound dissatisfaction with the shape and direction of one's own life are the most fundamental prerequisites for comprehending discourse about the Second Person of the Trinity. Individuals must admit to themselves that they cannot expunge their own guilt and are powerless to heal their own debility. They must come to appreciate the egregious extent of their own failure and lament their inability to transform themselves. This candid self-knowledge brings with it an enormous amount of suffering.[50] Only then can a person begin to understand that God the Redeemer enacts such an extravagant reconciliation and enables such a profound healing that this recreation rivals the divine munificence exhibited in the original act of creation. With that

[48] *SKS* 8, 325–6 / *UD*, 224.
[49] *SKS* 20, 328, NB4:81 / *KJN* 4, 329.
[50] *SKS* 25, 152, NB27:39 / *KJN* 9, 151–152.

mood of contrition as a foundation, the individual could then experience gratitude and wonder over the unfathomable depths of God's redemptive love. For Kierkegaard, Jesus' forgiveness of his enemies is a revelation of the unanticipated expansiveness of God's mercy. To encourage this pathos, Kierkegaard donned the persona of a penitent speaking with fellow sinners in order to comfort them with the promise of forgiveness. The mood of discourse about the Second Person must be suited to its content in order for genuine communication to be possible.

Much of Kierkegaard's explicitly Christian literature is intended to foster gratitude for God the Redeemer's mercy toward sinners and for God's gracious provision of a "Prototype" of genuine love for God and neighbor. Kierkegaard's authorship was saturated with the historic Lutheran conviction that the Incarnation is God's voluntary renunciation of power and glory in order to love humanity. Reflecting an emphasis deeply embedded in the Lutheran tradition, Kierkegaard's writings about the Incarnation were structured around the theme of *kenosis*, God's voluntary self-emptying in order to share human experience.[51] Paul's kenotic hymn in Philippians 2 was central for Kierkegaard. Like most Lutherans, Kierkegaard also concentrated on the Redeemer's "state of humiliation," rather than on Christ's exaltation to celestial glory. Most significantly, Jesus was the God who craved genuine solidarity with lowly and sinful human beings and was willing to abandon the prerogatives of divine majesty in order to pursue that relationship. The Son was willing to "leave heavenly glory" and even to "sacrifice his life" in order to save humankind from lovelessness.[52] The Son's condescension and self-emptying in the act of Incarnation was reflected in all the features of Jesus' earthly ministry of continuous self-sacrifice. The eternal Son voluntarily exposed himself to human misunderstanding, hostility, ridicule, unjust victimization, and even lethal persecution. In Christ, God even suffers the anguish of knowing that God's project of seeking fellowship with humanity might backfire by causing offense to all the persons whom God was trying to save from spiritual self-destruction.[53] In Christ God surrendered the serene blessedness of celestial self-sufficiency in order to enact the more glorious sublimity of a lowly life of unrestricted self-giving.

---

[51] See David Law, *Kierkegaard's Kenotic Christology* (Oxford: Oxford University Press, 2013).

[52] *SKS* 12, 173 / *PC*, 170–171.

[53] *SKS* 11, 69–71 / *WA*, 63–64.

To dramatize this kenotic pattern, the pseudonym Climacus narrated the tale of the king who yearned for loving mutuality with a peasant woman. Climacus writes:

> ...the king could have appeared before the lowly maiden in all his splendor, could have let the sun of his glory rise over her hut, shine on the spot where he appeared to her, and let her forget herself in adoring admiration. This perhaps would have satisfied the girl, but it could not satisfy the king, for he did not want his own glorification but the girl's, and his sorrow would be very grievous because she would not understand him.[54]

The happy union of the king and the maiden could not be accomplished by the ascent of the maiden, but only by the descent of the king. The king therefore surrenders all the privileges of royalty and becomes a lowly peasant, not in pretense but in reality, in order to make genuine mutuality possible. Analogously, God as the Redeemer does not relate to humanity as the exalted, mighty one, exercising control of human lives from a safe distance, but as the lowly and vulnerable one in the form of a servant. God's reconciling love is displayed in God's submission to the conditions of temporal life in order to enact solidarity with humanity. Climacus concludes, "For this is the boundlessness of love, that in earnestness and truth and not in jest it wills to be the equal of the beloved...."[55] Kierkegaard reiterated this theme in his own voice, writing in his journal, "[Christ's] degradation was in earnest."[56] The royal power highlighted in the parable accentuates the divinity of Christ in order to emphasize the magnitude of the self-emptying enacted in his life. This elaborate literary strategy is designed to encourage gratitude for God's extravagant self-giving, for only when this disposition is developed can the Second Person of the Trinity begin to be understood.

Other passions must also be nurtured in order to appreciate what it means to affirm that "God was in Christ." Most importantly, the sublime beauty of this divine self-emptying should awaken a loving response in the individual. It should elicit wonder, amazement, gratitude, and delight. God should be lauded not only for the gift of life but also for the gift of unconditional mercy. The beauty of this spectacle of radical kenosis should enflame the heart and draw it to the Redeemer. To illustrate this, Kierkegaard's pseudonym H. H. relates the story of a young boy who was shown a picture

---

[54] *SKS* 4, 236 / *PF*, 29.

[55] *SKS* 4, 238 / *PF*, 32.

[56] *SKS* 20, 226, NB2:223 / *KJN* 4, 226.

of a crucified man and was then told that the man in the picture was the most loving person who had ever lived. As the boy matured he developed a growing desire to offer his own life in love for humanity, just as the mysterious man in the picture had done. As Kierkegaard explains, the boy's heart was stirred by the sheer attractive power of the vision of unconditional love.[57] That attractive beauty is intensified when an individual realizes that the crucified one is not just a compassionate human being, but is God.

Paradoxically, understanding the Second Person of the Trinity also involves recognizing just how offensive the Incarnation really is. The suggestion that God does not want to be adored as an exalted cosmic potentate but rather seeks to be in fellowship with lowly, broken sinners is deeply offensive to ordinary human conceptions of God. Kierkegaard repeatedly highlighted the fact that Jesus' life of profligate self-giving triggered a response of virulent hostility and persecution. According to Kierkegaard, we humans desperately want God to be the perfect instantiation of the power to dominate others that we secretly covet for ourselves. We invent a deity free of the liabilities and limitations that constrain us, a God who is everything that we would like to be.[58] The prospect of God's humble self-emptying clashes with our own valorization of self-aggrandizement. Kierkegaard warns that it was Jesus' enactment of God's radically self-giving love that provoked the world's homicidal hatred. The crucifixion's stark exposé of humanity's allergic reaction to self-giving love should catalyze the individual's self-critique and remorse.

V. KIERKEGAARD ON THE PATHOS APPROPRIATE FOR THE HOLY SPIRIT

In Kierkegaard's writings the forms of pathos associated with the Holy Spirit are also depicted, sometimes overtly but more often subtly. He does provide a sustained discussion of the Holy Spirit in *For Self-Examination*, and references to the Spirit pervade his literature. His identification of the Holy Spirit with God is clear in a draft of a prayer intended for use in *The Sickness unto Death*.[59] Kierkegaard even uses traditional doctrinal formulae in regard to the Spirit, affirming that "(God) remains my Father, which he does

---

[57] *SKS* 11, 61 / *WA*, 55.

[58] *SKS* 16, 208–227 / *JFY*, 160–179.

[59] *SKS* 20, 286, NB4:2 / *SUD*, 141.

through the Spirit in the Mediator."[60] Throughout his authorship Kierkegaard refers to the Holy Spirit as a personal agent, and vehemently rejects the identification of this Spirit with the spirit of the age, the spirit of humanity, or any other immanent dynamic in the universe. The concept "Holy Spirit" is certainly not a pious-sounding name for humanity's own innate religious proclivities, for we humans are actually afraid of the transforming power of this disruptive Spirit. Kierkegaard insists that the Holy Spirit is not an enhancement of humanity's natural religiosity or "a direct heightening of the natural life in a person."[61] Rather, the Holy Spirit conveys to individuals an utterly novel form of life and a new, unanticipated set of concerns, passions, and dispositions.

Given his understanding of religious communication, Kierkegaard refrained from producing a neutral, seemingly analytic description of the Holy Spirit. He announced that the Holy Spirit can only be understood through the cultivation of "the existential element in Xnty" and obedient action rather than through disengaged reflection about the lightness of all burdens.[62] In Kierkegaard's pages the Holy Spirit is presented as that which must be invoked, trusted, and thanked for eliciting, goading, encouraging, and supporting the faith of the individual. The Holy Spirit is described as serving numerous roles in nurturing faith, stretching from its inception, through its maturation, and on to its blossoming. According to Kierkegaard, the Holy Spirit provokes the initial movements of faith by awakening individuals to the magnitude and gravity of their despair and slaying them spiritually before making them alive.[63] The Holy Spirit enables individuals to see themselves as nothing before God, which is a necessary part of becoming spiritually sober and a prerequisite for surrendering the illusion of autonomy and self-sufficiency. After the commencement of the striving to be a Christian, the individual's very ability to grow in faith, hope, and love is a gift of the Holy Spirit.[64] For example, Kierkegaard insists that it is the Holy Spirit who reminds the believer to love the neighbor as himself.[65] The Holy Spirit is also described as being the inner font of the believer's ultimate joy, which the world can neither give nor take away. Moreover, it is the Holy Spirit

---

[60] *SKS* 25, 140, NB27:23 / *KJN* 9, 142.

[61] *SKS* 13, 98 / *FSE*, 76.

[62] *SKS* 24, 469, NB25:48 / *KJN* 8, 475–476.

[63] *SKS* 13, 98–9 / *FSE*, 76–7.

[64] *SKS* 13, 102–4 / *FSE*, 81–3.

[65] *SKS* 9, 12 / *WL*, 3–4.

who inspires the believer's sincere prayers. Consequently, the faithful individual's apparent growth in Christian pathos should not be cherished and valued as her own achievement, nor should it be ascribed to her own religious prowess. According to Kierkegaard, as the Christian life continues the crucial capacity to die to the demands of self-love is an on-going gift of the Spirit.[66] The Holy Spirit, like a royal coachman, takes the reins of our lives, and replaces self-will with the blessed capacity to love.[67] The Holy Spirit enables the individual to embrace the reconciliation proffered by Christ the Atoner and to strive to be like Christ the Prototype.[68] Because human beings are powerless to persevere in following the path of Christ by themselves, the Holy Spirit must strengthen them to adhere to the way of the cross in spite of society's derision and hostility. The Holy Spirit enables the faithful to die to the spirit of this world and emboldens them to "suffer for the truth."[69] Moreover, the Spirit nurtures a wisdom that is at odds with ordinary sagacity because it flouts worldly tabulations of profit and loss. The ability of an individual to even begin to acquire any of these virtues is itself a gift of the Holy Spirit.[70] In all these instances, Kierkegaard was exhorting the reader to offer God thanks for every dimension of the inception and maturation of the reader's own religious pathos and to refrain from congratulating herself for any apparent internal progress.

As Leo Stan has shown, Kierkegaard most often highlights the Spirit's activity as the helper and comforter in times of trial and tribulation.[71] Kierkegaard writes, "...if the mark of the relationship to God is suffering, if the very expression of God's loving me is my having to suffer...then there must be a 'Spirit' in order to comfort."[72] The only antidote to the world's ferocious animosity to Christian love is the Spirit's succor.[73] The Holy Spirit also comforts the Christian as the Christian fails to live up to the daunting ideal of Christ as Prototype. The Spirit offers the reassurance of God's love when

---

[66] *SKS* 9, 24–95 / *WL*, 17–90.

[67] *SKS* 13, 107–8 / *FSE*, 87.

[68] *SKS* 25, 140–2, NB27:23 / *KJN* 9, 140–142.

[69] *SKS* 13, 52 / *FSE*, 24.

[70] *SKS* 5, 141–2 / *EUD*, 139.

[71] Leo Stan "Holy Spirit," in *Kierkegaard's Concepts,* Tome III: *Envy to Incognito*, ed. by Steven Emmanuel, William McDonald, and Jon Stewart (Ashgate: Farnham, 2014) (*Kierkegaard Research: Sources, Reception, and Resources*, vol. 15), 157–161.

[72] *SKS* 25, 46, NB26:40 / *KJN* 9, 43–4.

[73] *SKS* 13, 105 / *FSE*, 84–5.

the individual fears that she will falter in the future and fail to be a faithful disciple.[74]

VI. KIERKEGAARD AND THE IMMANENT TRINITY

The pervasiveness throughout Kierkegaard's corpus of these three families of different features of Christian pathos indicates that he did implicitly view the Christian life through the lens of the economic Trinity. The three-foldness in God is posited to account for the three-fold nature of Christian pathos. By doing so, Kierkegaard was exhibiting his roots in the Pietist heritage, and showing that he shared some aspects of the "subjective turn" in theological methodology with Schleiermacher. However, Kierkegaard's engagement with the doctrine of the Trinity was not confined to his rhetorical evocation of God's three-fold economy in the subjectivity of the believer. Kierkegaard, like many of his more speculative contemporaries, regarded the activities of God *ad extra* as manifestations of God's life of love *in se*. Consequently, while eschewing metaphysical speculation Kierkegaard sought to encourage yet another type of pathos, a pathos that would be appropriate to the concept of the immanent Trinity.

As we have seen, the speculative theologians like Martensen had borrowed and revised themes from Hegel, Markeineke, and Schelling to suggest that the doctrine of the immanent Trinity is an abstract way of affirming that God's most essential characteristic is love. In spite of his distaste for Martensen, Kierkegaard shared this view. Often Kierkegaard in his many different voices directly asserts that God's essence is love.[75] Divine love is so essential for Kierkegaard that he uses it as a lens to interpret God's other attributes, often referred to in the doctrinal tradition as God's metaphysical perfections. For example, God's omnipotence is described by Kierkegaard as being the awesome potency of God's love.[76] God's immutability is simply the constancy of God's love and the reliability of God's commitment to God's creatures.[77] The impassibility of God is not God's inability to empathically share human joys and sorrows, but is the unwavering nature of God's concern for God's children. Similarly, wisdom and justice are also characteristics of the more basic reality of God's compassion.

---

[74] *SKS* 25, 157, NB27:44 / *KJN* 9, 156–157.

[75] *SKS* 4, 129 / *FT*, 34; *SKS* 8, 365, 370, 373 / *UD*, 267–8, 274, 277; *SKS* 9, 263–4 / *WL*, 264–5.

[76] *SKS*, 10, 138 / *CD*, 127.

[77] *SKS* 5, 375 / *EUD*, 393.

The pivotal role of God's love in Kierkegaard's corpus has often been overlooked by readers who have been transfixed by his dramatic descriptions of anxiety and despair. But this allegedly melancholy and self-absorbed Dane often waxed exuberantly rhapsodic about the enchanting sublimity of the divine love. This is most evident when Kierkegaard describes God as that which is ultimately desirable, as the ultimate object of human yearning. In these contexts he makes it clear that the quality that is so desirable and attractive about God is the divine love. God does not just contingently decide to care for and cherish the world in three different ways; rather, God's disposition toward the world is rooted in the fact that *in se* God is loving relationality. This, of course, was articulated by Kierkegaard's more speculative contemporaries like Martensen through their retrieval of the doctrine of the immanent Trinity and their efforts to comprehend it in so far as they deemed that to be possible.

Kierkegaard, of course, did not take the speculative path. Faithful to his understanding of religious language, he refrained from trying to probe the mechanisms and dynamics of God's inner life. Rather, he attempted to exhibit the nature of God's intrinsic lovingness by enacting in his authorship the passions that should be a response to it. In order to accomplish this, he adopted the voice of an encomiast of love, for the joy and delight that are intrinsic to love can only be displayed through a mood of ecstatic celebration. Doxology is the most apt genre for discourse about God's love, for God's love cannot be discussed without praising it. God's love is reduplicated in Kierkegaard's rhetorical performance as he lauds God's love and seeks to inspire the reader to reflect God's love by loving the neighbor. That solicitude is itself an act of love for the reader, and aptly mirrors God's infinitely more profound concern for the reader. For example, *Works of Love* is an extended paean to divine love. Accordingly, Kierkegaard commences the book with a prayerful direct address to God as "the source of all love in heaven and on earth; you who spared nothing but in love gave everything; you who are love, so that one who loves is what he is only by being in you."[78] Kierkegaard's panegyric to God as the font of all love expresses the conviction that *in se* God is a dynamic of loving relationality.

When Kierkegaard rhapsodizes about divine love, he exults that God is both the source of all love and the true object of all love. God is the font of love, for "just as the quiet lake originates deep down in hidden springs no

[78] *SKS* 9, 12 / *WL*, 3.

eye has seen, so also does a person's love originate even more deeply in God's love."[79] As "Love's Hidden Life," the first chapter of *Works of Love* suggests, God's "economic" acts of creating, redeeming, and sanctifying are three different outpourings of God's immanent life of love. God is not motivated by a need for intimacy or fellowship, but solely by a gratuitous delight in and care for something other than God. In God's own self God eternally is the joyful perfection of love, even apart from God's relation to the universe. God's continuing love for God's creatures is not a response to their possession of attractive virtues or excellences; it is not even contingent upon their display of gratitude. God loves God's creatures simply because it is the nature of love to do so. Dispensing with the elaborate metaphysical apparatus typical of his contemporaries, Kierkegaard did inscribe in his authorship a functional equivalent of the theme that the economic Trinity is the manifestation of the immanent Trinity.

VII. CONCLUSION

In his own idiosyncratic way Kierkegaard did implicitly express the major motifs classically associated with the doctrine of the Trinity. Moreover, although he did not engage the trinitarian debates of his era directly, they informed his writing. Most surprisingly, he was sometimes in agreement with some of the affirmations of the very people he most vigorously polemicized against. He did share the belief of Martensen and other speculative theologians that God is essentially love. He even shared Martensen's conviction that this love should be understood primarily as the self-giving enacted in the Incarnation. He further echoed Martensen's critique of Hegel on the Trinity, and paralleled Martensen's insistence that the perfection of the divine love is logically prior to its enactment in creation, redemption, and consummation. Like Martensen and Sibbern, Kierkegaard sought to preserve God's freedom and to avoid collapsing the trinitarian dynamic into the spiritual evolution of humanity. For him, God's transcendent love is gratuitous, and is emphatically not governed by any necessity.

Kierkegaard also owed something to the legacy of the Enlightenment. As much as Kierkegaard diverged from theologians like Clausen, he shared Clausen's antipathy to speculative theories about doctrinal matters. Like them, he refused to engage in metaphysical speculation to clarify how God can be three persons in one nature. He resisted the temptation to illumine

[79] *SKS* 9, 17 / *WL*, 9.

the meaning of these traditional terms by trying to locate them on a conceptual map. He did not even search for metaphors to render the relationships of the persons of the Trinity to one another more intelligible. He did not try to probe the mystery of how exactly God could be loving in God's own self by ruminating about the necessity for some sort of divine self-othering. According to Kierkegaard that type of speculation would not be edifying, would violate the limits of our reasoning powers, and therefore would not be meaningful. This epistemological restraint owed a great deal to Kant and more broadly to the anti-metaphysical instincts of the Enlightenment. A more sophisticated ontology will not promote a deeper grasp of the concept "Trinity."

Kierkegaard was also certainly indebted to the legacy of Pietism and its survival in the theologians influenced by Schleiermacher. The "subjective turn," the attempt to explain the meaning of Christian concepts in terms of their desired impact upon the spirituality of the believer, is evident throughout Kierkegaard's work. However, unlike Schleiermacher and more like some of the earlier Pietist devotional authors, Kierkegaard was convinced that the pathos appropriate to a Christian concept was intrinsic to its meaning, and therefore could not be factored out in order to write about Christianity systematically and scientifically. Unlike Schleiermacher, he would not and could not construct a theological system, even one based on a phenomenology of Christian consciousness. Therefore, Kierkegaard could not follow Schleiermacher in regarding trinitarian language as a second-order (and possibly optional) codification of the believer's lived experience. Rather, for Kierkegaard the particular passions that trinitarian language should evoke must be inscribed into theological writing itself.

The unique thing about Kierkegaard is that in regard to the Trinity he shifted attention away from the construction of conceptual systems in order to refocus on the task of encouraging the reader to integrate in her own life a complex and rich set of interactive passions. In his authorship he rhetorically performs three different responses to three different aspects of God's love, and also a response to sheer sublimity of God as the font of all love. For Kierkegaard, the textual performance of the appropriate responses to God is the only way to clarify what "Trinity" means. Consequently, he eschews the genre of the philosophical treatise and restricts himself to the lyrical and provocative discourse. The Trinity can only be spoken of doxologically, gratefully, supplicatingly, ecstatically, and trustingly. To believe in the Trinity is to grow in all these forms of pathos. For Kierkegaard, the Trinity can be understood more fully as the divine love is reflected in the individual's own life.

Present Past: Traumatic Memory in Kierkegaard's *Repetition*

Nate Kramer

The editors of a recent collection of articles on the current state of memory studies, titled *Memory Unbound: Tracing the Dynamics of Memory Studies*, argue that there has been a recent and significant shift in the nature of memory (or at least our contemporary understanding of it).[1] Where memory was previously understood to be anchored and contained either in particular places or attached to specific communities, it now has become marked by an increasing fluidity and mobility. They write that "memory…is presently conceptualized as something that does not stay put but circulates, migrates, travels; it is more perceived as a process, as work that is continually in process, rather than as a reified object."[2] Though the editors theorize this new "mnemonic reality" as a result of contemporary and increasingly mobile individuals and communities, circulations of social and digital media, geographical, transcultural and transnational fluctuations, the unbinding of memory or its unmooring from place and domicile has been, this article will argue, been underway for some time. Søren Kierkegaard's *Repetition* may be read as a particularly important and early moment in the unbinding of memory.

Published in 1843 under the pseudonym Constantin Constantius, *Repetition* ostensibly reconsiders the Platonic mnemonic doctrine of *anamnesis* and advances in its place the more "modern" notion of repetition. Constantius writes on the very first page of *Repetition* "Say what you will…for repetition is a crucial expression for what 'recollection' was to the Greeks. Just as

I am pleased to be part of this *Festschrift* honoring Jon Stewart. Jon has been a formative and influential part of my career, and I thank him for his kindness and generosity to me as well as for the clarity and substance of his thinking on Kierkegaard.

[1] Lucy Bond, Stef Craps and Pieter Vermeulen, *Memory Unbound: Tracing the Dynamics of Memory Studies* (New York and Oxford: Berghahn Books, 2017).

[2] Ibid., 1.

they taught that all knowing is a recollecting, modern philosophy will teach that all life is a repetition."[3] Recollection is the Hong's English translation of Kierkegaard's Danish *erindring*, and the term most often used in English to translate the Greek concept of *anamnesis*. Though not the only theory of memory in the Classical world—Edward Casey remarks that generally "memory was a thematic, even an obsessive, concern of the early Greeks"—*anamnesis* has in large measure determined and set the agenda for thinking about memory in Western philosophy.[4] Literally an "unforgetting," Plato associated *anamnesis* with the very possibility of knowledge which describes a process by which knowledge is not discovered outside of ourselves, somewhere out there in the world or through experience with the world, but internally by remembering it amongst already acquired memories. What one remembers or "unforgets" is essentially those eternal forms and ideas that for Plato formed the basis of true knowledge. Thus memory became the faculty for knowing and self-knowing and the mode for understanding the true nature of reality.

Despite Constantin's assertion that he will take aim at Platonic *anamnesis*, there is in fact very little if any direct philosophical polemic leveled against it in the course of *Repetition*. In fact, Kierkegaard does not use the Greek term throughout the entirety of the book, using instead the Danish *erindring* as noted above. Though *erindring* can be understood as more or less equivalent to *anamnesis* within *Repetition* (both the Hong translation and the commentary accompanying the new *SKS* insist on this equivalency) the word also implies a rather different, broader conception of memory.[5] At its most basic, *erindring* can be and often is simply and directly translated as memory, however, the term does not denote the general and abstract faculty as the Danish *hukommelse* does.[6] The Danish term *erindring* indicates a more

[3] *SKS* 4, 9 / *R*, 131.

[4] Edward S. Casey, *Remembering: A Phenomenological Study*, 2nd ed. (Bloomington and Indianapolis: Indiana University Press, 2000), 13. Plato deals explicitly with *anamnesis* in the *Meno* and *Phaedrus*.

[5] The Hong translation of *Repetition* prefers, by and large, the term "recollection" to translate *erindring* and its meanings. Recollection is, of course, a perfectly acceptable and even preferred term when discussing *anamnesis*, but, to my mind, seems slightly more technical than, for example, remembering or even reminiscing. This technical range of recollection is due in part to recollection's associations with *anamnesis*. Translation can be often a thankless job, but I do think the preference for a more philosophical and technical jargon has obscured the more natural and everyday experience of remembering that Kierkegaard addresses in *Repetition*.

[6] In *Stages on Life's Way*, William Afham makes a distinction between *at erindre* and *at huske*, both of which can be translated as "to remember." The substantive *erindring* is differenti-

specific form of memory that today would be called in cognitive- and neuropsychology episodic memory or autobiographical memory. This kind of memory describes events and situations personally experienced by the individual that come to establish a sense of self that persists and continues over time. Such memories thus come to form the basis of one's identity.[7] Though there are clear overlaps with Platonic *anamnesis*, *erindring* does not imply, at least on the surface, the epistemological problems and suspicion of sense experience that underlie Platonic *anamnesis*. Furthermore, and perhaps most important for Constantius, *erindring* is not to be understood as the recollection of the Platonic *eidos,* but rather the remembering or recollecting of one's own past so as to have a sense of self. *Erindring* thus forms a crucial role in the formation of identity insofar as it connects or relates the self back to its past and creates a sense of identity or sameness over time. In doing so *erindring* provides a sense of coherence and stability to the self.

Why this need for repetition then? By announcing repetition as a replacement for recollection, Constantin seemingly asserts some disturbance in the field of memory (*erindring*) such that the function of recollection as that which provides this sense of identity and coherence has been compromised. Kierkegaard's *Repetition* has rarely been considered in terms of memory or as a "memory text" with memory usually treated as a nominal concern of the text, however, this article will propose that memory is in fact the central issue at stake in *Repetition* and that Constantin identifies the past as a problem such that access to it and its meaning has been lost. Constantin thus "invents" repetition as a new and modern form of memory in order to reestablish a connection to a lost and unremembered past. The first part of this article will attempt to account for the sense of historical and memorial rupture that pervades *Repetition* by situating its claims in the context of nineteenth-century Denmark. *Repetition* can be read as a response to what Richard Terdiman has called the memory crisis of the nineteenth century:

---

ated in Danish from another word, also translated as memory, *hukommelse*. This memory, however, is a more general designation for memory and lacks the personal and autobiographical associations. *Hukommelse* designates the faculty of memory as such and is absent from Kierkegaard's *Repetition*.

[7] See *Den Store Danske*'s entry on *erindring*, for example, which also mentions Kierkegaard's interest in the term. F. J. Billeskov Jansen, Steen Folke Larsen: erindring i *Den Store Danske*, Gyldendal. Accessed May 16, 2018 at http://denstoredanske.dk/index.php? sideId=71893.

the "massive disruption of traditional forms of memory" that arose out of the social, economic, political, and cultural upheavals that mark the period.[8]

Of course, repetition is hardly the solution to the loss of *erindring* that Constantin initially claims. As I will argue in the following, the past has not only become a "foreign country" for Constantin, but has in fact become threatening and even malevolent, "uremittingly and treacherously retak[ing] everything it had given without providing a repetition."[9] Although I will deal only cursorily with the complexity of the narrative strategy in *Repetition*, part of the foundation for this paper rests on the claim that the curious form *Repetition* takes is symptomatic of the very disturbance in the coherence of time and memory Constantin explores. *Repetition*'s strangeness may be owed to the fact that, as Niels Nymann Eriksen notes "repetition is not so much a philosophical doctrine as it is a paradigm of thought, and as such it is something that cannot be grasped as an object for thought."[10] Instead, we are offered a narrative or rather a series of nested narratives that run the gamut from the biographical to the autobiographical to the epistolary to the travel narrative. Divided into two parts written by Constantin, seven letters from the Young Man, a brief "Incidental Observation by Constantin Constantius," yet another letter by the Young Man and a final letter by Constantin addressed to the reader, *Repetition* is a meandering, and often bewildering work. The very form *Repetition* takes suggests that repetition and the general reflection on the function and purpose of memory cannot be articulated in so straightforward a manner. What I aim to address with regard to its narrative strategy and what may well strike the reader of *Repetition* is the arrival of a certain figure of blockage that stops short and prevents the narrative from moving forward. This is most evident in the concluding scene of Constantin's experiment when he returns home to his apartments in Copenhagen. Constantin's visit to Berlin thus results in a dramatic reversal in which the past is encountered as traumatic insofar as trauma denotes a pathological past that exceeds or lies beyond Constantin's ability to manage or control it. In accounting for this sense of the past as traumatic in *Repeti-*

---

[8] Richard Terdiman, *Present Past: Modernity and the Memory Crisis* (Ithaca and London: Cornell University Press, 1993), 5.

[9] *SKS* 4, 45 / *R*, 172. See also David Lowenthal, *The Past is a Foreign Country* (Cambridge: Cambridge University Press, 1999).

[10] Niels Nymann Eriksen, *Kierkegaard's Category of Repetition: A Reconstruction* (Berlin and New York: Walter de Gruyter, 2000) (*Kierkegaard Monograph Series*, vol. 5), 2.

tion, I suggest that this results in what might be called the unbinding of memory from its traditional moorings, from its being "there."

I. THE NINETEENTH-CENTURY CRISIS OF MEMORY IN DENMARK

The reader of Kierkegaard is no doubt familiar with the often rehearsed historical circumstances leading up to and engulfing the Denmark in which Kierkegaard wrote: the significant agricultural reforms of the previous century that increased the power of the rural farm owners and peasants throughout Denmark and the emergence of the constitutional monarchy in the middle of the nineteenth century; the late entry of Denmark into the Napoleonic Wars alongside France, the defeat of which led to Denmark being divested of Norway and other territories; the bombardments of Copenhagen in 1801 and 1807 by the British which destroyed large sections of Copenhagen, but also lead to the city's subsequent rebuilding and fueled the movement toward urbanization; the financial devastation wrought by state bankruptcy in 1813, to say nothing of the religious and broad cultural changes of the period.[11]

No doubt responding to this sense of upheaval, Johan Ludvig Heiberg, the Danish playwright and man of letters, declared in his *On the Significance of Philosophy for the Present Age* (1833) that the then present age was an age in crisis.[12] This crisis for Heiberg, however, was not geo-political or economic or social, these being but the manifestations of a deeper crisis. The source rather was precisely historical. The Danish Golden Age was a decisive break from the past not because of the overwhelming changes it faced, but because Heiberg following Hegel believed that the generation of the Golden Age had failed to grasp the essential meaning of its historical moment. History had always undergone periods of instability and stability according to Heiberg via Hegel. Denmark, reeling from these crises, Heiberg

---

[11] See Bruce Kirmmse's landmark *Kierkegaard in Golden Age Denmark* (Bloomington and Indianapolis: Indiana University Press, 1990) and George Pattison's *Kierkegaard, Religion and the Nineteenth-Century Crisis of Culture* (Cambridge: Cambridge University Press, 2002). Jon Stewart's herculean contributions to the historical, philosophical, and cultural context of the Danish Golden Age and Kierkegaard's place in the culture has been enormously influential. See among so many other works his *Søren Kierkegaard: Subjectivity, Irony, and the Crisis of Modernity* (Oxford: Oxford University Press, 2015).

[12] *Heiberg's On the Significance of Philosophy for the Present Age and Other Texts*, ed. and trans. by Jon Stewart (Copenhagen: C. A. Reitzel, 2005) (*Texts from Golden Age Denmark*, vol. 1).

writes "strives powerfully forward in manifold directions. However, it does not itself know where many of these directions will lead it."[13] This had led to not a "fixed existence but only a becoming, in which what is old ends and what is new begins, an appearance of existence, destined to take the place of a real condition."[14] Heiberg's criticism of the "becoming" character of the age and his clear preference for a "fixed existence" led to what he sees as a forgetting, a forgetting of the Idea that grounds history itself.[15] Heiberg claims that "It may seem that ideas are sometimes subjugated by force and sometimes cunning, but one forgets that both force and cunning themselves are forms of the eternal Idea or reason."[16] The solution to such a forgetting and the crisis of history that marks the Danish Golden Age will be philosophy and more particularly a Hegelian dialectics of Spirit since "[p]hilosophy is nothing other than the knowledge of the eternal or speculative Idea."[17] Thus to grasp the ebbs and flows of history in order to chart the way forward in the present moment is to remember and thus secure the Idea that lies at the heart of history.

Kierkegaard's *Repetition* can likewise be seen as addressing the ominous changes afoot, even echoing in many ways Heiberg's own diagnosis of the modern age. The analysis of the crisis as Kierkegaard sees it, however, is not to be found in Hegel's Idea but in what Richard Terdiman calls the "present past." Terdiman in his 1993 *Present Past: Modernity and the Memory Crisis* argues that the long nineteenth century, the period from 1789 to around 1920, is marked by a memory crisis. Terdiman claims that if the past had always been uncertain terrain it became especially so during the nineteenth century. There was, he notes, a growing sense that the past had "somehow evaded memory, that recollection had ceased to integrate with consciousness. In this memory crisis the very coherence of time and of subjectivity seemed disarticulated."[18] This massive rupture that separated the past from

[13] Stewart, *On the Significance*, 87.

[14] Ibid.

[15] Jon Stewart notes in the introductory material to his translation that "History moves through periods of stability and crisis. In the stable times there is a universally acknowledged system of fixed beliefs. When contradictions arise in it, a period of crisis or evolution is initiated, which only ends once the age has found a new truth upon which it can base its belief and institutions," ibid., 29).

[16] Ibid., 88.

[17] Ibid.

[18] Terdiman, *Present Past,* 4.

the present and disrupted traditional forms of memory became a critical and theoretical preoccupation of the long nineteenth century.

Terdiman attributes this disruption of memory to dramatic shifts in social relations caused by the industrial revolution and arrival of protocapitalist economies, and modernity itself: the tremendous jump forward in the productive power of human labor, the reorganization of production in nineteenth-century Europe that altered the very social rhythms of the period. The rise of the media and an increasingly "programmed collective experience in shopping, in entertainment, in sports, and in the national political ceremonial" combined to create a sense of deep unease and uncertainly about the present moment's relationship to the past.[19] The "epochal transition" from community (*Gemeinschaft*) to society (*Gesellschaft*), as described by Ferdinand Tönnies, quickly rendered obsolete traditional family and villages structures as these were quickly transformed into an urban existence.[20] Where traditional forms of human interaction and relations had looked to the past for security and certainty, the past traditionally understood was simply gone. If memory "is the modality of our relation to the past," then in the long nineteenth century that relation to the past, the modality of memory itself, became hopelessly vexed.[21]

Although schematic, Terdiman's memory crisis as a description of the consequences of the broad social, economic, political and cultural upheavals of the long nineteenth century provides a helpful way to think about the world to which Kierkegaard's *Repetition* is responding. Terdiman's observations may therefore helpfully redescribe the Danish Golden Age and its own discontinuities and upheavals as part of a broader European crisis of memory. *Repetition* thus participates alongside (though it predates) other texts of the period coming to terms with the shattering of traditional forms of memory. To do so would therefore also situate Kierkegaard's authorship more generally and *Repetition* in particular in the broader European response to such a crisis and place it among the works of the nineteenth century's fascination with memory. For Terdiman, it is the francophone litera-

[19] Ibid., 30.

[20] Jon Stewart notes in the introductory material to his translation that "History moves through periods of stability and crisis. In the stable times there is a universally acknowledged system of fixed beliefs. When contradictions arise in it, a period of crisis or evolution is initiated, which only ends once the age has found a new truth upon which it can base its belief and institutions," *On the Significance*, 29).

[21] Terdiman, *Present Past*, 7.

ture of memory in the poetry of Charles Baudelaire, Alfred de Musset's *Confessions*, and Marcel Proust's *In Search of Lost Time*. Henri Bergson's *Matter and Memory* from 1896 would also be emblematic for the memory crisis.

II. REPETITION AS MODERN MEMORY

Repetition as both a philosophical idea and a psychological one looms large in the intellectual history of the twentieth century, and Kierkegaard's influence on the philosophical idea of repetition, whether explicitly acknowledged or not, is significant. Gilles Deleuze sees both Kierkegaard and Nietzsche as vested in creating a "philosophy of the future" based on repetition as the fundamental category.[22] Heidegger may have denied Kierkegaard's influence on him for the most part, yet his conception of *Wiederholung* articulated in *Being and Time* certainly owes a great deal to Kierkegaard. In such an accounting one might also point to Theodor Adorno's cultural critique as rooted in a conception of repetition and Derrida's own interest in repetition that occurs throughout his entire *oeuvre*, and who gives due acknowledgement to Kierkegaard. As for the psychological/psychoanalytic interest in repetition, a reconsideration of Kierkegaard's "existential psychology" is certainly in order, especially that popularized in the '70s and early '80s. And while there are significant differences between Freud's conception of repetition and Kierkegaard's, the differences I would like to believe are less than sometimes claimed. Freud's *Beyond the Pleasure Principle* (1920) and the idea of repetition compulsion could be read, I think, fruitfully alongside Kierkegaard's *Repetition*.[23] Freud's essay "Remembering, Repeating and Working-Through" (1914) as the earliest formulation of the compulsion to repeat would also bear some further scrutiny in this regard, to say nothing of Jacques Lacan's own interest in Kierkegaard and the concept of repetition. But, by and large, Kierkegaard's repetition as explicitly related to memory as

---

[22] Gilles Deleuze. *Difference and Repetition*, trans. by Paul Patton (New York: Columbia University Press, 1994).

[23] See Eriksen's *Kierkegaard's Category of Repetition* and in particular his discussion of Don Juan in *Either/Or* and Freud's repetition compulsion on p 25ff. Whereas Eriksen sees Freudian repetition as only dealing with "one particular point in the history of the individual," the repetition compulsion, especially in the context of trauma has rather to do with at least two historical points in the life an individual that become coordinated in the experience of trauma. Hence, one could make the argument that Freud's repetition compulsion is about "historicality" rather than only the "history" of one moment.

such has been rarely treated in either the philosophical or the psychological literature, let alone that of memory studies.

Kierkegaard's repetition is at once more subtle and banal than the history of repetition in the twentieth century might concede. The Danish for repetition—and for which Constantin takes delight in congratulating the Danish language—is *gentagelse*, the verbal form of which (*at gentage*) literally means "to take again." Defining repetition, Constantin explains "that which is repeated has been—otherwise it could not be repeated—but the very fact that it has been makes the repetition into something new."[24] What is "taken again" is obviously the past, what "has been." Taking the past again might suggest, at first glance, that one simply re-members it. However, this fails to properly distinguish the difference in remembering the past found in *erindring* and that of repetition. The active "taking again" found in repetition implies that the remembering in recollection is conceived of as relatively passive. Furthermore, Constantin insists that the active form of remembering in repetition turns or transforms what is remembered into something new.[25]

The difference between recollection and repetition (*erindring* and *gentagelse*) as well as the shift spoken of at the beginning of this article, from memory as something bounded and restricted to one more active, can be thought of in terms of a difference between an "active model" of memory and a "passive" one described in Edward Casey's *Remembering: A Phenomenological Study.* Although, according to Casey, there has never been a clear historical division between the two, the "passivist paradigm" has often been associated with Plato and Aristotle and the understanding of remembering as "reduced to a passive process of registering and storing incoming impressions."[26] Casey continues

> The passivist paradigm is still very much with us, whether it takes the form of a naive empiricism or of a sophisticated model of information processing. In fact, since Aristotle's position was first formulated, passiv-

---

[24] *SKS* 4, 25 / *R*, 149.

[25] Though the issue of the unconscious is not at stake here, Freud's models of memory fit quite well the active model in which memory has itself become pathological. One might think of *Studies in Hysteria* from 1897, a scant fifty years after *Repetition* in which Freud and Breuer make the breakthrough assertion that hysterics suffer not from physiological damage of one sort or another but from memories.

[26] Casey, *Remembering*, 15.

> ism has been the predominant, and typically the 'official'...view of memory. On the other hand, and as a consequence of this very fact, there has grown up a countervailing tradition of 'activism,' according to which memory involves the creative transformation of experience rather than its internalized reduplication in images or traces construed as copies.[27]

Recollection or *anamnesis* (*erindring*) depends on a view of memory in which memories as "images or traces construed as copies" are inscribed in the mind which thus functions as a kind of repository or container for such memories. The act of remembering in this view retrieves or calls up from the storehouse of the mind these representations of the past. As Casey notes, not only do Plato and Aristotle depend on such a view for their theory of knowledge but this has become the popular understanding of how memory works. One need only remind oneself of the many metaphors for memory including ones of more recent vintage in which the mind is imagined as a kind of database with both short term and long storage sectors.

Kierkegaard, however, appears to eschew such a model of how memory works when it comes to repetition. Repetition reimagines the past not as a collection of stored images to be retrieved but as a dynamic process of exchange. In such a view, memories are not simply there in one's mind to be retrieved nor are memories merely faithful copies of past experiences. One returns to the past or remembers in such a way that the very act of remembering alters and transforms the past. This focus on the presentness of the past is captured quite neatly in Constantius' formulation that "[r]epetition and recollection are the same movement, except in opposite directions, for what is recollected has been, is repeated backward, whereas genuine repetition is recollected forward."[28] Whereas the past is imagined to be something already given and determinate in recollection and the rememberer merely "returns" to such past memories, repetition brings the past into the present, takes the past again into the present moment and for reasons that are described by Constantius as futural, "recollected forward." The making of the past present in this way alters the past, renders it no longer determinate but susceptible to the purposes for which it is being recollected. Zofia Rosinska,

---

[27] Ibid. Casey is quick to note that while the activist theory of memory is detectable in Plato and Aristotle, the activist model has been developed more completely during the modern period. Casey notes for example Janet's idea of the retroactive transformation of memories through narrative and Freud's ideas surrounding remembering as an act of interpretation and construction. Kierkegaard certainly belongs in this company as well.

[28] *SKS* 4, 9 / *R*, 131

for example, in her "Philosophical Psychology of Memory," follows Casey's distinction between passive and active memory, and states it this way:

> The active model does not treat the content of memory as a recorded image, as an object that can be recollected, reminisced or recognized. According to this model, the content of memory is subject to transformations and relocations, it forms a dynamic structure, which apart from recollecting, reminiscing and recognizing also includes the following processes: repetition, narration and evaluation and feelings.[29]

Reexamining, evaluating, and narrating the past make the past present and in doing so, for Kierkegaard, they repeat the past in the present. Repetition as an active form of memory does not treat the past therefore as inscribed or localized in the storage places of the mind, but as something fluid and necessarily altered in its being called up for reasons and purposes (even if these reasons and purposes remain in one way or another unknown to the rememberer) that actively transform and reshape the past memory. Remembering in this way is as much about the present as it is about the past. In repetition's rejection of the past as something contained and bounded to something liberated and creative, one also imagines such a past, to echo a phrase, to be a "usable past" in which the past becomes serviceable or functional for the present purpose or moment.

Having articulated what might be possible in Constantin's consideration of repetition, Constantin's trip to Berlin presents a deeply ironic view of the above. Towards the middle of Part One of *Repetition*, Constantin Constantius speaks of an "investigative journey...to test the possibility of and meaning of repetition."[30] The experiment takes him to Berlin, a city he had traveled to before, with the intent of reconstructing, viz. repeating, the exact journey to Berlin he had undertaken some years earlier. The irony of devising an experiment to test the possibility of repetition should not be lost on readers of *Repetition*. Despite Constantius' earlier claims about repetition, there now appears something of a curious mistaking of the nature of repetition. Samuel Weber has suggested that the return to Berlin is to see "whether or not the kind of blissful moment [Constantius] describes, in which

[29] Zofia Rosinska, "Philosophical Psychology of Memory," in *Memory Work: The Theory and Practice of Memory*, ed. by Andreas Kitzmann, Conny Mithander, and John Sundholm (Frankfurt am Main: Peter Lang, 2005), 31.

[30] *SKS* 4, 27 / *R*, 150.

temporal bodily existence is transcended by a being in which 'everything [is] prescient,' can be *maintained*, *repeated*—that is, *recovered*—in more than just memory."[31] Repetition in such a view denotes a conception of the past that surpasses memory, lies beyond it in a fantasy of memory outside of time.

Despite this, there are good reasons for remaining with Constantius as key to understanding the problem of repetition. Robert Pogue Harrison, for example, calls Constantius "the voice of repetition" since it is from Constantius that we learn as much if not more than from the Young Man and his infatuation with the beloved about the name and nature of repetition.[32] Constantius' trip to Berlin is or will be revelatory, for repetition does indeed take place (as it always does), though not in the way Constantius imagines or understands repetition to be. In contrast to his previous declarations on repetition, Constantius now seemingly literalizes the idea of "taking again" and seems to believe that repetition is a repetition of the past verbatim, that is as the same thing reoccurring precisely and without difference. And the trip to Berlin indeed disconfirms the possibility of such absolute identity and sameness as it begins to slip wildly out of control.

The trip starts out well enough with Constantius claiming that "everything…repeated itself" on his journey to Berlin, that is except for him choosing a seat in the forward compartment.[33] However, the disorienting and jumbled travel experience to Berlin where Constantius fears the "memory of…being a limb on a larger body" so jostled is he in the coach on its way to Berlin anticipates, if humorously, the potential for chaos found in this more "active" model of memory.[34] And of course this is only the beginning of the discombobulation that accompanies Constantin's experience. Though the hotel room is very much like the one he had upon his first visit, the landlord has since married to Constantius' chagrin and the city is now engulfed in a dust storm. Undaunted for the time being, Constantius' thoughts turn to the theater when he finds an advertisement in the newspaper that Johann Nestroy's farce *Der Talisman* will be performed at the Königstädter Theater. Constantius notes that "the recollection of it awakened in my soul; the first time I was there, it seemed as if the first impression

[31] Samuel Weber, *Theatricality as Medium* (New York: Fordham, 2004), 206.

[32] Robert Pogue Harrison, "Heresy and the Question of Repetition: Reading Kierkegaard's Repetition," in *Textual Analysis: Some Readers Reading*, ed. by Mary Ann Caws (New York: MLA, 1986), 150.

[33] *SKS* 4, 27 / *R*, 151.

[34] Ibid.

evoked in my soul only a recollection that pointed far back in time."[35] All of the elements of *erindring* are here (rather than those of repetition), including the idea of an impression left on his soul of his first experience at the theater. This memory causes an avalanche of other memories to occur to Constantius and for the next several pages the reader is carried along in Constantius' reminiscences. Emerging from his reveries, Constantius determines to attend the performance. However, upon arriving at the theater, his present experience does not match his recollections: the girl that sat on the third row the first time he attended *Der Talisman* is not there. And Beckmann's performance that was originally a source of wild hilarity Constantius now finds uninspiring and dull. Disillusioned, Constantius returns to his apartment only to find everything there to be a disappointment as well. Resolved to test the possibility of repetition one more time (that is, repeating it), Constantius returns again to the theater the next evening only to be rebuffed once again: "The only repetition was the impossibility of a repetition. Unter den Linden was unbearably dusty; every attempt to mingle with people and thus take a human bath was extremely disappointing. No matter how I turned and shifted, all was futile."[36]

Robert Pogue Harrison remarks that "the lover thinks he discovers repetition, but in truth ...only discovers more poetry."[37] I would add that Constantius thinks he fails to discover repetition, but in truth does. Both the Young Man and Constantius are self-deceived when it comes to repetition, but Constantius *experiences* repetition though he does not realize it, does not *know* that he does. What Constantin experiences is that the past is not something that can be taken again as if it was some object or collection of objects to simply be taken hold of since the past is always colliding with present concerns and expectations such that the past is itself never stable but is an ongoing process of transformation. Constantius' palpable disappointment that the past cannot be "taken again" as it were does not reveal that there is no repetition but rather that there is no "beyond memory" as Samuel Weber described it, nothing outside of time and the self's relation to time, i.e., memory. Constantius thus perceives a rupture to his dismay between past and present, a lack of continuity wherein the past has become something alien for Constantius such that he no longer recognizes it as his, as a past that can be "taken again."

---

[35] *SKS* 4, 30 / *R*, 154.
[36] *SKS* 4, 44 / *R*, 170.
[37] Harrison, "Heresy and the Question of Repetition," 150.

The disturbing sense of loss that a past that once seemed stable and "there" to simply retrieve is no longer possible suggests that Kierkegaard's *Repetition* can be taken as an important intervention into this dramatic historical shift articulated by Richard Terdiman but found in so many other authors of the rapidly changing world and seemingly dramatic upheavals of the nineteenth century. Namely, the past has been rendered inaccessible and thus precipitated a certain crisis of memory. Surprised and unnerved by this realization, Constantius retreats only to be surprised again by a past, a past that is not only not his but now a traumatic one, when he returns home. Constantius' return home brings the traumatic nature of the past acutely to the fore in which repetition seemingly escapes, as it were, the contained experimental conditions of Berlin and follows Constantius to his own home in Copenhagen, as if repetition had infected everything and was not the kind of object for scientific analysis he seemingly believes it to be.

III. REPETITION WITH A VENGEANCE

After experiencing such frustrations in Berlin, Constantius beats a quick retreat back to the presumed safety of his home in Copenhagen only to find that his servant, taking advantage of his master's trip to do some much needed cleaning, has moved all of the furniture:

> My hope lay in my home....I arrive. I ring my doorbell. My servant opens the door. It was a moment eloquent with meaning. My servant turned as pale as a corpse. Through the door half-opened to my rooms beyond I saw the horror: everything was turned upside down....In his perplexity, he did not know what to do; his bad conscience smote him—and he slammed the door in my face. That was too much. My desolation had reached its extremity, my principles had collapsed....I perceived that there is no repetition, and my earlier conception of life was victorious.[38]

Yes, the moment is eloquent with meaning, and eloquent with humor besides. The language of the scene in his own doorway is no doubt exaggerated for comedic effect, even bordering on the farcical in its extremity: a point to which I will return. However, the exaggerated nature of Constantius' rhetoric prevents the reader too from knowing how to read the scene.[39]

---

[38] *SKS* 4, 45 / *R*, 171.

[39] One cannot tell in Constantius' recounting of the scene from a later moment in which he sits down to write this whether or not it happened in the way that he describes, whether the scene is simply dressed up for comedic effect or if there isn't something almost confessional in Constantius' reaction.

The reader, just as Constantin, is left wondering what to think. The moment is rife with death, confusion, and chaos: the servant turns pale as a corpse upon seeing his master, Constantius, glimpsing the jumble of furniture and disarray of his apartment, sees what he describes as the horror. Prevented from viewing the state of his apartment by the stunned servant who shuts the door in his face but also prevented from seeing the scene because he cannot bear to see it in its entirety, Constantius collapses. He is deserted by not only his principles, as he says, but by the past itself and left stunned and helpless on his very doorstep.

To describe this moment as traumatic would not, I think, stretch the limits of what we have come to describe as trauma. Trauma, of course, has been used in such varied contexts and has come to designate almost any response of the mind to an overwhelming or catastrophic event. In its more psychoanalytic valence, trauma is linked to the repetition of such events in the form of flashbacks and nightmares and repeated acting-outs of the original trauma against the will of the victim. The key symptom of trauma then is a rehearsal, re-presentation, re-performance of some original trauma-event. We are not given the original trauma-event and yet there is enough in *Repetition* to suggest that Constantius is working through some kind of trauma. His relationship to the Young Man suggests as much, with some scholars noting that the Young Man might even be Constantius himself. In reflecting on the failure of his Berlin experiment, Constantius writes "How humiliated I was: I, who had been so brusque with that young man, had now been brought to the same point. Indeed, it seemed as if I were that young man myself, as if my great talk, which I now would not repeat at any price, were only a dream."[40] Of more interest to me is the fact that Constantius is himself "brought to the same point" and that he himself feels as if he is living in repetition, the repetition of a kind of fugue state. Fearful of the kind of disorientation that takes place on his doorstep, Constantius had apparently taken prior steps to insure that such things would not happen. Constantius notes the hope he found in his home was not ill-placed because he had "left the strictest instructions that my conservative principles should be maintained in my absence" by his servant.[41] Constantius refuses the servant to perform any sort of housecleaning, "especially floor scrubbing with soap" because he "mistrusts all upheavals."[42] Constantius' careful planning,

[40] *SKS* 4, 45 / *R*, 172.
[41] *SKS* 4, 44 / *R*, 171.
[42] Ibid.

however, is to no avail. He is disarmed and overcome by surprise that repetition in its negative sense has followed him even to his own home, his presumed sanctuary and retreat from such disorder.

Villy Sørensen, the noted Danish modernist writer, reads Kierkegaard's *Repetition* as dealing with this sense of trauma and blockage in terms of Constantius' misplaced reliance on scientific and philosophical explanation. "Constantin cannot reclaim himself in memory (*erindringen*) because the absurd continues to remain in force. And exactly because he cannot overcome (*komme over*) it, he philosophizes over it."[43] What Sørensen means by the absurd is more or less synonymous with trauma—a term he himself uses throughout his *Poets and Demons*—but Sørensen's point here is that Constantius attempts to compensate for the repeated trauma by way of philosophy and science. Constantius attempts to manage the traumatic by subjecting it to the methodologies and disciplinary practices that come to form a rational understanding of the world. Cathy Caruth, whose *Unclaimed Experience* from 1996 effectively launched trauma studies notes, however, that "[c]entral to the very immediacy of this experience is a gap that carries the force of the event and does so precisely at the expense of simple knowledge and memory. The force of this experience would appear to arise precisely, in other words, in the collapse of its understanding."[44] Crucially, not only does trauma undo the knowledge and understanding that Constantius seeks, but memory itself.

The attempt to neutralize the trauma experience by defending the psyche against it through conceptualizing the experience and repressing it is precisely the memory crisis of modernity. Returning to Terdiman's argument, he connects this traumatic experience to "the pervasive and continuing perception at the heart of the memory crisis: that rather than being subject to our recapture, the past in fact malignantly captures us."[45] The reversal Terdiman discovers in the memory crisis is also what Constantius discovers: the active *gentagelse* as a "taking again" on the part of the subject is assumed now by the past, a past that now "unremittingly and treacherously retake[s] everyone it had given without providing a repetition."[46] This is what defines

[43] Villy Sørensen, *Digtere og dæmoner. Fortolkninger og vurderinger* (Copenhagen: Gyldendal, 2003), 34.

[44] Cathy Caruth, *Unclaimed Experience: Trauma, Narrative, and History* (Baltimore and London: The Johns Hopkins University Press, 1996), 7.

[45] Terdiman, *Present Past*, 225.

[46] *SKS* 4, 45 / *R*, 172.

the traumatic experience in Kierkegaard's *Repetition*: that the past has seemingly split itself off from the subject, Constantius in this case, and [**"has"**] become an agent unto itself.

The past is thus not something that can be known in an objective sense, in which things are simply "there" to be recalled at will, but now marks a rupture within such a possibility and elicits a form of memory that must deal with a past as no longer available as it had heretofore been. The perturbations of memory that thus mark the crisis of memory in the modern period maroon the self in its relation to the past. The subject who wishes to grasp its past and take it back has now become subject to the very past it wants to control. Kierkegaard's *Repetition* is thus a significant text in articulating the nature of the memory crisis and functions as an early text in the unbinding of memory.

The Diaries of P. C. Kierkegaard: An Overview

Finn Gredal Jensen

If in the Danish Golden Age someone referred to "Dr. Kierkegaard," most people would think of Peter Christian Kierkegaard (1805–88) and not of his younger brother Søren, who had only published some awkward books and whose fame would be posthumous. Leif Grane begins a fine article on P. C. Kierkegaard with this observation, which is very true.[1] It is equally true that today he is mostly considered as an "appendix" to Søren Kierkegaard, however interesting he is in his own right. This approach is of course unfair. His great importance in his own age should not be underestimated as should not his vast intellectual capacity.

Unfortunately, however, he had at least two problems. First and most important, his close relation to N. F. S. Grundtvig *de facto* prevented him from pursuing an academic career at the University of Copenhagen, where he only tutored and was allowed to give some lectures but was never appointed professor. From 1842 he became isolated far away from Copenhagen, first as a vicar in Pedersborg near Sorø and later as bishop in Aalborg 1857–75. But he was nonetheless influential among his ecclesiastical colleagues, in the Grundtvigian circles, and also in political life as member of *Landstinget* 1849–52 and briefly as cabinet minister 1867–68.

Secondly, although he was rightly praised as a brilliant orator—*der Disputierteufel aus dem Norden* ("Disputing devil from the North") being his nickname in Germany—he was not capable of writing as fluently as his more renowned brother. Nevertheless, his authorship is quite voluminous, including many contributions to theological periodicals, some of which he

---

[1] Leif Grane, "Sørens Broder. Om Peter Christian Kierkegaard (1805–1888)," in *Fra Egtvedpigen til Folketinget. Et festskrift til Hendes Majestæt Dronning Margrethe II ved regeringsjubilæet 1997*, ed. by Poul Lindegård Hjorth, Erik Dal and David Favrholdt (The Royal Danish Academy of Sciences and Letters, Copenhagen: Munksgaard, 1997), 81–108.

also edited himself. These materials were all later collected in *Samlede Skrifter*, vols. 1–6, which appeared from 1902–05.[2] Somewhat surprisingly, though, this edition of collected writings left out his two principal works, the philosophical doctoral dissertation on the concept of the lie, *De notione atque turpitudine mendacii* ("*Concerning the Baseness of Lies*, Göttingen 1829), and the controversial theological licentiate dissertation, *De theologia vere christiana, præcipue autem philosophica ejus parte, rite construenda* (*On True Christian Theology, Principally of a Philosophical Kind, Solemnly Considered*, Copenhagen 1836). The reason for this, according to the editors, was that these two dissertations were "unsuitable for this edition which is intended for the general public."[3] As academic works they were in Latin, demonstrating P. C. Kierkegaard's exceptional skills in this language, which Poul Martin Møller highly praised in a review:

> The author's proficiency in the Latin language demonstrates his wide reading and knowledge of Roman literature. This is far from implying, however, that his treatise displays any signs of a vain pursuit of Ciceronian repetitions. On the contrary, he masters the art of handling the old language as a living one and of completely letting it enter the service of thought.[4]

When it comes to the diaries, the general judgment about the readability must be modified a bit. There is a difference between P. C. Kierkegaard's published texts, the style and cryptic syntax of which was worked out carefully, and his private manuscripts not meant for publication. In his juvenile years, particularly when travelling, the account is very lively and even entertaining to read. At any rate, the diaries are important sources that certainly deserve to be edited and published.

---

[2] P. C. Kierkegaard, *Samlede Skrifter*, vols. 1–6, ed. by Poul Egede Glahn and Lavrids Nyegård (Copenhagen: Karl Schønbergs Forlag, 1902–05). A bibliography of P. C. Kierkegaard's authorship can be found in Otto Holmgaard, *Peter Christian Kierkegaard. Grundtvigs Lærling* (Copenhagen: Rosenkilde og Bagger, 1953), 139–142 ("Kronologisk Fortegnelse over litterære Arbejder").

[3] P. C. Kierkegaard, *Samlede Skrifter*, vol. 1, 1902, xiii.

[4] P. M. Møller, "De Notione Atque Turpitudine Mendacii Commentatio. Autore Petro Christiano Kierkegaard, Phil. Doct., Gottingæ Typis Dieterichianis. MDCCCXXIX. (133 S.)," *Maanedsskrift for Litteratur*, vol. 7, 1832, 65–85; 85. The review was reprinted in *Efterladte Skrifter af Poul M. Møller*, vols. 1–3, ed. by Christian Winther, F. C. Olsen, and Christen Thaarup (Copenhagen: C. A. Reitzel, 1839–43), vol. 2, 1842, 84–104.

I. THE DIARY MATERIAL AND THE LACK OF AN EDITION

The relevant diary material comprises a number of manuscripts all located at the Royal Library in Copenhagen. The three main sources to be considered as P. C. Kierkegaard's diaries in a strict sense are the following: (1) Ny Kongelig Samling (NKS) 2656 4° I, 184 pages, covering the years 1828 and 1830–50; (2) NKS 907 8°, 186 pages, describing the years abroad 1829–30; and (3) NKS 3013 4° II, 223 pages, covering the years 1850–83. P. C. Kierkegaard died in 1888, but his diary stops in the year 1883. Apart from this there are numerous letters and other manuscripts to be found (e.g., in the P. C. Kierkegaard archive NKS 3174 4°). It should be mentioned that as a vicar in Pedersborg and Kindertofte near Sorø he carefully documented his official acts and correspondence on a daily basis, and from April 1844 he was officially obliged to do so. From this period a journal covering the years 1842–49 is preserved (NKS 3005 4° I, 158 pages), which cannot, however, be regarded as a "diary" in a private sense, although it is of course an important source of information not only about his ordinary daily work as a vicar, but also about more unusual matters such as the crisis that arose vis-à-vis the higher authorities when he refused to carry out compulsory baptisms.

I will try in the following to cast some light upon the contents especially of the three main manuscripts listed above. Surprisingly, this material has never been published before in its entirety. It has only been quoted here and there in the Kierkegaard literature, for instance in Bruce H. Kirmmse's *Encounters with Kierkegaard: A Life as Seen by His Contemporaries* (1996),[5] in Peter Tudvad's *Kierkegaards København* (2004),[6] and in Jon Stewart's *A History of Hegelianism in Golden Age Denmark*, Tome I, *The Heiberg Period: 1824–1836* (2007).[7] The largest excerpts, but hardly philologically reliable, are found in Carl Weltzer's monograph, *Peter og Søren Kierkegaard* (1936).[8]

---

[5] *Encounters with Kierkegaard: A Life as Seen by His Contemporaries*, collected, edited, and annotated by Bruce H. Kirmmse (Princeton, New Jersey: Princeton University Press, 1996); Danish edition, *Søren Kierkegaard truffet. Et liv set af hans samtidige* (Copenhagen: C. A. Reitzel, 1996).

[6] Peter Tudvad, *Kierkegaards København* (Copenhagen: Politikens Forlag, 2004). In his diary quotations Tudvad used my transcriptions of the manuscripts.

[7] Jon Stewart, *A History of Hegelianism in Golden Age Denmark*, Tome I, *The Heiberg Period: 1824–1836* (Copenhagen: C. A. Reitzel, 2007) (*Danish Golden Age Studies*, vol. 3).

[8] Carl Weltzer, *Peter og Søren Kierkegaard* (Copenhagen: G. E. C. Gads Forlag, 1936). At the time of his death in 1961 Weltzer had not finished another monograph he had been working on until 1955, describing P. C. Kierkegaard's spiritual development; the manuscript, com-

In this work, however, Weltzer did not include the travel diary NKS 907 8°, to which he had no access, since this was donated to the Royal Library much later, in 1949, from the estate of Professor Victor Kuhr, who is maybe best known as co-editor of *Søren Kierkegaards Papirer*.

During some of my years spent at the Søren Kierkegaard Research Centre at the University of Copenhagen (1999–2008), while working on the edition of *Søren Kierkegaards Skrifter*, I had the opportunity to use some research time on transcribing and encoding P. C. Kierkegaard's diaries. This took place now and then in the years 2002–05, and I completed a large part of the material. In collaboration with Niels W. Bruun I also began writing commentaries, but after this the project came to a standstill. Some of the transcriptions were later used in *Søren Kierkegaards Skrifter*, particularly in the commentary volume to the letters, K28 (published 2012), which also included the relevant information taken from a special feature of the diaries, namely P. C. Kierkegaard's monthly surveys or lists of his private correspondence. From a Søren Kierkegaard perspective this information is also interesting in the sense that it documents letters which are now lost, the main reason being that Søren Kierkegaard burned the letters he received from his elder brother.[9]

In the future, hopefully, the diaries of P. C. Kierkegaard will be published in full, at least digitally on the internet, by the Society for Danish Language and Literature, Copenhagen.

II. "MEMORIES OF YOUTH"

At the beginning of the earliest diary, P. C. Kierkegaard gives an overview of the past years under the heading "Memories of Youth" ("*Ungdoms Minder*").[10] This is done by naming a number of persons important to him and, mostly by means of keywords, different personal landmarks or incidents from earlier in his life. From his time at the Borgerdyd School (the School of Civic Virtue) in Copenhagen, the most important names mentioned here

prising 506 pages, with the working title *En Uværdig. P. C. Kierkegaards religiøse Udvikling* (*An Unworthy One: P. C. Kierkegaard's Religious Development*), is now at the Royal Library (acc. 1994/41); cf. the mention of this as a forthcoming work in Weltzer, *Grundtvig og Søren Kierkegaard* (Copenhagen: Gyldendal, 1952), 45.

[9] This information from the diaries is available in *SKS*, vol. K28, 44–47. In general, see also the commentaries of the same volume to the extant letters from Søren Kierkegaard to P. C. Kierkegaard.

[10] Royal Library, NKS 2656 4° I, 2.

are possibly those of two of his schoolmates, Ludvig Christian Müller (1806–51) and Theodor Wilhelm Oldenburg (1805–42), both theologians and life-long friends. At the very beginning of the same diary P. C. Kierkegaard a few years later, on December 15, 1832, entered a number of pathetic poems he had received from Oldenburg back in 1826, and added in Latin, *quanto melius Brorson* ("How much better Brorson!"), demonstrating this by quoting some lines from H. A. Brorson's famous hymn "Den yndigste Rose er funden" and noting that "on the same occasion the monuments of his and my poems were burnt."[11] However, this did not prevent Oldenburg from later writing some fine hymns, and Kierkegaard from publishing a selection of poems by him when he passed away at an early age.[12]

In general, early deaths were very common at the time: In the "Memories of Youth" one learns, for instance, about the deaths of the brother Søren Michael in 1819, following his tragic accident in the schoolyard, and of the oldest sister Maren Kirstine in 1822. Another tragic incident is the death of Carl Lund (not to be confused with the nephew of the same name), with whom P. C. Kierkegaard made a short trip to Sweden in the summer of 1824, where he got drenched with rain, fell ill and eventually died. Generally, the close relations between the Kierkegaard and Lund families are of course evident from the diary: the engagements and marriages of the two surviving Kierkegaard sisters, Nicoline Christine and Petrea Severine, with two of the other brothers, J. C. and H. F. Lund (in 1824 and 1828), but more interesting to observe, between the lines, is the importance (both to Søren and P. C. Kierkegaard) of yet another brother, the natural scientist P. W. Lund, although the diary only notes his name and the fact that he went to Brazil in the autumn of 1825.

P. C. Kierkegaard had left the Borgerdyd School in October 1822, but only to return later as a teacher. In an excellent school testimony headmaster Michael Nielsen described him as a distinguished example, shining as "a light for others to regard with admiration and to imitate" (*lumen cæteris ad intuendum imitandumque*).[13] This was, of course, also an ideal and high standard to be aspired to by his brother Søren, who had started at the school the year before, in 1821. In only three-and-a-half years, P. C. Kierkegaard completed his studies in theology at the University of Copenhagen in April

---

[11] Royal Library, NKS 2656 4° I, 1.

[12] *Mindeblade om Theodor Wilhelm Oldenburg, Præst til Sorterup og Ottestrup. Smaadigte af den Afdøde*, edited and published by P. C. Kierkegaard (Copenhagen: J. C. Scharling, 1844.)

[13] The last part of the testimony is quoted in Weltzer, *Peter og Søren Kierkegaard*, 17.

1826 with the best grade *laudabilis*, and after this he was teaching, mostly Greek and Latin, at his old school until 1828 when he decided to go abroad. The diary does not say much in detail about what happened during these years at school and university, but, as already mentioned, only gives the "headlines" and sums up the main or most impressive occurrences such as the serious fire of April 1–2, 1826, which had also severely damaged the Kierkegaard family residence (2 Nytorv), his suffering from typhus in the summers of 1826 and 1827, his travels to Vesterborg on the island of Lolland in the year 1826, where he met his future first wife, Elise Marie Boisen, daughter of Bishop P. O. Boisen, and to Jutland in the summer of 1827. On January 22, 1827, a Latin-speaking society or *disputatorium*, a *societas eristica*, was founded, in which he participated and to which he would later send a long letter in Latin from Berlin.

While teaching at the Borgerdyd School P. C. Kierkegaard hardly knew precisely what he was heading for. He was, so says the first diary, "eagerly studying philosophy, but in lack of the outlook or specific points of view, drowned in Kantianism."[14] At the same time the diary reports a few recreational activities: "During this summer [of 1827] I was riding a lot, either together with Christian Lund or using his horse," and at the end of December of the same year it says, maybe surprisingly, that he had "begun to learn fencing."[15] Eventually, in March of 1828, he turned to his close friend Johannes Ferdinand Fenger (1805–61) and suggested that they travel together. There were still some necessary things to attend to before they could leave, as when in April 1828 "Søren was confirmed on the 20th and received my watch; I [received] Father's."[16]

III. YEARS OF TRAVELLING 1828–30

Then, finally, on May 30, 1828, the journey began. After spending a few days in Hamburg, P. C. Kierkegaard together with Ferdinand Fenger (in the diaries always abbreviated "FF") arrived in Berlin on June 9, 1828, where he would stay for over a year. From this point on, after the heading "Journey" ("*Reise*") on p. 3, the diary is kept in detail on a daily basis, recording all information concerning whom he met and with whom he corresponded, what he was reading and what he saw. In the last case, one even finds a

[14] Royal Library, NKS 2656 4° I, 2.
[15] Royal Library, NKS 2656 4° I, 3.
[16] Ibid.

number of small sketches that he made to assist his memory. The first part of the diary NKS 2656 4° I ends on August 14, 1828 with the very short and rather atypical entry: "August 13 being lazy, *item* August 14."[17] After this follow a survey of correspondence, "Letters since I left Copenhagen," and a list of *personalia familiæ*, birthdays, deaths etc., but more important the following remarks which will clarify the complex chronology of the earliest diaries:

> *The journey to Silesia and Saxony* is contained in two quarto volumes, of which the last one also continues my stay in Berlin until the end of the year 1828. *The continuation* of my stay in Berlin, the further journey and my stays in Germany, the Netherlands and France, is contained in a third quarto volume, which goes until the beginning of "the great week" 1830. *The following* is contained in the present volume when read from the reverse.[18]

Unfortunately, the two volumes mentioned at the beginning, covering the rest of the year 1828, have never turned up at the Royal Library and are presumably lost. In this case gaps must be filled out from other sources, primarily from letters. The volume covering "the continuation" in Berlin, the travels in Germany, the Netherlands and France, is the extant manuscript NKS 907 8°, which begins joyously in Berlin just after midnight on New Year's Eve, January 1, 1829: "The year 1829 was initiated by FF and myself in the room of his brother, the consul, in Hotel de Rome with a friendly conversation about boys and merry pranks of youth, touching glasses of punch as it stroke 12 and wishing each other a happy new year."[19] This diary ends in Paris on July 27, 1830 and, with a small overlap, "the following" is continued on July 26, 1830, *in medias res* of the French July Revolution ("the great week"), in the very same manuscript, NKS 2656 4° I, as the earliest part of the diary, but now written starting from the opposite side of the volume.

But let us now return for a while to Berlin. It is evident both from letters and from the diaries that P. C. Kierkegaard attended lectures by a number of prominent people at the university, Hegel, Schleiermacher and others, although he seems to have preferred the church historian August Neander, with whom he also had a more personal relation. Just a few days after his

---

[17] Royal Library, NKS 2656 4° I, 14.
[18] Royal Library, NKS 2656 4° I, 15.
[19] Royal Library, NKS 907 8°, 1.

arrival, on the 10th of June, he visited Neander, with a letter of recommendation from A. G. Rudelbach, and afterwards noted in his diary, "from him I received *eine allgemeine Bürgschaft* so that I could borrow books from the great royal library, and an invitation to his Sunday *soirées*."[20] An example of such a private *soirée* was on June 15, "where a sleepy entertainment had as its subject a creed that a number of Don Cossacks considered as inherited from their ancestors."[21] Soon he had access to library books and started working on his philosophical dissertation on the concept of the lie, first concentrating on Patristic literature, St. Augustine in particular. He also took advice from Neander concerning what to read and excerpt. On June 11 he attended the first lectures, Schleiermacher on pastoral theology and Neander on church history, and the next day he and Fenger paid Schleiermacher a visit: "Schleiermacher, whom we visited with a recommendation from H. C. Ørsted, was exceedingly polite, but nothing more."[22] The little spare time left was spent playing chess, whist, billiards, going to the opera or taking short excursions to Charlottenburg and Potsdam (in July), or being sick: "The 21st unwell, the 22nd of June sick, presumably from the water I was drinking in vast amounts in this heat. I was lying for a whole week..., nursed by FF, who supplied me with Lessing, Klopstock, Herder, Körner, Bürger, Hölty, Wieland."[23]

To get a proper impression of P. C. Kierkegaard's view of Hegel, we will have to move to the next diary, NKS 907 8°, beginning in January 1829.[24] (As already mentioned there is a gap caused by the two diary volumes missing for the last part of 1828, which also included the travels to Silesia and Saxony, where Neander had provided him with letters of recommendation to Breslau and Leipzig.) I will just mention a few instances: On January 12, 1829, P. C. Kierkegaard wrote a long letter in Latin, quoted in the diary on pp. 5–7, to the aforementioned *societas eristica* in Copenhagen, containing the following remarks: "*Audivi Hegelium, miratus sum ingenii acumen, insanam sapientiam non potui concoquere*," that is, "I heard Hegel, I was astonished at the acumen of his intellect, but I could not digest his mad

[20] Royal Library, NKS 2656 4° I, 7.

[21] Royal Library, NKS 2656 4° I, 8.

[22] Royal Library, NKS 2656 4° I, 7.

[23] Royal Library, NKS 2656 4° I, 9.

[24] See also Jon Stewart, "Peter Christian Kierkegaard's Stay in Berlin," in his *A History of Hegelianism in Golden Age Denmark*, Tome I, *The Heiberg Period: 1824–1836*, 327–331.

philosophy."[25] In the month of March 1829 Hegel had been ill for a while and was about to reappear: "Hegel, who would have lectured today [March 18], has cancelled. As a token of courtesy, Marheineke likewise cancelled his own lecture and, consequently, the auditorium was empty and 2–300 people had shown up in vain in order that the two Dalai-lamas could flatter each other."[26] About a week later P. C. Kierkegaard heard Hegel again and was impressed, but entirely rejected his understanding of Christian dogmatics. This becomes even clearer from a letter he completed on May 16, 1829 to his old headmaster Michael Nielsen. The letter, according to the diary, included "a detailed account of my opinions concerning Hegel's philosophy (*in specie* the lectures by him that I attended) and the essential reason why I do not want to listen to him."[27] Luckily, this important letter has previously been published by Holger Lund.[28]

The diary contains several reflections on P. C. Kierkegaard's troublesome working process. Mostly, this is concerned with the problem of pulling himself together and concentrating (a problem familiar to most people). This is a typical entry: "Indisposed I went to bed at 11 and on Sunday January 4 I got up, indisposed, at 9. After lazing for a couple of hours, however, I felt better…."[29] To illustrate the problem of concentration I will also quote a passage from March 9, 1829 (the "*m.*" referred to is *mendacium*, the concept of lying, and his abbreviation for the dissertation):

> Since Hegel is still sick and Ritter's lectures have come to an end, I had all of the day ahead of me to work on *m.* I did write something, but in the afternoon I felt so dull and, as I wanted to force it, so dizzy that I was compelled to stop and to continue with some easy reading (Strauss, *Glockentöne*), whereupon it passed over. I am not sure exactly how to explain this spiritual discomfort, which really scared me, whether it was caused by the tension yesterday or too intense reflection today. I have noticed that reflection on these abstract matters is much more tiring when you are not writing than when the pen is in motion.—Moreover, to pre-

---

[25] Royal Library, NKS 907 8°, 5.

[26] Royal Library, NKS 907 8°, 30.

[27] Royal Library, NKS 907 8°, 54.

[28] Holger Lund, *Borgerdydsskolen i Kjøbenhavn 1787–1887. Et Mindeskrift i Anledning af Skolens Hundredaarsfest* (Copenhagen: Otto B. Wroblewskis Forlag, 1887), 175–179; summarized in Holmgaard, *Peter Christian Kierkegaard*, 20f.; Grane, "Sørens Broder," 83.

[29] Royal Library, NKS 907 8°, 2.

> vent such occurrences I must be careful to vary my activities more, to write about *m.* mainly in the morning.[30]

Despite his diligence the pen was not sufficiently "in motion," and he decided to finish the manuscript in Göttingen. On September 1, 1829 he left Berlin for Wittenberg and Halle; he spent almost two weeks in Glauchau, visiting Rudelbach, and after this detour arrived in Göttingen on October 1. Here he worked intensely on the dissertation, which he successfully defended on December 14. After this promotion he wrote "*Telos*" in Greek in his diary.[31] In general, it is worth emphasizing that the diary is of course an important source of information about the genesis of the dissertation, supplying all the reflections made while he was writing it, and documenting the daily progress.

From Göttingen P. C. Kierkegaard sent a copy of the dissertation to Jacob Peter Mynster, explaining in the letter enclosed that he needed the doctoral degree in order to achieve an easier access to Catholic libraries for further studies, since the philosophical dissertation was only meant as the first part (on the concept of the lie and its morality from a philosophical perspective) of a research project on "the doctrine of the duty of truthfulness and its limits, philosophically, biblically and historically."[32] Insofar as Mynster, who later became bishop of Copenhagen, was also a board member of the university, it is obvious that P. C. Kierkegaard's intention was to establish a good standing for himself, in preparation for an academic career in Copenhagen. In his diary he had planned his continued studies abroad in detail, writing that he would first focus on *doctrinæ de mendacio historia* (the history of the doctrine of the lie), on morality in general and biblical studies.[33] On February 26, 1830 he left Göttingen and travelled north alongside the Rhine, which he enjoyed (he was also a tourist and liked to describe what he experienced), spending time in a number of German cities, especially Bonn, and arriving in the Netherlands on April 11, mainly in pursuit of scholastic literature in the libraries of Utrecht and Leiden. In the month of June he was in Louvain and Brussels, and then proceeded to Paris, arriving there on July 1, 1830, where a few days later, on July 6, he celebrated his 25th birthday.

---

[30] Royal Library, NKS 907 8°, 27.

[31] Royal Library, NKS 907 8°, 119.

[32] Royal Library, NKS 2312 4°; the letter is quoted in Weltzer, *Peter og Søren Kierkegaard*, 29–31.

[33] Royal Library, NKS 907 8°, 117.

Apart from studying and making excerpts in libraries he found time for museums, churches, theater, and social duties; for instance, on July 8 he paid "the poor [P.A.] Heiberg" a visit.[34] At the end of the same month he was an eyewitness to the dramatic July Revolution. On Tuesday July 27 he writes: "As I left the dinner table with Mourier, everything was in motion, Palais Royal and a fair he would show me were blocked, gendarmes on foot and on horseback were in motion, likewise people and stones, and it was only with difficulty and by detours that I reached my home, where I wrote a letter to Father...."[35] At this point the manuscript NKS 907 8° comes to an end, but the account continues in the diary NKS 2656 4° I (now written starting from the opposite side of the volume) and for some reason with a repetition of the entries for July 26–27. This might be explained by the possibility that the material was entered in the volume later and then edited slightly; a hint that this could be the case is an entry from August 12, 1830 where it says: "arranged my notes since Paris (however, not in the present volume, in which I am entering them on November 30, 1831)."[36] In the new version the account is now even more dramatic and elaborate, which is really worth reading, but unfortunately too long to quote here. In this context one also finds the famous scene often referred to from July 29 saying that "in the evening the construction of new barricades was begun, for instance, one just in front of my home, in which I was forced to participate and where a person passing by, with an expressive smile, handed me two bullets."[37]

This whole experience made P. C. Kierkegaard decide to leave Paris quickly, but he had to wait until August 5 since he was ill, although encouraged by the arrival of his friend Fenger on July 31. He then travelled to Strasbourg, Baden, Tübingen, Stuttgart, Augsburg, Munich, Nuremberg, Erlangen, and after this spent the first half of September at Rudelbach's in Glauchau as he had done the year before; then, after stays in Berlin and Hamburg, with a steamship he reached Danish soil on September 29. He did not return directly to Copenhagen, however, but dwelt two months in Vesterborg, Bishop Boisen's residence on the island of Lolland, where he was ill some of the time, but also helped the bishop with delivering sermons. Although the diary does not say so explicitly, without even mentioning her,

---

[34] Royal Library, NKS 907 8°, 182.

[35] Royal Library, NKS 907 8°, 185.

[36] Royal Library, NKS 2656 4° I, 5. In this and the following instances of quotations from this diary the pagination referred to is from the reverse direction of the volume.

[37] Royal Library, NKS 2656 4° I, 2.

he saw Marie Boisen again. Earlier while still in Göttingen, on January 13, 1830, he had sent a letter to his friend Oldenburg from which he quotes in the diary, reflecting on love and marriage in general and stressing that "such a thing is easier said than done. It is not enough that I fall in love, in which case it was no big deal, but it must involve some one (*una*) who would be able to love me, and that is the knot."[38]

IV. LIFE IN COPENHAGEN 1831–42

Above I have been focusing much on the travels, not only because of their great importance, but also because proportionally these few years take up quite a lot of space in the diaries, about 220 of 593 pages or 38 per cent, and with the two missing travel diaries of 1828 added, this percentage would be even bigger. There is also a significant difference: in the treatment of the remaining 52 years, from 1831 until the last diary stops in 1883, the entries are now kept in a briefer style and not as elaborate as earlier. Of course, this may not be surprising at all; when people travel, they are more inclined to document what happens, whether this be in writing or in modern times with photography, etc.

On Christmas Eve 1830 P. C. Kierkegaard finally arrived in Copenhagen after an absence of more than two-and-a-half years. With this his juvenile *Wanderjahre* had come to an end. On his way back to Denmark he had considered Poul Martin Møller's position as professor in philosophy at the University of Christiania (today Oslo), which was vacant when Møller moved back to Copenhagen, but Møller in a kind letter, dated October 17, 1830, had answered his inquiry and advised him not to apply for it. In this letter Møller also thanked Kierkegaard for a received copy of his doctoral dissertation (which he would later review thoroughly in *Maanedsskrift for Litteratur*)[39] and "for the friendly disposition with which you have preserved the memory of our social life in Copenhagen."[40]

---

[38] Royal Library, NKS 907 8°, 126.

[39] See the reference above in note 4.

[40] *Poul Møller og hans Familie i Breve*, vols. 1–3, ed. by Morten Borup (Copenhagen: C. A. Reitzel, 1976), vol. 2, 20f., letter no. 116; on P. C. Kierkegaard's relation to Møller see also my article "Poul Martin Møller: Kierkegaard and the Confidant of Socrates," in *Kierkegaard and His Danish Contemporaries*, Tome I, *Philosophy, Politics and Social Theory*, ed. by Jon Stewart (Farnham and Burlington: Ashgate, 2009) (*Kierkegaard Research: Sources, Reception and Resources*, vol. 7), 101–167; 117 with note 68.

Instead P. C. Kierkegaard now resumed his old work, teaching Greek, Latin and religion, at the Borgerdyd School, and from 1833 onwards he also tutored students of theology. Meanwhile he proceeded with his work on the continuation of the dissertation, but never finished the project. Soon after his return to Copenhagen he had frequented the Theological College of Education (i.e., the school for hopeful clergymen), but was in serious doubt whether he should become a priest or a teacher, if possible at the university. The problem was his deep feeling of not being worthy of joining the clergy. This is illustrated in an almost grotesque manner when in 1833 he applied for a vicarage on the island of Mors in Jutland, "according to Father's wish," says the diary; "whether it was according to mine I hardly know myself."[41] However, he got it, but when on March 6 he had reported at the bishop's for ordination, his scruples increased seriously:

> I began to worry more and more about all sorts of things, what I ought to do and promise, but particularly about my unworthiness of the holy office. I spent two days in deep agony until Friday the 8th where I informed Father about my sentiment and then, on his advice, turned to G. [Grundtvig]. When he had completely convinced me that my anxiety was not, as Father believed, caused only by physical weakness and hypochondria, with the help of God I reached the decision to resign, and this decision, to my great surprise and joy (praise the Lord!), Father tried to move only to a small extent.[42]

A few days later, on March 11, he had an audience of King Frederik VI and reports in the diary: "God gave me the courage to propose my commission, briefly and firmly. He also bent the heart of the king so that I could leave with a light reprimand and a permission to apply for my resignation. *Soli deo gloria!*"[43] This was a sort of repetition on a larger scale of what had happened the year before when he had applied for a seat at Borch's College, but was very happy to learn that he did not receive it, and thus was not compelled to renounce it again with the risk of being regarded as insane. He writes, "This is what comes from making plans without seriously, in the sight of God, considering if you have other than false, crooked, and fleshly motives."[44]

The very fact that P. C. Kierkegaard consulted Grundtvig in this highly personal matter shows what great importance he had to him already at this

---

[41] Royal Library, NKS 2656 4° I, 33.
[42] Royal Library, NKS 2656 4° I, 35.
[43] Ibid.
[44] Royal Library, NKS 2656 4° I, 23.

time. He had visited Grundtvig in January 1831, not long after his arrival back in Copenhagen. He afterwards became increasingly involved with him, and subsequently he was a faithful ally (more than a "disciple") of Grundtvig for many decades to come, although they never became personal friends in a strict sense. In the 1830s the Kierkegaards, including the father and Søren, attended Grundtvig's sermons in Frederik's German Church (today Christian's Church) in Christianshavn, and P. C. Kierkegaard had very close relations to several of Grundtvig's supporters, especially J. C. Lindberg, L. C. Müller, and A. G. Rudelbach, who was in "exile" in Germany. Quite significantly, he was so supportive of Grundtvig that he now decided to write a licentiate dissertation in strong defense of his theology and understanding of the church, entitled *De theologia vere christiana, præcipue autem philosophica ejus parte, rite construenda* (1836). He finished this work at the end of August 1835, but then became very sick and experienced what seems to have been a deep religious crisis. This might be what Søren Kierkegaard had in mind in the *Journal NB8* from 1848, looking back at the time when they were both still living at Nytorv, and when Peter "was morbidly seized by religiosity."[45] In the month of October 1835 P. C. Kierkegaard writes the following in his diary:

> On the 2nd [of October] I had come so far that I dared to visit Grundtvig, who in the wildest rage of my sickness had tried to comfort me two or three times, but without my mental anxiety allowing a proper conversation at the time. Also now, at this visit, I was really completely confused, since on the whole an immense tension, anxiety and confusion in my mind and will, although decreasing, lasted the rest of the month. In the middle of the month, however, I spoke to him again. Likewise to Oldenburg, who travelled to Bornholm to attend his brother's wedding and on the 31st (after 14 days) returned to me. On the 16th Father wanted me to take communion, but although I had promised it and was determined, this was entirely in vain. Shower every second day.[46]

In the diary one can follow the difficult genesis of the licentiate dissertation in 1835 and the circumstances surrounding its approval. Especially the *vota* of the professors M. H. Hohlenberg and H. N. Clausen were very negative,

[45] *SKS*, 21, 159ff., NB8:36 / *KJN* 5, 166.
[46] Royal Library, NKS 2656 4° I, 68.

and the thesis was more or less regarded as nonsense.[47] Despite this severe enmity, however, P. C. Kierkegaard was allowed to defend it, on the condition that he make some alterations and additions. The successful defense lasted 9 hours. Afterwards he notes in the diary: "[January] 29 I defended the thesis from 10 a.m. until about 2 p.m., and again from 4 until about 9. The adverse judgment of the dissertation had created a stir among the students so that all day long the house was packed."[48] The reason why so many students appeared was that P. C. Kierkegaard was a very popular teacher. Initially he was a tutor (until 1842), and in 1834 he had been permitted to lecture at the university, albeit only in moral philosophy. At the Theological Faculty he was now *persona non grata* in the sense that the doors were shut for a permanent position as professor. However, with his new degree he had achieved the right to lecture in theology, which he did in 1836–38 (on the Gospel of John, Catholic Letters, Hebrews) and in 1839 (on church history).

In 1839, together with Grundtvig, he was one of the founders of the "Danske Samfund" (Danish Society), inspired by Grundtvig's famous lectures, "Mands Minde" (Within Living Memory) at Borch's College in 1838. In this society P. C. Kierkegaard also gave popular lectures on church and world history, and in 1840–42 he even repeated them privately for Caroline Amalie, the Grundtvigian-minded queen of the new King Christian VIII. After Grundtvig had become established as pastor at Vartov Church in 1839, P. C. Kierkegaard attended services regularly and also gave some sermons there himself as his substitute. Meanwhile he was writing a lot, contributing to the Grundtvigian periodical *Nordisk Kirke-Tidende*, edited by J. C. Lindberg, and from 1840 to his own periodical, *Nordisk Tidsskrift for christelig Theologi*, edited together with his close friend T. W. Oldenburg until his early death in 1842. All of these many activities can of course be followed at close hand in the diary.

Later in 1836 P. C. Kierkegaard finally married Marie Boisen. She was a lively woman and undoubtedly brought some joy into the gloomy Kierkegaard residence at Nytorv with the two peculiar brothers, Peter and Søren, and their dominant father, until she died only a year later on July 18, 1837. Soon after her death Peter writes about her feelings: "Earlier she had once

[47] For an analysis of the theological licentiate dissertation and its evaluation, see especially Leif Grane, "Omkring Peter Christian Kierkegaards teologiske disputats," *Kirkehistoriske samlinger*, 1976, 122–149; see also Grane, "Sørens Broder," 86–95.

[48] Royal Library, NKS 2656 4° I, 71.

said that she would hate to die, and that she loved me so much; and at other times she had also complained that I felt so sad."[49] This proved to be the happiest year of P. C. Kierkegaard's life, and this was also his greatest sorrow. Apart from this there were plenty of other family tragedies in the 1830s: the deaths of the two last Kierkegaard sisters in 1832 and 1834, of the brother Niels in America in 1833, of the mother in 1834, and probably most important, of the domineering father M. P. Kierkegaard on August 9, 1838. Especially the death of the old father is described in detail quite dramatically in a long passage of the diary.[50] The doctors worked with a number of different means at their disposal: leeches, leaven, a Spanish fly, but all in vain. Afterwards P. C. Kierkegaard reflects as follows:

> My tension during his sickness was overwhelming, and I must thank God, both for his and for my sake, that he did not remain lying for longer time in his terrible death struggle, without our being able in the slightest way to make ourselves understood by him or to do something for him; but especially [I must thank God] for the great grace with which he comforted me, both regarding everything by which I had sinned against him, and regarding what had so often worried himself and by which he had worried me: the condition of his soul. I did not obtain what I had highly wanted for a while, a calming utterance by him [sc. the father], but this was replaced thoroughly by an abundance of comfort and relief from above. It was also very comforting to me that he had just been to church with me on the 5th and, as he had longed, he saw me take communion after M.'s [Marie's] death. I also found it comforting that on Monday evening he was very well satisfied with Søren and was in agreement with him, despite the fact that he had scolded Søren during the day and had refused him something.[51]

Søren Kierkegaard had left home at Nytorv in September 1837 in what was one of the most critical years of his life. In August of the same year his older brother had expressed his deep concern about his condition: "Lately Søren has been depressed perhaps more than ever by brooding, most likely over his health, but it makes him unhappy and unfit, and it is close to making him mad. To judge from recent days, when things really began to go wrong, the pleasure trip he took on the very day of the burial [of Marie] did

[49] Royal Library, NKS 2656 4° I, 88.

[50] Royal Library, NKS 2656 4° I, 101; quoted in Weltzer, *Peter og Søren Kierkegaard*, 126–128.

[51] Royal Library, NKS 2656 4° I, 102; the translation of the last two sentences of this quotation, "It was also" etc., is taken from Kirmmse, *Encounters with Kierkegaard*, 143.

not benefit him at all."[52] Throughout the diaries there is plenty of evidence of P. C. Kierkegaard's constant worries about Søren, e.g., in March 1835: "Søren does not seem to be studying for his examinations *at all* now. May God help him to find a good way out of all this inner ferment and to the salvation of his soul."[53]

It should be mentioned that the diary contains a number of poems and hymns by P. C. Kierkegaard; this number is especially great in the year 1838. Another recurrent phenomenon to be observed in the diaries is his use of dreams and bibliomancy: he looks up random verses of the Bible, taking them as omens and regularly noting them in the diary, although he is seriously in doubt whether this practice is Christian, as when on one occasion in 1833 he writes: "Is this superstition or not? ...God forgive me if it is wrong, but I hope even more that this, too, according to His fatherly guidance, will be of benefit to me, to my warning, comfort and encouragement."[54]

V. VICAR IN PEDERSBORG 1842–56

In 1841, after some years as a widower, P. C. Kierkegaard married Sophie Henriette Glahn (called Jette), who was a niece of Grundtvig's wife. Until her father Poul Egede Glahn became perpetual curate at Garnison's Church in 1824, she had even been raised in Grundtvig's home, to which she felt closely connected. In 1842 she gave birth to a son, Poul (Pascal Michael Poul Egede Kierkegaard), but after this she became permanently sick with an unknown condition and spent much of her long life in bed. In a way, this was a sad replacement of Marie Boisen, but P. C. Kierkegaard was devoted and now had a family of his own. Possibly tired of being "freelance" and with no realistic possibility of a real academic career, he decided to leave the capital and become a priest. In September 1842 he was appointed to the vicarage of Pedersborg and Kindertofte near Sorø.

In the 1840s P. C. Kierkegaard's daily duties and correspondence are documented in great detail in the aforementioned official journal, 1842–49 (NKS 3005 4° I), while he simultaneously kept his private diary (still in the same manuscript, NKS 2656 4° I). From October 1850 onwards the private diary is continued in a new volume (NKS 3013 4° II). All of these sources

---

[52] Royal Library, NKS 2656 4° I, 90; trans. by Kirmmse, *Encounters with Kierkegaard*, 142f.

[53] Royal Library, NKS 2656 4° I, 64; trans. by Kirmmse, *Encounters with Kierkegaard*, 142.

[54] Royal Library, NKS 2656 4° I, 34f.

show that the new life as *pastor rusticus* was indeed a practical challenge. His generally poor financial circumstances are evident from extant household account books.[55] Presumably for economic reasons P. C. Kierkegaard was still tutoring, but now in his vicar's residence in Pedersborg with a number of different students lodging there over the years. In the two parishes there were many duties that needed his attention, but his rural parishioners did not seem to appreciate their very erudite vicar sufficiently, since often the churches were almost empty. This was in spite of the fact that he was quite accommodating to the local environment, for instance by establishing a "book club" (*læseforening*) in Pedersborg where he gave popular lectures, in a Grundtvigian popular spirit. It must have been a relief that there were sometimes visitors from Copenhagen, such as his brother Søren, and a few friends living in the neighborhood, for instance, Ferdinand Fenger, who was now a vicar in Lynge south of Sorø, and he also saw B. S. Ingemann at Sorø Academy.

The greatest challenge in the Pedersborg years was the conflict that arose soon after P. C. Kierkegaard had begun as a vicar when he refused to carry out compulsory baptisms of Baptist children. This almost cost him his job. Both the diary and the official journal (which was private until April 1844) contain all the material to clarify the case; in the journal there are also copies of P. C. Kierkegaard's fruitless letters to the authorities: the Chancellery, Bishop Mynster, and Prime Minister A. S. Ørsted.[56] In March 1843 he was in Copenhagen for an audience with King Christian VIII, who strongly advised him to obey the decree, but also added, according to the diary, "that he would possibly have a word with the bishop, and that I could also approach him [the bishop]; however, he would not tolerate that any stir were created (and disobedience?)."[57] The following day, March 21, P. C. Kierkegaard saw Bishop Mynster, who was rather hot-tempered. He did not want to discuss the matter and said that he had not issued the decree. Kierkegaard replied that the bishop himself had motivated the decree by stressing that compulsory baptism should be an official duty of the clergy; "this insinuation that I knew to what extent, in truth, he could deny being the legislator led him to lose his patience to such a degree that he said that I made use of the

[55] The account book NKS 2656 4° II covers the years 1836–43 and NKS 3005 4° II covers the years 1843–83.

[56] Royal Library, NKS 3005 4° I, 4–8 (February 1843).

[57] Royal Library, NKS 2656 4° I, 128.

same sophistic inclination in life as I did in science."[58] In the time that followed, P. C. Kierkegaard solved the problem by letting another priest execute these baptisms, but when two years later, in 1845, he had to do it himself and refused, the authorities threatened to dismiss him. However, this never happened since he was strongly supported by several other clergymen, including Grundtvig. In all probability, his personal relation to the king and queen, who held him in great esteem, was of decisive importance. In 1847 the decree of compulsory baptism was repealed, and eventually, in 1849, with the Danish constitutional act and its provision of freedom of religion, the problem vanished.

P. C. Kierkegaard needed to escape from Pedersborg once in a while, and there were several ways to do this. Of course, he could keep his intellectual focus and write, first and foremost in his new periodical 1849–53, *Fortsættelser fra Pedersborg. Et kirkeligt Tidsskrift.* (It was entitled *Fortsættelser*, "continuations," because it was regarded as a continuation of his and Oldenburg's periodical, *Nordisk Tidsskrift for christelig Theologi.*) He regularly went to Copenhagen. In 1850 he made use of his *jus docendi* and lectured in the ceremonial hall of the university with a large audience, and in the next year there was a petition signed by 53 theologians encouraging him to apply for a vacant professorship, but this application was in vain, and so it was in 1854 when H. L. Martensen left his professorship to succeed Mynster as bishop of Zealand. The Theological Faculty cunningly avoided Kierkegaard, and an incompetent applicant was appointed instead.

There were other ways of escape, of which I will briefly mention three: politics, conventions, and holidays. P. C. Kierkegaard's political career began unsuccessfully when in 1848 he was not elected to the national constituent assembly, and the year after he failed in a bid to become a member of the *Folketinget*, the lower house of the parliament. However, he was elected to the upper house, *Landstinget*, and was a member from 1849–52. He was also member of a church commission, which was a disappointment. At home he had hired a curate to take care of his ministerial duties while he was away.

His participation in conventions, clerical conferences, was more important to him—and also more important, in a very negative sense, to his brother Søren with the conflict between them escalating because of Peter's political and Grundtvigian activities (as is well known, Søren despised de-

[58] Royal Library, NKS 2656 4° I, 129.

mocracy and Grundtvig).[59] P. C. Kierkegaard was a successful speaker in both the Southwest Zealand and Roskilde conventions. When in an improvised lecture in the Roskilde Convention of October 30, 1849, which took place in Ringsted, Peter, in a comparison with Martensen, had characterized Søren as "ecstatic," the younger brother was really hurt.[60] The diary does not say much about this; there is only the information in November that he is preparing the lecture on Søren and Martensen for print. On the next very critical occasion, in 1855, he notes in the diary: "Spoke against the pseudonymous (Sørenish) literature and theory at the Roskilde Convention on July 5."[61] This attack was not printed,[62] although decades later P. C. Kierkegaard published a statement in *Dansk Kirketidende*, 1881, explaining his public utterances concerning his brother, and also the speech at his funeral.[63] Søren could not forgive him and on his deathbed did not want to see him: "on the 19th [of October] tried to see him at Frederik's Hospital, but in vain."[64] Some entries in November concern Søren's death and funeral. He also notes: "The scene at the grave. The considerations of the newspapers I ignored during my own inner struggle, [heading: December] grief and loneliness."[65]

A fine example of P. C. Kierkegaard taking a holiday is his very long journey abroad in the summer of 1856. The diary only supplies us with the following sparse information:

---

[59] I will not treat the complex relation between the two brothers in detail here since this has been done so often in the Kierkegaard literature. For a survey I will refer to Thorkild C. Lyby, "Peter Christian Kierkegaard: A Man with a Difficult Family Heritage," in *Kierkegaard and His Danish Contemporaries*, Tome II, *Theology*, ed. by Jon Stewart (Farnham and Burlington: Ashgate, 2009) (*Kierkegaard Research: Sources, Reception and Resources*, vol. 7), 189–209, especially 197ff. See also the bibliography of that article for further literature on P. C. and Søren Kierkegaard.

[60] The lecture was later printed in *Dansk Kirketidende*, no. 219, 16 December 1849 (vol. 5, no. 11), cols. 171–193; reprinted in P. C. Kierkegaard, *Samlede Skrifter*, vol. 4, 1903, 99–120; selections translated in Kirmmse, *Encounters with Kierkegaard*, 256–259.

[61] Royal Library, NKS 3013 4° II, 14.

[62] P. C. Kierkegaard's notes, Royal Library, NKS 3005 4° VII, were later published in Otto Holmgaard, *Exstaticus. Søren Kierkegaards sidste Kamp, derunder hans Forhold til Broderen* (Copenhagen: Nyt Nordisk Forlag Arnold Busck, 1967), 23–84; selections translated in Kirmmse, *Encounters with Kierkegaard*, 259–268.

[63] "En Meddelelse fra P. Chr. Kierkegaard," *Dansk Kirketidende*, 1881, no. 22, cols. 337–345; reprinted in P. C. Kierkegaard, *Samlede Skrifter*, vol. 4, 1903, 120–128; translated in Kirmmse, *Encounters with Kierkegaard*, 146–150.

[64] Royal Library, NKS 3013 4° II, 15.

[65] Ibid.

> On Sunday the 6th [of July] in the evening (my birthday) I then travelled via Korsør away from my home once more and was stranded in the same night in bright moonlight and fair weather south of Langeland. The journey to Hamburg, Halle, Prague, Vienna, Salzburg, Innsbruck, Zillertal, Bregenz, Switzerland, Geneva, Milan, Switzerland again, via Basel, Frankfurt, Kassel, Göttingen, Hanover until [heading: September] on Tuesday the 9th at 9 o'clock I was standing at the vicar's residence again—all of this I will skip here.[66]

A reader of the diary might of course feel disappointed, but fortunately, this surprising gap of two months in the diary can be filled out with a series of interesting and wonderful travel letters from P. C. Kierkegaard to his dear wife Jette, who was staying at home, most probably in bed.[67]

VI. BISHOP IN AALBORG 1857–75 AND THE FINAL YEARS

Later in 1856, P. C. Kierkegaard was suggested as bishop of the diocese of Aalborg. Surprisingly, Bishop Martensen had recommended this promotion, but presumably only to avoid having P. C. Kierkegaard in Copenhagen, since he had now been seriously considering to return to the capital to become a priest there or even professor. Regarding Aalborg he hesitated, as always, but after consulting different authorities, in particular Grundtvig and Scripture, he agreed, also when seeing that "almost like a wonder, Jette, who was frightened of Copenhagen, is so calm about going to the Siberia of North Jutland."[68] In February 1857 he was ordained by Martensen in the Church of Our Lady, and in March he reached Aalborg, where he was joined by his wife in September.

Before his consecration as bishop he had composed a short vita, two pages in manuscript, which is important because it is a personal assessment of his life so far.[69] In his youth he was, "so bless the Lord, not able to forget completely the faith that dwelled in the hearts of his parents…but for many years was blinded by dead, inflating knowledge," and since he was often caught in earthly desires, his course of life was insecure and spineless.[70] His

[66] Royal Library, NKS 3013 4° II, 17.

[67] These letters are located at the Royal Library, as the late diary also in NKS 3013 4° II.

[68] Royal Library, NKS 3013 4° II, 19.

[69] The manuscript is in the Royal Library, NKS 3013 4° II; partly quoted in Weltzer, *Peter og Søren Kierkegaard*, 22f. and 297f.

[70] Ibid., fol. 1r; quoted in Weltzer, *Peter og Søren Kierkegaard*, 23.

judgment of the years in Pedersborg was more positive, and now, in his own way, he was quite confident about the future:

> Having a vocation to an even bigger and more responsible duty than before, he is heading for this and the few more years that might be left for him, confident in the Lord, who calls workers even in the eleventh hour and who forgives them, not only for being idle and not serving him for so long, but also for having misused the time and the strength he endowed them with, for too long, according to the will of his adversary—to the Lord, with whom there is forgiveness, that he may be feared (*Psalms* 130:4).[71]

The late diary tells of many busy years with heavy official duties, visitations, etc.,[72] but also of the shadows of the past being constantly present. On the back of the front cover of the volume P. C. Kierkegaard had fastened, with seals, a copy of a hymn (presumably by M. F. Liebenberg) in his father's handwriting, which he would possibly see every time he opened the diary. But the late Søren Kierkegaard was omnipresent when his posthumous papers arrived at the bishop's residence, apparently at the end of May 1857, which is evident not from the diary, but from a letter from the brother-in-law J. C. Lund.[73] The papers lay untouched for some time before P. C. Kierkegaard published *The Point of View for My Work as an Author*, but then left it to H. P. Barfod and after him Hermann Gottsched to publish *Af Søren Kierkegaards Efterladte Papirer*, vols. 1–9, 1869–81. Barfod became the bishop's secretary and diocesan treasurer, and one not only finds his handwriting in Søren Kierkegaard's papers, but even in the bishop's private diary where in a number of cases Barfod was authorized to enter copies of letters.[74]

While still in Pedersborg in November 1856, P. C. Kierkegaard had had a dream about Søren a year after his death, in which Søren, in the square Amagertorv, expressed his appreciation that he left politics and

[71] Ibid., fol. 1v; quoted in Weltzer, *Peter og Søren Kierkegaard*, 298.

[72] See especially Carl Weltzer, "Biskop P. C. Kierkegaard. Nogle Linier i hans Bispegerning," *Kirkehistoriske Samlinger*, 6th series, vol. 4, 1942–44, 436–534.

[73] See my article "Two Letters Discovered: From J.C. Lund to P. C. Kierkegaard and from Regine Schlegel to Henrik Lund," *Kierkegaard Studies Yearbook*, 2006, 261–270.

[74] The first example of this is NKS 3013 4° II, 75–79: letter to Henrik Lund, 2–4 October 1865, regarding the publication of Søren Kierkegaard's papers; quoted in Weltzer, *Peter og Søren Kierkegaard*, 312–317.

agreed with him in certain religious matters.[75] However, the bishop would not leave politics entirely, although in June 1861 he had a dream which made him refuse to be a local candidate for the *Folketing*.[76] But in 1867–68, somewhat reluctantly, he was in Copenhagen as minister of ecclesiastical affairs and public instruction (*kultusminister*); in September 1867 among the terms of his employment which he himself set was that he should have no responsibility for the Royal Theater and Orchestra and "be exempt from social duties" (*selskabelighed*).[77] The main issue at stake was the bill regarding voluntary congregations within the established church (*valgmenigheder*), but the opposition from the bishops, except P. C. Kierkegaard, and the clergy was enormous.[78] This intensified his general depression and made him resign in February 1868 before the bill was passed. The half year as minister was a long tale of woe, of which, however, the diary is silent; the pressure must have been so great that he found no time do update it, except for entering the usual lists of correspondence.

Back in Aalborg life became increasingly sinister in the bishop's residence. The son Poul had studied theology, became an atheist and eventually insane.[79] After two years of hospitalization he returned and got a light job as diocesan librarian. P. C. Kierkegaard could only experience this as yet another clear sign of the curse on the family. His old feeling of unworthiness and sinfulness became worse. In 1875 he resigned and the following year moved to a smaller house in Aalborg, but was still quite active, as is evident from the diary, exemplified for instance by his preaching in the poorhouse. In 1879 he refused an honorary doctorate in theology and tried, in vain, to be relieved of his episcopal rank and to return his decorations.[80] In the years following the death of his wife in 1881, his mental condition grew worse, and in 1884, on his own initiative, he was declared legally incapacitated. The final years were spent in mental darkness until he died on February 24,

[75] The dream, which also involves Bishop Mynster, is reported in the diary, Royal Library, NKS 3013 4° II, 18.

[76] Royal Library, NKS 3013 4° II, 48.

[77] Royal Library, NKS 3013 4° II, 92.

[78] For the general point of view of the clergy, see for instance H. L. Martensen's memoirs, *Af mit Levnet*, vols. 1–3 (Copenhagen: Gyldendal, 1882–83), vol. 3, 76–78.

[79] On his destiny and diagnosis see Ib Ostenfeld, *Poul Kierkegaard. En skæbne* (Copenhagen: Nyt Nordisk Forlag Arnold Busck, 1957).

[80] A copy of his letter to the king, in Barfod's handwriting, is inserted after the last leaf of the diary. See also H. P. Barfod, *Til Minde om Biskop Peter Christian Kierkegaard* (Copenhagen: Karl Schønbergs Forlag, 1888), 21–23.

1888. The last diary had already come to an end in March 1883, probably also due to the fact that P. C. Kierkegaard was increasingly blind.[81] Some of the entries in 1882–83 are written by another hand, maybe after dictation,[82] but the last entries in 1883 are made by himself in a very big and unsteady handwriting. In January he writes, for instance, "Brooding and increasing anxiety [because of] the royalties for Søren's writings" (which was a continuous source of self-reproach), in February again, "growing anxiety," and in March, "the strongest scruples."[83] With these and a few further remarks the diary ends.

[81] The proper part of the volume actually ends in April 1878, on 185, but P. C. Kierkegaard added a number of extra leaves, fastened with stitching threads: in the back of the volume 12 leaves (23 written pages) and in the front of the volume a "second continuation" of 7 leaves (13 written pages).

[82] Weltzer, *Peter og Søren Kierkegaard*, 357, wrongly assumes that this handwriting is Barfod's.

[83] Royal Library, NKS 3013 4° II, 222.

Kierkegaard's Relations to Idealism Demystified

María J. Binetti

For decades, Kierkegaardian studies have been on the lookout for Idealist and Hegelian ghosts, as if Idealism were a sort of specter haunting the healthy unfolding of thinking. The Danish zeal for distinguishing itself from the German colossus of philosophy, together with the postmodern zeal for distinguishing itself from speculative modernity, have created the hallucinatory effect of the Idealist phantom and set up Kierkegaard in the sacramental position of the grand anti-Idealist and anti-Hegelian champion. In accord with this particular trajectory of Kierkegaardian interpretation, Existentialism and post-modernity have also been laid in the anti-metaphysical and irrational ground of non-philosophy. In short, the historiographical destiny of Kierkegaardian studies has been the construction of the grand Idealist myth together with its anti-Idealist counterpart.

In the course of recent years, Jon Stewart has the merit of having denounced this historiographical myth, about which he says: "This is a nice dramatic story to tell undergraduate students and to rehearse in introductory textbooks but in the end, instead of providing a useful framework for further studies, it gives rise to a series of misunderstandings and outright myths about the Hegel-Kierkegaard relation and thus about the development of philosophy in general."[1] The dramatic story of modern and contemporary philosophy has broken the essential continuity of thinking, and introduced instead a dualistic paradigm made by exclusions, equivocations, and conceptual distortions of all kinds. The oppositions of Existentialism vs. Idealism, irrationalism vs. rationalism, and anti-philosophy vs. metaphysical thinking are the outcome of such a confusion.

Jon Stewart's work tries to deconstruct this great drama of contemporary philosophy in order to restore the historical and speculative continuity

[1] Jon Stewart, *Idealism and Existentialism. Hegel and Nineteenth- and Twentieth-Century European Philosophy* (London: Continuum, 2010), 1; see also Jon Stewart (ed.), *The Hegel Myths and Legends* (Evanston: Northwestern University, 1996).

of thinking, untangle conceptual ambiguities, and show the deep confluence between Kierkegaard and the Idealist project. His patient reconstruction of Danish Hegelianism tries to check the uncritical oversimplifications of the historiographical mainstream and provide one of the main supports on which to set up a positive approach to the relation of Kierkegaard to Idealism in general, and to Hegel in particular.[2] In contrast to the dominant story, Stewart has shown the way in which "many of Kierkegaard's best-known concepts such as 'repetition,' the theory of stages, and 'the leap' originally come from Hegel."[3]

Following Jon's Stewart landmark works, this paper aims to explain the positive influence of absolute Idealism on Kierkegaard's existential thinking. It does not mean that Kierkegaard would be only and merely an Idealist philosopher; he is also many other things in many different ways, even contradictory ones. But among all those things, he is also an Idealist thinker in his singular and unique way.

I. WHAT DOES IDEALISM MEAN?

The attempt to exorcize Idealist ghosts supposes, first and foremost, an explanation of what Idealism means, historically and conceptually speaking. From a historical point of view, Idealism arises as an emancipatory project inspired by the political atmosphere of the French Revolution. It was developed in two main centers: Tübingen University, where Friedrich Schelling, Friedrich Hölderlin and Georg W. F. Hegel studied, and the Jena Athenaeum, established by the Schlegel brothers and attended by Friedrich Schleiermacher, Novalis and Ludwig Tieck, among others.

In addition, from a speculative standpoint, Idealism means a type of metaphysical thinking; that is, not an epistemological or knowledge theory, but a theory of reality according to which actuality means subject, free creation, spirit and the concrete becoming of the absolute. In general, Idealist metaphysics could be conceptualized by four main determinations, namely: 1) monism—instead of the classic dualism, 2) immanence—instead of ab-

---

[2] Cf. Jon Stewart, *A History of Hegelianism in Golden Age Denmark*, Tome I, *The Heiberg Period: 1824–1836*, and Tome II, *The Martensen Period: 1837–1842* (Copenhagen: C. A. Reitzel, 2007) (*Danish Golden Age Studies*, vol. 3).

[3] Jon Stewart, *Kierkegaard's Relations to Hegel Reconsidered* (New York: Cambridge University Press, 2003), 623; see also his "Kierkegaard as Hegelian," *Enrahonar. Quaderns de Filosofia*, vol. 29, 1998, 147–152; "Kierkegaard and Hegel on Faith and Politics," *Kierkegaardiana*, vol. 20, 1999, 251–254.

stract transcendence, 3) negative potency—instead of the perfect and immobile supreme act, and 4) free subject—instead of substance, as the concrete becoming of the absolute, dialectically differentiated in a self-contradictory process.

The movement of self-consciousness shows the reflective structure of the actual, according to which the immediacy of the substance is mediated by the infinite reflection of thought, and resolved in a third relational and reciprocal subject, both real and ideal, contingent and necessary, existential and rational. This movement entails freedom to the extent that it depends on its own inner reflection realized in the negative self-determination of being. Because the absolute idea that defines Idealism is not a mere representation or an abstract image or mental sign, but the self-expression of freedom, that is, the consciousness of the creative potency, it results essentially in action, real becoming, and an effective ability to be. Given this, the Idealist subject is not a fixed and positive entity, but rather a reflexive action negatively determined by its absolute difference as other.

The Idealist subject is determined by a dialectical-speculative constitution, according to which affirmation becomes negation, identity becomes difference, and itself becomes otherness in the very oneness of the absolute. The absolute subject is structurally wounded by an inner negation that defines its self-contradictory dynamism, and triggers its positive creativity. It is not a matter of a mere simple and immediate negation, but rather of a determinate and double one, negating itself in a third positive and creative movement, that is, a middle term that overcomes all differences. Thus, the dialectical-speculative constitution of the Idealist subject coincides with its medial or reciprocal actuality, always reduplicated in a new mediate identity. Other names for this absolute mediation can be love, life, reason, or concept, depending on varying contexts and authors, but they all coincide in the production of the unity in and by the non-unity.

In the last resort, the Idealist subject is resolved into its individual or singular actuality, conceived as a synthesis between identity and difference, universality and particularity, infinity and finitude, eternity and time, and ideality and reality. The essential *desideratum* of Idealism, i.e., the fulfillment of God's Kingdom on earth, is achieved in the individual becoming of the absolute. Actual existence turns out to be, Idealistically considered, the *Dasein* of the absolute: its time, finitude, and historical *Bildung*.

These general determinations are shared by the major expressions of absolute Idealism, namely, Romanticism, Hegelian philosophy, post-

Hegelianism, and Kierkegaard, who also assumes the self-reflective, negative, and singular dynamism of the Idealist subject. That is what I will try to show in the following lines.

II. THE GREAT MYTH OF AN ANTI-IDEALIST AND ANTI-HEGELIAN KIERKEGAARD

As Jon Stewart has pointed out, Kierkegaard's presumed polemics against Idealism is fraught with vagueness and inaccuracies. He seldom names his interlocutor and mostly writes indefinitely against "Hegelians," "speculation," "modern culture," or simply "philosophers" or "philosophy," as if they were all equivalent. He avoids proper names and textual analysis, offering instead a personal and visceral reaction rather than an analytical and conceptual account. The polemics allowed Kierkegaard to measure himself and set forth his own existential thinking. However, the evaluation of his polemic as a consistent, accurate and rigorous portrayal of speculative Idealism is, as Stewart has demonstrated, untenable.

On the one hand, from a historical perspective, Stewart has shown that "Kierkegaard never had the grand polemic with Hegel that commentators have attributed to him."[4] His criticism is rather addressed to a heterogeneous group of contemporary Danish Hegelians, using code and nicknames to preserve their anonymity. On the other hand, from a conceptual standpoint, there are major disagreements between what Kierkegaard understands by Idealism, and what Idealism means in itself, particularly as understood by Hegel.

The main Kierkegaardian misunderstanding is to assume the point of view of the abstract and finite understanding—the *Verstand*—with its representative logic and dualistic ontology, as if that were the speculative perspective of Idealism, whereas it is just the point of view of Kierkegaardian criticism. According to this point of view, Kierkegaard fixes, opposes and excludes terms such as being and thinking, reality and ideality, time and eternity, finitude and infinity, human being and God, and so on, in order to attribute one of the abstract opposites to Idealism—namely, the universal and eternal side of the reason's system—and the other to his own existential philosophy—i.e., the concrete and historical side of actual becoming.

But the true story of Idealism is indeed the overcoming of abstract understanding—the *Verstand*—by the speculative reason. It asserts, instead of

[4] Stewart, *Kierkegaard's Relations to Hegel Reconsidered*, 623.

the intellectualist dualism, the identity of the contradiction in the immanence of a mediated becoming that Hegel calls the Concept, and attributes to reason—*Vernunft*—as absolute conception. The rational consistency of Idealism radically differs from its characterization by Kierkegaardian intellectualism. Unlike the substantial world of self-subsisting and independent entities, the speculative conception encompasses a relational subject in continual self-differentiation. What abstract understanding excludes as irreducible opposites, conceptual reason conceives as reciprocal action.

It would seem that the naïve dualism that Idealism endeavored to overcome is back with Kierkegaard, who, anachronistically enough, pretends to ignore the dialectics of identity, and blames Idealism for a pantheistic totality that dissolves the singularities into the bare darkness of indifference. The kind of identity that Kierkegaard attributes to the rational system corresponds to the abstractions of the finite understanding, ruled by the logic of non-contradiction. According to the principle of non-contradiction it is impossible for "A" to be "A" and "non-A" at the same time and in the same respect. By contrast, according to Idealism in general and Hegel in particular, it is necessary for "A" to be "A" and "non-A" at the same time and in the same respect, to the extent that identity is difference, negation is self-contradiction, and the same is always other.[5] Idealist identity, whose dynamism overcomes the immobile and tautological identity of the self-subsisting *res*, drives an active, temporal and finite process of self-differentiation that determines the core of actuality.

Another Kierkegaardian objection to the supposed system of pure reason—namely, *Verstand*—concerns the beginning out of nothingness, without any presupposition. However, the true story of Idealism begins with being in the reflexive action that reduces it to nothing, for recovering it as becoming. To Hegel—and indeed to Idealism in general—the beginning presupposes and posits the same that results from it, because the system is circular. The Idealist beginning is not a first principle of representative understanding, but the first action of freedom, capable of reflecting the absolute in any difference as the repeated center of an infinite circle. Philosophical concepts conceive the *medium*, the effective mediation, and they pursue the dialectical becoming of an absolute presupposed by its own creation.

---

[5] See Jon Stewart, "Hegel, Kierkegaard and the Danish Debate about Mediation," *Bulletin of the Hegel Society of Great Britain*, no. 61, 2010, 61–86. See also his translation: *Mynster's "Rationalism, Supernaturalism" and the Debate about Mediation*, ed. and trans. by Jon Stewart (Copenhagen: Museum Tusculanum Press, 2009) (*Texts from Golden Age Denmark*, vol. 5).

Insofar as the beginning reflects the absolute, its action is free, and freedom reflects on itself as idea. The ideal identity of actuality and intelligibility constitutes the deepest ground for the essential convergence between consciousness and action, theory and praxis, and reason and becoming. Because the idea is the reflective subject-object of freedom, its self-consciousness results in concrete, effective action, creation, and the actual becoming of the subject. The ideal reflection of the absolute unfolds in existence, and that is why the system of reason—*Vernunft*—has much less to do with the rigorous deductions of abstract understanding than with the potency of freedom and its creations.

Moreover, Kierkegaard's criticism concerns the Hegelian category of mediation, which Hegel conceives as the dynamism of overcoming the contradiction into the contradiction itself. Kierkegaard misunderstood it as a third fixed state in between two opposite things, mixing or without mixing them. Also in this case, Kierkegaardian mediation belongs to the representation of finite understanding and follows the logic of abstract identity—which fixes and excludes independent substances—rather than the dialectical-speculative logic of reason, which overcomes the contradiction in itself. Hegelian mediation expresses the becoming of an absolute that presupposes, posits and overcomes each of its self-differences in the middle/third of itself.

Mediating the universal and particular, the eternal and temporal, the necessary and contingent, and the singular individual emerges as relational dynamism. The primacy that Idealism grants to the individual has little in common with the abstract and impersonal pantheism Kierkegaard ascribes to Hegel, or with the mere emotional subjectivity he assigns to Romanticism. On the contrary, the Idealist primacy of the individual is strictly metaphysical, and from it follows the Kierkegaardian primacy of the individual, focused on emotional terms. Thus, there never existed any pantheist forgetfulness of the individual in Idealism in contrast to its heroic vindication, but rather two levels of analysis—metaphysical and psychological—arising from the same self-reflective and negative structure.

The existing individuality by which Kierkegaard is supposed to have overcome the pantheism of mere reason expresses indeed—metaphysically speaking—the great achievement of Idealism. In fact, Idealism turns the individual into the absolute while breaking the absolute into the immanence of finitude. This qualitative difference in the immanence of the absolute is the framework of Kierkegaardian existence.

III. KIERKEGAARD'S RELATIONS TO IDEALISM DEMYSTIFIED

When Kierkegaard leaves aside his reputed polemic against Idealism to focus on the existing individual in itself, he gives up the dualist paradigm of his criticism and assumes the speculative pattern of a self-reflective absolute mediated by its absolute difference. Like Idealism, Kierkegaardian metaphysics entails a dynamical monism, interrupted by the force of the contradiction, and reconciled by the unity of faith and love. In order to conceive the existing individual, Kierkegaard takes on the Idealist principles mentioned above, namely, the starting point of self-consciousness, the idea as the self-reflection of freedom, the dialectical becoming of spirit, the mediation of identity by difference, and the reciprocal action of the absolute. In the following lines, I will try to show how these principles articulate Kierkegaard's philosophy.

Concepts such as anxiety, irony and the aesthetic life in general evidence the beginning of Kierkegaard's thought in the self-consciousness of freedom as negative reflection. The action of freedom is an absolute beginning because it arises in its own ideal reflection without any other presupposition than its position. The *Ansich* of freedom, as Kierkegaard called it,[6] constitutes a positive reality from which it is not possible to abstract, an immediate and indeterminate substratum in which *logos* and reality, concept and phenomenon, idea and existence are one and the same.

At the beginning there is only freedom in its absolute possibility containing at any instant the ability for a new start. The infinite possibility of freedom reflects on itself as idea, which is not an intellectual representation, but an effective potency capable of unfolding its concrete content in the dialectics of time, contingency and finitude. Once the idea emerges from the self-reflection of consciousness, it needs to become concrete by repeating its eternity into the finite reality.[7]

Much has been said about the singular existence as a core category of Kierkegaardian philosophy. Less attention has been paid, however, to the idea that supports and enhances it. In fact, Kierkegaardian existence is the concrete achievement of the ideal, its effective actualization through a dia-

---

[6] Cf. *SKS* 4, 410 / *CA*, 108.

[7] See Jon Stewart, "Kierkegaard's Criticism of Abstraction and His Proposed Solution; Appropriation," in his *Idealism and Existentialism. Hegel and Nineteenth- and Twentieth-Century European Philosophy*, 94–119.

lectical process that repeats the immediate in a negative and infinite movement. The reduplication of the idea as *logos* and potency, consciousness and action, concept and praxis enables that kind of knowledge that Kierkegaard denominates essential or existential, and the *Concluding Unscientific Postscript* attributes to the subjective thinker. As the synthetic organ of the absolute, this sort of knowledge does not mean an abstract way of thinking but a concrete way of acting and, as such, it is speculative knowledge. The subjective thinker becomes his own idea, his knowledge is essentially action, and its content is its own freedom.

Kierkegaard endorses the Idealist assertion about the ideality of the finite to the extent that the immediacy relates to itself in the idea,[8] and that relationship determines the essence of actuality. In this respect, Kierkegaard shares the main concern of Idealism: how to re-unite the ideal and factual, the eternal and temporal, and thinking and being, after reflection has opposed them. Such a reunion is impossible for the abstract understanding, but infinitely possible for the essential knowledge of freedom, although that action is not direct but dialectical.

Kierkegaardian freedom is a dialectical becoming, a self-differentiating process mediated by the counter-movement of any movement, and the negative of any position. At any stage of freedom, affirmation becomes negation, potency becomes impotence, identity becomes difference, immediacy becomes reflection, and itself becomes absolutely other. However, the negative movement does not stop with a pure nothing, but with the second reflection of the negative which determines its positive result. In that sense, Stewart asserts that "the existential realm of freedom is compatible with Hegel's philosophy and his speculative doctrine of contradiction,"[9] that is, with a double negation reflected in itself. According to the diverse levels and intensities in the way of life, Kierkegaard classifies the negative path of becoming as anxiety, guilt, despair or sin, all of which are consistent with a free *neg*-action.

Insofar as Kierkegaardian negation remains immanent to its own reduplication, it subsists in a second immediacy that follows reflection, and unfolds its creative energy as the positive result of its dialectical becoming. This is what Kierkegaard calls a "positive third"[10] as a mediate action that takes on the differential and self-contradictory character of Idealist identity in

---

[8] Cf. *SKS* 6, 384 / *SLW*, 303.

[9] Stewart, *Kierkegaard's Relations to Hegel Reconsidered*, 202.

[10] *SKS* 11, 127 / *SUD*, 13.

order to overcome the dualistic paradigm of abstract intellectualism and actualize the paradox of an absolute reunion. Then, contrary to the ontological dualism for which A is simply A, the Kierkegaardian subject dialectically is and is not itself. It conceives its identity in a self-contradictory movement that finally is resolved in an absolute difference.

It is well known that Kierkegaard's philosophy is a dialectical one, articulated around a qualitative difference that never stops becoming. However, it is not so well known that, to the same extent, Kierkegaard's philosophy is a medial one: the eternal repetition of the *medium* as the reciprocal action of all differences. Jon Stewart has pointed out the equivalence between Kierkegaardian repetition and Hegelian mediation, both identified with the speculative result of freedom in a positive third.[11] As in the case of mediation, the third moment of repetition is not a substantial entity, self-subsisting and independent of the action of repeating, because there are no substances to repeat, but just a relational subject whose concrete dynamism synthesizes what the representative understanding excludes.

It might be objected that even though Kierkegaard would endorse the mediation of relative terms, he definitely refuses the mediation of the qualitative difference between God as transcendent and the human being as immanent. This objection understands God as an infinite substance independent of the human substance, according to the representation of the abstract intellect. If that were the case, the divine consciousness that determines the self-consciousness as individual would be so remote and alien as that faraway horizon of an unreal abstraction. In that case, God and the human being would be the substantial abstraction to which Kierkegaard denies any possible mediation, represented as two opposing and excluding entities and fantasized as a distant ideality.

But the true story is that, insofar as it is existing, the singular individual is always and everywhere the immanence of both: the redoubling of the negative into the positive, and the conversion of the absolute difference into the reconciled identity. In Kierkegaardian categories, that new re-unity is named faith, or even better: love. The second immediacy of faith reconciles the absolute difference in a positive dynamism, as well as love does.[12] Since Kierkegaardian faith abandoned the remote transcendence of the immobile substance in order to undertake the immanent production of the subject, the

[11] Cf. Stewart, *Kierkegaard's Relations to Hegel Reconsidered*, 299ff.

[12] *SKS* 20, 362, NB4:159 / *KJN* 4, 362.

kingdom of God became flesh, anxiety and freedom. The paradox of such a faith turns the absolute into time, finitude, and singular existence.

Overcoming the mere abstract and fixed representation of a substantial God, Kierkegaard aims to conceive a dynamic absolute, immanent to the consciousness of its own qualitative difference. Thereby the Kierkegaardian absolute results in the neg/action of the subject: its infinite reduplication as other along with its speculative recovering of itself. It can never be the object of abstract knowledge but only the subject of freedom, i.e., the act of faith. In other words, according to Kierkegaard, "God himself is indeed this: how one involves oneself with him. In relation to sensory and external objects, the object, the matter, is something other than the mode, the manner; there are many modes—perhaps one stumbles upon a lucky mode, etc. In relation to God, 'How' is 'What.'"[13] Then, neither is God a transcendent entity nor is the individual an abstract substance. The only real and concrete is a differential, relational, and mediate action, that Kierkegaard conceives as "pure reciprocity,"[14] and as "intermediate determination,"[15] creating *inter-esse* or *mellemværelse* ("inter-existence) of human and divine being, the self and the other, and the other and the neighbor. Pure reciprocity is one of the names for that dynamical subject reduplicated in its absolute difference; another name for it is the singular individual.

The individual is, for Kierkegaard, the only effective and concrete determination of the absolute, its concrete neg/action which is both identity and contradiction, and absolute difference and repetition. The abstract representation of the individual as a substantial entity in front of a substantial and immutable God is the objective and intellectualist caricature of what only the free action of faith can produce in its actual existence. I point out three main determinations of the Kierkegaardian individual in basic agreement with Idealist metaphysics. First, it is determined by a subjective relation, or better, by a self-relation repeated in its absolute difference. Secondly, as a concrete synthesis of opposites, the individual encompasses universality and particularity, finitude and infinity, time and eternity, humanity and divinity, and self, other and neighbor. Third, the singular *is* not a substantial entity but *becomes* an absolute *Bildung*, always expectant of the existential novelty and open to an unpredictable singular history.

---

[13] *SKS* 23, 215, NB17:70 / *KJN* 7, 219.
[14] *SKS* 9, 377 / *WL*, 385.
[15] *SKS* 9, 111 / *WL*, 107.

In the last resort, Kierkegaardian metaphysics is resolved into a sort of monism of love: the radical determination of the absolute, proper name of God, and the perfect bond of unity. In its infinite reduplication, the relationship of love turns out to be always three, never two, and this dialectical-speculative third is the very first one actively differentiated. In a nutshell, the absolute difference of love, subsisting in the immanence of its perfect unity, enables the emergence of the individual as the only possible absolute of Kierkegaardian thought.

IV. AN ORIGINAL IDEALISM

Kierkegaard's Idealism is *sui generis*. It selects, combines, and balances traits and nuances of the three major Idealist expressions, namely, Romanticism, Hegel's philosophy, and post-Hegelianism. His original synthesis is driven by two main assumptions: the primacy of the existing individual and the final goal of becoming a Christian, to which Kierkegaard tries to adjust an Idealist metaphysics.

In accord with Romanticism, Kierkegaard defines the essential core of his singular thinking. Romantic categories such as individuality, nostalgia, *pathos*, poetry, possibility, progressive infinity, and love compose the conceptual framework of Kierkegaardian philosophy. The absolute immanence that enables the metaphysical emergence of the Romantic individual also supports the radical dialectics of Kierkegaardian existence, redoubled in its own reflection and confronted with its qualitative difference. But despite his clear Romantic roots, Kierkegaard misread Romanticism as an aesthetic and subjectivist thinking, and resorts to Hegel as the objective and universal rescuer from Romantic fancies and arbitrariness.

Hegel himself is a Romantic, and precisely the most systematic of all Romantics. Kierkegaard endorses the Hegelian dialectics of actuality and follows the triadic structure of spiritual becoming articulated in three main stages: 1) the subjective-aesthetic spirit: pure abstract possibility and extrinsic necessity; 2) the objective-ethical spirit: effective potency and inner necessity; 3) the absolute-religious spirit: capable of everything, even its absolute difference. According to Stewart, "Hegel was one of Kierkegaard's most important sources of inspiration for the development of the theory of stages,"[16] consistent with the dialectical scheme of immediacy, mediation, and mediated or second immediacy. The third stage actualizes the abstract pos-

[16] Cf. Stewart, *Kierkegaard's Relations to Hegel Reconsidered*, 231–232.

sibility of the aesthete as well as the concrete potency of the ethical person by the free omnipotence of the absolute, emerging as the single individual in the synergistic action of itself and the other. The Kierkegaardian singular individual gains from Hegel the objective and mediated consistency that is lost with Romanticism. However, it regains from Romanticism the passionate inner emotion that is supposed to be lost with Hegelian metaphysics.

With regard to post-Hegelianism, Kierkegaard's religious thinking takes sides in the debate that arose in the Hegelian school after Hegel's death, and tries to redefine Christian religion in the new framework of speculative self-consciousness. In that context, Kierkegaard presupposes the validity of Christian dogmatics, as right-wing Hegelianism does, and at the same time he assumes the immanence of the divine into the human self-consciousness, as left-wing Hegelianism asserts. Precisely, the immanent reflection of the singular consciousness in the absolute determines Kierkegaard's attempt to re-found Christianity.

One of the most original traits of Kierkegaard's Idealism consists in applying the speculative metaphysics of the immanent subject to a new foundation of the Christian religion, now redefined by the principle of the Idealist self-consciousness. Kierkegaard tried to idealize Christianity in a sort of synthesis of the religious Middle Ages and speculative modernity. But the fact is that from the historical and speculative point of view, Christianity has been born and articulated around a dualistic paradigm, according to which God is a transcendent substance, the final object of human knowledge and freedom. Thus, the attempt to refound a dualistic and substantialist dogmatic on a new monistic and immanent framework turns out to be a square circle and causes the main inconsistencies and ambiguities of Kierkegaard's thinking.

In short, Kierkegaard wanted to be conservative and revolutionary at the same time, and both only to a certain extent? He wanted to be an authentic Christian, devoted to support the established order of the official church without external changes, but also to set up a primitive stage of Christianity which ignores doctrines, creeds or clerical institutions, and which actually never existed. For the traditional establishment, faith means an act of understanding based on dogmatic commandments and objective representations. For the modern subject, Christianity is a matter of self-consciousness and absolute freedom, without any dogmatic or objective content. What is strange is that Kierkegaard tried to justify the former by the latter.

As a result, Kierkegaard's religious consciousness ends up denying more than 1800 years of historical Christianity and arguing for a primitive Christianity that never existed or ever will exist. It collapsed into a kind of Christianity without church and history, without traditions and dogmas. The clearest result of this ambiguity in Kierkegaard, who wanted to found Christianity on Idealism, is the post-modern "religion without religion,"[17] radicalized by the latest Post-theological thinking.[18]

V. CONCLUSION

There is a before and after Jon Stewart in Kierkegaard studies. His work has laid the groundwork to the demystification of Idealism and a serious reconsideration of Kierkegaard's philosophy. It has demonstrated why "this widely accepted picture of the development of European thought is fundamentally incorrect and is in fact based on a misunderstanding in its initial premise, namely, that Kierkegaard issued a straightforward critique of Hegel."[19] Deconstructing this initial premise, Stewart makes it possible to reconsider the historical continuity between the Idealist project and contemporary thinking.

The new speculative turn of the twenty-first century along with the Hegel renaissance and the latest advances in Kierkegaard studies, have come to endorse Jon Stewart's judgment. Indeed, the hex of the hegemonic historiography seems to have been broken and the new century begins to resignify Idealism not only as the past but also as the present and future of thinking. The new metaphysical speculation considers itself as "the latest system-program of German idealism,"[20] and this becoming involves Kierkegaard as a forerunner and medium between the first and last system-program.

In accordance with Stewart, the most recent Kierkegaard studies indicate a kind of Idealist turning point in authors like Slavoj Žižek, Alison Assiter, Michael O'Neill Burns, and Steven Shakespeare, who in one way or another read Kierkegaard into the framework of the Idealist tradition. From

---

[17] Cf. Jacques Derrida, *Donner la mort* (Paris: Galilée, 1999), 75; see also John Caputo, *The Prayers and Tears of Jacques Derrida: Religion without Religion* (Bloomington: Indiana University Press, 1997).

[18] Christopher Watkin, *Difficult Atheism: Post-Theological Thinking in Alain Badiou, Jean-Luc Nancy and Quentin Meillassoux* (Edinburgh: Edinburgh University Press, 2011).

[19] Stewart, *Kierkegaard's Relations to Hegel Reconsidered*, 622.

[20] Adrian Johnston, *Adventures in Transcendental Materialism: Dialogues with Contemporary Thinkers* (Edinburgh: Edinburgh University Press, 2014), 13.

that reading, Kierkegaard is reinterpreted as a thinker of immanence, radical contingency and the absolute fracture of actuality. He is understood to have overcome the abstract foundationalism of the first cause by the virtual post-foundationalism of the free subject.

Reading Kierkegaard today means to open a new speculative horizon—neither conclusive nor closed—that began with the idealistic dream of achieving the kingdom of God on earth and turns now into the challenge of actualizing the world as divine potency for which everything is possible.

"Hidden Inwardness" and "Subjectivity is Truth": Kant and Kierkegaard on Moral Psychology and Religious Pragmatism

Roe Fremstedal

In the *Concluding Unscientific Postscript*, Kierkegaard (the pseudonym Climacus) complains that we have "forgotten what it is to exist and what inwardness means."[1] Hidden inwardness is described as the true religiousness, which uses all its tricks (*Kunst*) to prevent it from being noticed.[2] Still, the meaning of "inwardness" is hardly clear, perhaps precisely because it is forgotten or hidden. In this paper, I will try to make sense of "hidden inwardness" by arguing that it concerns morality rather than legality, and character rather than actions. The idea is that our characters ground our actions, although we only know our characters from our actions.

Alastair Hannay describes Kierkegaard's concept of inwardness as follows:

> "Inwardness" is by no means a perfect translation of "Inderlighed." As with Hegel's *Innerlichkeit*, the sense is not that of inward-directedness... [but of] an inner warmth, sincerity, seriousness and wholeheartedness in one's own concern for what matters, a "heartfeltness" not applied to something but which comes *from* within. However, since "inwardness" has become a standard translation for Kierkegaard's "Inderlighed" and in this sense even finds a place in the *Oxford English Dictionary*, it has been retained here.[3]

---

[1] *SKS* 7, 226 / *CUP1*, 249.

[2] *SKS* 7, 430 / *CUP1*, 475.

[3] Alastair Hannay, "Note on the Translation," in Søren Kierkegaard, *Concluding Unscientific Postscript to the Philosophical Crumbs*, ed. and trans. by Alastair Hannay (Cambridge: Cambridge University Press, 2009), xxxvii–xl, xxxviii–xxxxix.

The Danish Wolffians and Kantians coined many Danish philosophical terms in the late eighteenth century.[4] *Inderlighed* in particular is a Danish equivalent of the German *Innerlichkeit* and *Innigkeit*, terms Kantians associated with the moral-religious character or disposition (*Gesinnung*) that is hidden. Although Kant repeatedly uses the term "inward [*innerlich*],"[5] he prefers the term *Innigkeit* instead of *Innerlichkeit*. Still, he uses *Innigkeit*, not in the sense of intimacy, but in the sense of inwardness. For instance, he speaks of "the inwardness of a benevolent disposition [*der Innigkeit der wohlwollenden Gesinnung*]."[6] Like Kierkegaard, he claims that "the outer...does not disclose the inwardness of the [moral] disposition [*der innern sittlichen Gesinnung*]."[7] We do not know hearts and reins—either in our own case or in the case of others.[8]

It seems that instead of merely resorting to idiosyncratic terminology, Kierkegaard uses the same terms as Danish Kantians (and Fichteans) used in order to describe the distinction between the free moral disposition and intersubjective phenomena, as well as the related distinction between internal freedom (*homo noumenon*) and external freedom (independence from

---

[4] Cf. Harald Høffding, *Danske Filosofer* (Copenhagen: Gyldendal, 1909), 16, 21, 26f.; Anders Thuborg, *Den Kantiske periode i dansk filosofi 1790–1800* (Copenhagen: Gyldendal, 1951), 17f., 121–49, 181; Søren Holm, *Filosofien i Norden før 1900* (Copenhagen: Munksgaard, 1967), 13, 33–43; Carl H. Koch, *Dansk oplysningsfilosofi 1700–1800* (Copenhagen: Gyldendal, 2003) (*Den danske filosofis historie*, vol. 3).

[5] Cf. Immanuel Kant, *The Metaphysics of Morals*, in Immanuel Kant, *Practical Philosophy*, ed. and trans. by Mary Gregor (Cambridge: Cambridge University Press, 1999), 6:222, 6:306, 6:354, 6:357, 6:377, 6:418, 6:441, 6:463, 6:470. References to Kant use the volumes and pagination of Immanuel Kant, *Gesammelte Schriften* (Berlin: Reimer, later de Gruyter, 1900ff.), vols. 1–29.

[6] Kant, *The Metaphysics of Morals*, 6:456.

[7] Immanuel Kant, *Religion within the Boundaries of Bare Reason*, in Immanuel Kant, *Religion and Rational Theology*, ed. and trans. by Allen Wood and George di Giovanni (Cambridge: Cambridge University Press, 2001), 6:63, cf. 6:95, 6:99. Dieter Henrich argues that in the *Inquiry concerning the Distinctness of the Principles of Natural Theology and Morality* Kant admired Francis Hutcheson's recognition of the "original inwardness of the ethical [*ursprünglichen Innerlichkeit des Sittlichen*]." See Dieter Henrich, "Hutchinson und Kant," *Kant-Studien*, vol. 49, 1957–58, 49–69, 64.

[8] Kant, *Religion within the Boundaries of Bare Reason*, 6:47f.; cf. *SKS* 20, 325, NB4:78 / *KJN* 4, 326. Kant presents his account of the disposition or character as a philosophical reconstruction of the biblical idea of that only God knows hearts and reins. See Kant, *The Metaphysics of Morals*, 6:438f. I prefer "hearts and reins" (King James Bible) to "hearts and minds." The former is closer to Kant and Kierkegaard, since "reins" means not only the seat of feelings and passions but "kidneys," like Kant's "*Nieren*" and Kierkegaard's "*Nyrer*."

being constrained by another's choice).[9] The distinction between the inner (*det Indvortes*) and the external (*det Udvortes*) in Kierkegaard (and Climacus in particular) seems to correspond to Kant's distinction between the supersensible (*übersinnliche*) disposition (*Gesinnung*) and phenomena that are intersubjectively available, including the consequences of our acts.[10] For both Kant and Kierkegaard, "inwardness" refers not so much to the lower-level maxims that underlie various actions, as to the moral character (the supreme maxim) that underlies these maxims. Finally, as we will see, Kierkegaard (and the pseudonym Climacus) often reserve "inwardness" for an ethico-religious character based on neighbor-love.[11]

I. LEGALITY, MORALITY, AND CHARACTER

Like Kant, Kierkegaard distinguishes between doing the right thing and doing the thing for the right reason. Kierkegaard writes: "even if people did *what* duty commands, they would still not [necessarily] be doing their duty."[12] *Works of Love* stresses that "No one can decide" "whether it is actually out of love" that one acts or not; "it is possible that it is vanity, pride—in short something bad, but it is also possible that it is love."[13]

---

[9] For examples of how external and internal freedom were rendered inward (*indvortes*) and external (*udvortes*) freedom by the Danish Kantians and Fichteans, see Thuborg, *Den Kantiske periode i dansk filosofi 1790–1800*, 125. My Kantian approach to inwardness in this chapter is partially anticipated by Wimmer and Palmquist. Wimmer takes Kierkegaard's concepts of inwardness and subjectivity to correspond to Kant's noumenal *Gesinnung*, something that is also suggested by Palmquist. Harbsmeier, by contrast, focuses on the importance of Romanticism and Pietism for Kierkegaard's "inwardness." See Reiner Wimmer, *Kants kritische Religionsphilosophie* (Berlin: de Gruyter, 1990), 207 (*Kantstudien-Ergänzungshefte*, vol. 124); Stephen Palmquist, "The Paradox of Inwardness in Kant and Kierkegaard: Ronald Green's Legacy in the Philosophy of Religion," *Journal of Religious Ethics*, vol. 44, no. 4, 2016, 738–51; Eberhard Harbsmeier, "Der Begriff der Innerlichkeit bei Søren Kierkegaard," *Kierkegaardiana*, vol. 20, 1999, 31–50.

[10] Cf. Kant, *The Metaphysics of Morals*, 6:237, 6:418, 6:340; Immanuel Kant, *Critique of Practical Reason*, in Kant, *Practical Philosophy*, 5:161. See also n17 below. Palmquist argues that *Gesinnung* should be translated as "conviction" rather than "disposition" or "attitude." However, I focus on our fundamental *Gesinnung* in the sense of our supreme maxim, which is identical to our moral character or personality. See Palmquist, "The Paradox of Inwardness in Kant and Kierkegaard," 748.

[11] Judge William describes the choice of the ethical in terms of inwardness (*SKS* 3, 164 / *EO2*, 167). But his use of the term seems somewhat loose, sporadic and non-technical, whereas the use in the *Postscript* is more consistent and systematic.

[12] *SKS* 10, 215 / *CD*, 206.

[13] *SKS* 9, 367 / *WL*, 374.

It is clear that Kierkegaard distinguishes between *legality* and *morality*, between acting in accordance with the law and acting out of respect for the law. We can know the legality of actions based on experience, but we do not know their morality in any straightforward manner. Because of this, legality is compatible with egoism *and* altruism, with radical evil *and* morality.

Still, we can know that acts without legality are *not* moral. Since legality is necessary, Kierkegaard (Climacus) concludes that "the religious person's incognito...does not mean that his...is the actuality of a robber, a thief, a murderer."[14] This appears to be a formal point to the effect that one cannot possibly have the right reasons or motivation (e.g. faith) if one does the wrong thing (e.g. kill). In this sense, legality is necessary. Nevertheless, Kierkegaard (Climacus) fails to specify whether he is thinking of moral or juridical legality (i.e. whether the law in question is moral or juridical). Still, on balance we can infer that the former seems more likely than the latter, since the discussion centers on ethics, religion, and character. The concept of ethics, both here and elsewhere in Kierkegaard, is not secular but religious, since the good and the divine are regarded as identical.[15]

Perhaps because he focuses on character rather than actions (and the formal aspects of morality rather than its material aspects), Kierkegaard tends to be vague (if somewhat traditional) about the content of morality. It is therefore difficult to ascertain what accepting legality would amount to on Kierkegaardian terms. Surely, it should not mean that we always ought to accept whatever practice is established by society. Kierkegaard is clearly opposed to an ethics that justifies and deifies the established order, attributing such a view to the pseudonym Judge William.[16]

Nevertheless, it is even more complicated with *characters* than actions, since characters are only known from actions (while also being the source of actions). For this reason, characters are more hidden, or less explicit, than the motives and causes of actions. For Kant, an action presupposes a lower-level maxim, which again presupposes a character (supreme maxim). Indeed, Kant describes character as a disposition (*Gesinnung*), which is supersensible

---

[14] *SKS* 7, 453n / *CUP1*, 500n. Kierkegaard also relies on the distinction between legality and morality in his journals (*SKS* 23, 384, NB19:86 / *KJN* 7, 392). Like Kant, he even contrasts Jewish legality with Christian morality (*SKS* 18, 381, KK:11 / *KJN* 2, 348; *SKS* K18, 558, see also *SKS* 11, 196 / *SUD*, 82; *SKS* K11, 216).

[15] *SKS* 4, 160 / *FT*, 68; *SKS* 6, 439 / *SLW*, 476; *SKS* 7, 133–43 / *CUP1*, 142–54; *SKS* 8, 151–3, 364 / *UD*, 39–41, 268.

[16] Cf. Merold Westphal, *Kierkegaard's Concept of Faith* (Grand Rapids: Eerdmans, 2014), 48f.

and therefore not directly accessible to us.[17] Kierkegaard also denies that we have any direct access to our own disposition or character (although he seems less explicit about whether the disposition is supersensible).

Like Kant, Kierkegaard insists that we have an unconditional obligation to be moral, irrespectively of how others act towards us. Still, it is very difficult, if not impossible, to avoid assumptions about our moral characters and personalities. In many situations, for instance, we need to choose who we are to trust and who we should not. It seems impossible to do this, unless there is a way to distinguish a life of virtue from evil that stays within the bounds of legality. It thus seems that inwardness cannot be entirely hidden. Jack Mulder writes:

> [T]he problem with hidden inwardness is not that it is inward, the problem with hidden inwardness is that it is *hidden*. To hide something one necessarily contains it. And this is the problem. An inwardness that confines itself (in order not to be seen for what it is) is not in fact inwardness, but negative outwardness.[18]

An entirely hidden inwardness seems to be a false inwardness, a negative outwardness. Kant thinks that we need many observations in order to confirm that someone has a moral character, but only one observation to know that there is no (moral) character.[19] One act without legality (e.g. killing) indicates an underlying evil character, whereas acts that appear good need not involve a good character.[20]

Like Kant, Kierkegaard holds some acts to be incompatible with morality (and genuine religiousness). *Works of Love*, which provides a notable example, describes several types of behavior that are incompatible with neighbor-love. In the case of bitter mockery, poisonous distrust, and cold

---

[17] Kant, *Religion within the Boundaries of Bare Reason*, 6:63, 6:67; Robert B. Louden, *Kant's Impure Ethics: From Rational Beings to Human Beings* (Oxford: Oxford University Press, 2002), 136, 152. See also n10. In his 1833–34 lecture notes, Kierkegaard refers to Kant's view of moral rebirth, whereby moral character is established. See *SKS* 19, 57, Not1:7 / *KJN* 3, 52.

[18] Jack Mulder, Jr., "Re-Radicalizing Kierkegaard: An Alternative to Religiousness C in Light of an Investigation into the Teleological Suspension of the Ethical," *Continental Philosophy Review*, vol. 35, 2000, 303–24, 317.

[19] Immanuel Kant, "Reflexionen zur Anthropologie," in Kant, *Gesammelte Schriften*, 15:55–654, especially 15:541, *Reflexion* 1230; cf. 15:526, *Reflexion* 1191; Kant, *Religion within the Boundaries of Bare Reason*, 6:20, 6:68.

[20] Cf. Kant, *Religion within the Boundaries of Bare Reason*, 6:71, 6:63. This presupposes the doctrine of moral rigorism at the level of character, i.e. that characters are either good or evil. See 6:22–5.

callousness, he says that "it will be recognizable from the fruits that there is no love within."[21] And someone who accuses and condemns others is thereby said to reveal and condemn himself indirectly.[22] After this, Kierkegaard emphasizes that one must forgive one's neighbor if one is to be forgiven by God, since "the forgiveness you give is the forgiveness you receive."[23]

Furthermore, he adds: "[T]here is nothing, no 'thus and so,' that can unconditionally be said to demonstrate unconditionally the presence of love or to demonstrate unconditionally its absence."[24] Nevertheless, Kantians could concede that there is nothing that unconditionally demonstrates the presence of charity (practical love). Still, some acts *are* incompatible with morality (e.g. murder) and would seem to demonstrate the absence of love (given sanity and accountability). Despite this, Kierkegaard is probably right that the absence or presence of love cannot be demonstrated unconditionally with a single proof or consideration. To know this we would not only need to know the nature of an individual act, but also the relevant context, intentions, reasons, causes, and whether the person was sane or not. We need not only an act, but also an autonomous action and relevant character traits. We must then rely on inferences from the outer to the inner that involve judgments that are uncertain, as Kant points out.[25] These judgments are conditioned on many different fallible considerations about the agent and the context, as Kierkegaard in turn suggests.[26]

In the case of neighbor-love, Kierkegaard contrasts the hiddenness of love with its visible fruits.[27] Words and deeds indicate something about the underlying disposition or character, even if the character is hidden. Rather than being absolutely hidden, inwardness is the disposition or character that grounds ethico-religious actions.[28] The "inner" and "inward"—"*det*

---

[21] *SKS* 9, 15 / *WL*, 7.

[22] *SKS* 9, 373f. / *WL*, 380f. *Practice in Christianity* makes a similar point by claiming that condemning a Christian for confessing his faith, is to condemn yourself (*SKS* 12, 215f. / *PC*, 220).

[23] *SKS* 9, 373 / *WL*, 380.

[24] *SKS* 9, 22 / *WL*, 14. Ferreira writes that "inner does not always reveal outer and vice versa…Any act can be done lovingly or unlovingly." M. Jamie Ferreira, *Love's Grateful Striving: A Commentary on Kierkegaard's* Works of Love (Oxford: Oxford University Press, 2001), 253.

[25] Kant, *Religion within the Boundaries of Bare Reason*, 6:63–7; Louden, *Kant's Impure Ethics*, 136–52.

[26] *SKS* 9, 15 / *WL*, 8f.

[27] *SKS* 9, 15ff. / *WL*, 8ff.

[28] The exception to this is the private revelations discussed in *Fear and Trembling* and *The Book on Adler*. By definition, such revelations are private, even if they involve inwardness and

Indvortes" and "*det Inderlige*"—therefore do not need to refer to a private, inner space, life, or experience that is available through introspection. (For this reason, the translation of "*det Indvortes*" as "the inner world" seems questionable.[29])

Still, "inwardness" is better described negatively than positively, because it is easier to make the case that "inwardness" is lacking than to make the case that it exists. The concept of hidden inwardness need, then, not be as problematic as it seems, since it mainly involves the broadly Christian and Kantian idea that we do not know the hearts and reins of others—or even ourselves.[30] It is only God, as a scrutinizer (knower) of hearts, who knows our innermost being,[31] including whether we have attained inwardness or not.[32] Gordon Michalson comments:

> [J]ust as there is a noumenal shield protecting the Kierkegaardian object of faith, there is a corresponding noumenal shield protecting the inner recesses of this all-important subject of faith, the true disciple. This becomes clear in Kierkegaard's claim that we can never truly "know" or recognize an authentically religious person, the presumptions of Christendom notwithstanding. The Kantian attitude toward the profound concealment of the true moral worth of another person is recapitulated almost exactly in Kierkegaard's idea of the "knight of faith," whose identity remains forever hidden from the scrutiny of others.[33]

---

lead to outward acts (e.g. the sacrifice of Isaac). *The Book on Adler* discusses whether Adler's deeds and words are compatible with a putative private revelation, something Kierkegaard denies.

[29] See *SKS* 3, 96 / *EO2*, 94.

[30] See n8.

[31] *SKS* 10, 244 / *CD*, 237.

[32] Harbsmeier, "Der Begriff der Innerlichkeit bei Søren Kierkegaard," 31ff.

[33] Gordon Michalson, *Lessing's "Ugly Ditch": A Study of Theology and History* (London and University Park: The Pennsylvania State University Press, 1985), 90. Marilyn Piety writes: "Kierkegaard clearly holds something like a Kantian view of the relation between the phenomenal and noumenal view of a person. This view can be found, for example, in the section of *Either-Or Part II* entitled "The Aesthetic Validity of Marriage." It may be challenging to make sense of how the phenomenal and noumenal aspects of a person can be brought together in such a way as to preserve human freedom, but Kant asserts they can be, and Kierkegaard appears to follow Kant in this respect. In fact, Kierkegaard distinguishes between 'rationalism' and 'naturalism' in a journal entry that examines this aspect of Kant's thought (*SKS* 19, 159 [Not 4:11 / *KJN* 3, 139f.])." See Marilyn G. Piety, "Kierkegaard on Nature and Miracles: A Reply to Hampson," 2017, https://pietyonkierkegaard.com/tag/kierkegaard-on-kant/ (2018/02/01).

Kierkegaard does not seem to accept Kant's transcendental Idealism.[34] But he does accept associated Kantian ideas about the finitude and limits of human cognition, denying that we can have knowledge of the *Gesinnung* in particular and the supersensual in general (as suggested by Platonists and rationalists). He also accepts Kant's related critique of theoretical proofs for the existence of God. Even if Kierkegaard is not a transcendental Idealist, he nevertheless accepts broadly Kantian points about the limits and finitude of human cognition, sketched by Kant in *Dreams of a Spirit-Seer* prior to his more celebrated transcendental Idealism in *The Critique of Pure Reason*.[35]

II. DID KIERKEGAARD'S VIEW OF INWARDNESS CHANGE?

Many scholars have pointed out that Kierkegaard's earlier works tend to defend hidden inwardness, whereas his later works tend to attack it.[36] In 1846, he in the guise of Climacus calls for inwardness, whereas he takes up the persona of Anti-Climacus when he calls for outwardness in 1850.[37] Kierkegaard sketches the following historical narrative. First, medieval Christianity over-emphasizes outwardness by privileging the monasteries. As a corrective, Protestantism and the *Postscript* emphasize worldliness *and* inwardness. Finally, Kierkegaard's later writings react against the latter by stressing outwardness in the form of Christian suffering, martyrdom and imitation of Christ.[38]

The late Kierkegaard is worried that Christendom uses "hidden inwardness" as an excuse for moral laxness and mere legality. If inwardness is essentially hidden, nobody can know whether I am moral or not. Keeping up appearances, or negative outwardness, would suffice. To counteract moral

---

[34] Ulrich Knappe, *Theory and Practice in Kant and Kierkegaard* (Berlin: de Gruyter, 2004) (*Kierkegaard Studies Monograph Series*, vol. 9), Chapters 1–2; Roe Fremstedal, *Kierkegaard and Kant on Radical Evil and the Highest Good: Virtue, Happiness, and the Kingdom of God* (Basingstoke: Palgrave Macmillan, 2014), 229.

[35] Kierkegaard quotes *Dreams of a Spirit-Seer*, see *SKS* 18, 198, JJ:179 / *KJN* 2, 182f.; *SKS* K18, 312.

[36] Joachim Bold, *Kierkegaards "Furcht und Zittern" als Bild seines ethischen Erkenntnisbegriffs* (Berlin: de Gruyter, 2006) (*Kierkegaard Studies Monograph Series*, vol. 13), 108ff. referencing Garff and others.

[37] Ferreira, *Love's Grateful Striving*, 254. Even Anti-Climacus is originally described as an extraordinaire Christian in hidden inwardness. See *Pap.* X–6 B48 / *JP* 6, 6349.

[38] Cf. *SKS* 22, 241, NB12:162 / *KJN* 6, 243; *SKS* 23, 435, NB20:74 / *KJN* 7, 443; *SKS* 24, 368, NB24:78; *KJN* 8, 373; *SKS* K26, 243.

laxness, the late Kierkegaard emphasizes the moral need for action and for renouncing self-interest, holding that neighbor-love must either express itself outwardly or die.[39] Although love as such is hidden, its presence is still indicated by its visible fruits.[40] Christian discipleship in particular involves confessions, suffering, and martyrdom that is polemical against worldliness. The late Kierkegaard therefore stresses the scandalous nature of Christianity as a corrective against "hidden inwardness." Nevertheless, this change in the use of the term need not involve a radical change of theoretical position; it is best considered to be a change of emphasis, which counteracts the misuse of "hidden inwardness" in Christendom.

In 1844, Kierkegaard (now using the persona of Haufniensis) stresses that inwardness is *in* action, and that inwardness can only be achieved *through* action.[41] In 1846, he (now as Climacus) admits that inwardness without outwardness can easily involve self-deception.[42] Nevertheless, inwardness as such cannot be seen or contemplated, since it can only be expressed or realized.[43] For this reason, the point is that inwardness can only be achieved through ethico-religious words and deeds.

III. INWARDNESS AND SECOND-ORDER VOLITIONS

Judge William describes "the inner [*det Indvortes*]" as a "will [that] is directed towards itself."[44] Rather than referring to an "inner world" (Hongs' translation), *det Indvortes* are second-order volitions, wills to will something. It does not concern first-order volitions (that is, the different objects or events I desire). Rather, it concerns my will (or desire) to act on first-order volitions (or desires) or not. Putting it in Kantian terms, it requires different incentives (*Triebfedern*) that are prioritized and incorporated into my maxim by the power of choice (*Willkür*). Putting it in contemporary terms, "the inner" concerns *volitional identification* with, or alienation from, first-order volitions and desires. This second-order volition also separates selfhood (and spirit) from human nature, since the self is a reflexive self-relation that relates actively to the human synthesis (of necessity and freedom, finitude and

[39] Ferreira, *Love's Grateful Striving*, 253; cf. Palmquist, "The Paradox of Inwardness in Kant and Kierkegaard."

[40] *SKS* 9, 15ff. / *WL*, 8ff.

[41] *SKS* 4, 439 / *CA*, 138.

[42] *SKS* 7, 369 / *CUP1*, 406.

[43] *SKS* 7, 292 / *CUP1*, 320.

[44] *SKS* 3, 96 / *EO2*, 94.

infinitude) by identifying with some first-order states, while alienating itself from other such states.[45]

In this respect, "inwardness" is like "the inner" and selfhood, since all these concepts concern second-order volitions. Still, not just any second-order volition or desire would qualify as genuine inwardness or authentic selfhood. Proper inwardness and selfhood require unconditional ethico-religious commitments that are *long-term*, by being grounded on one's very character. For this reason, Judge William describes the categorical choice of the ethical in terms of inwardness,[46] whereas Climacus reserves inwardness for natural religion and Christian faith. Both see it, however, as being based in one's fundamental attitude towards one's life as a whole

Inwardness can then be interpreted either as a perfect moral character or as a character that is fundamentally committed towards morality by wholeheartedly engaging in self-improvement. At least, one must be unconditionally striving for the good if one is to achieve wholeheartedness.[47] The process of moral improvement can be interpreted both as a never-ending temporal process of reform (a process of sanctification that gradually improves moral behavior), or as a sudden rebirth or conversion at the level of character. Unlike many Pietists, Kierkegaard thinks that it is unimportant to specify a point in time for conversion.[48] He emphasizes that being good is a never-ending task, and that it is always possible to lapse back into evil. Judge William describes the process of moral improvement in terms of human effort, whereas Kierkegaard focuses on the dialectics between human effort and divine grace (which is not irresistible). As we will see, even Climacus, who is a mere humorist, sees moral improvement and eternal happiness, as lying beyond our human ability.

---

[45] *SKS* 11, 129 / *SUD*, 13. See also John Davenport, "Selfhood and Spirit," in *The Oxford Handbook of Kierkegaard*, ed. by John Lippitt and Georg Pattison (Oxford: Oxford University Press, 2013), 230–51.

[46] *SKS* 3, 164 / *EO2*, 167.

[47] *SKS* 8, 139f. / *UD*, 24.

[48] *SKS* 10, 225 / *CD*, 217; Patrick Stokes, *The Naked Self: Kierkegaard and Personal Identity* (Oxford: Oxford University Press, 2015), 213.

IV. IRONY AND HUMOR IN *CONCLUDING UNSCIENTIFIC POSTSCRIPT*

Kierkegaard (Climacus) does not just connect religiousness to "hidden inwardness," but also to humor. Religious inwardness is not entirely hidden but expressed as humor, whereas the ethical is expressed as irony.[49] Irony here refers to a specific way of existing that requires (1) legality (a point that seems implicit); (2) personal awareness of unconditional moral responsibility; and (3) that one ironically comprehends all the relativities of life by seeing the conflict between the infinite ethical requirement and everything finite or relative.[50] Not only does irony require first-order representation of the ethical task and reality, but it also requires a second-order representation of how these first-order representations conflict. Nevertheless, the ethicist goes beyond mere irony by being unconditionally committed towards morality. Since we cannot verify if someone is fully committed towards morality, we cannot then know whether he is an ethicist or a mere ironist.

Humor, on the other hand, goes beyond irony (although it may presuppose it) by requiring that one "joins the conception of God together with everything [else] and [then] sees the contradiction."[51] Instead of focusing on the conflict between ethical ideals and reality, the humorist focuses on the conflict between a transcendent (or hidden) God and reality. Humor requires not only first-order representations of God and everything else, but also a second-order representation of how these first-order representations conflict.

Still, humor does not require inwardness.[52] Neither does it require theistic belief, since humor need not involve natural religion or Christian faith;[53] the mere humorist is said to have an abstract relation to God.[54] Presumably, he relies on a regulative idea of God as a transcendent idea,[55] or sees God as possible rather than actual.

---

[49] *SKS* 7, 457ff. / *CUP1*, 504ff.

[50] *SKS* 7, 455–8 / *CUP1*, 502–5.

[51] *SKS* 7, 458 / *CUP1*, 505.

[52] *SKS* 7, 458ff. / *CUP1*, 505ff.

[53] *SKS* 7, 483n / *CUP1*, 531f.n.

[54] *SKS* 7, 408n / *CUP1*, 448n.

[55] Kierkegaard's notes from H. L. Martensen's lectures refer explicitly to the regulative status of God as a transcendent ideal that we should strive to approximate. See *SKS* 19, 140, Not4:11 / *KJN* 3, 139.

Nevertheless, humor does require the concept of infinite guilt. "Infinite guilt" is the rigorist idea that any immoral action involves total guilt. Any moral failure involves a radical and essential failure, not a partial one.[56] To the humorist, any finite human attempt to improve the human condition appears to be a jest, given the infinite ethical task (or God's will) and our infinite guilt.[57] The humorist is aware of "infinite guilt," but he revokes it with jest, despite being committed towards morality. He has some awareness of his guilt but does not take it seriously, something that separates him from the religious believer who sees himself as infinitely guilty and therefore totally in need of divine forgiveness. But since we cannot verify if someone is a believer or serious about his personal guilt, religiousness expresses itself as humor that takes as its object the contrast between God and world.[58]

Unlike *Either/Or*, the *Postscript* is clear that inwardness requires religious suffering. Both natural religion and Christian religiousness require religious suffering, in which one suffers by virtue of being separated from the highest good (eternal happiness), one's final end.[59] By its very nature, the highest good is impossible to realize fully in this life (as Augustine maintained),[60] which results in the fact that faith in it cannot find a suitable external expression either.[61] While happiness and virtue coexist in the afterlife, this is not the case in this life. For this reason, in the *Postscript* Kierkegaard (Climacus) claims: "the specific sign that one relates oneself to the absolute [*telos*, the highest good] is that not only is there no reward to expect but suffering to endure."[62] Suffering involves both general passivity and more specific *Qual* (agony, anguish, or torment). We are passive insofar as we

---

[56] Fremstedal, *Kierkegaard and Kant on Radical Evil and the Highest Good*, chapter 2. See also n20 on Kant's doctrine of moral rigorism at the level of character.

[57] John Lippitt, *Humour and Irony in Kierkegaard's Thought* (Basingstoke: Palgrave Macmillan, 2000), 94.

[58] Neither the religious believer nor the ethicist want to appear better outwardly than other humans do. See C. Stephen Evans, *Kierkegaard's* Fragments *and* Postscript*: The Religious Philosophy of Johannes Climacus* (New York: Humanity, 1999), 193, 205.

[59] Merold Westphal, *Becoming a Self: A Reading of Kierkegaard's* Concluding Unscientific Postscript (West Lafayette, IN: Purdue University Press, 1996), 161–5.

[60] John D. Glenn, Jr., "'A Highest Good … An Eternal Happiness': The Human Telos in Kierkegaard's *Concluding Unscientific Postscript*," in *Concluding Unscientific Postscript to 'Philosophical Fragments,'* ed. by Robert L. Perkins (Macon, GA: Mercer University Press, 1997) (*International Kierkegaard Commentary*, vol. 12), 247–62; Fremstedal, *Kierkegaard and Kant on Radical Evil and the Highest Good*, chapters 4–9.

[61] *SKS* 7, 446 / *CUP1*, 492.

[62] *SKS* 7, 366 / *CUP1*, 402, cf. *SKS* 5, 326–8 / *EUD*, 337–9.

cannot save ourselves, being dependent on divine assistance in order to realize the highest good.[63] We are subject to *Qual* insofar as we experience injustice, hardship, or loneliness, since virtue in this life guarantees neither happiness nor the communion of the saints.

Suffering requires relinquishing our natural tendency to relate unconditionally or absolutely to finite, lesser goods. Only the highest good, eternal happiness, has unconditional and infinite value.[64] Nevertheless, this means that we must give up our self-assertiveness and pride, and accept our passivity, since we are not capable of saving ourselves. We are not even able to understand sin without Christian revelation.[65]

V. "SUBJECTIVITY IS TRUTH"—AND UNTRUTH

The concept of hidden inwardness sheds light on the controversial theses "Subjectivity is truth" and "Subjectivity is untruth" in *Concluding Unscientific Postscript*. Indeed, the former thesis is formulated "Subjectivity, inwardness, is truth,"[66] whereas the latter is described as a more inward expression of the former.[67] Note that Kierkegaard (Climacus) is not giving a general account (or theory) of truth here. He is only concerned with the cognition of truth *essential* to ethical and religious existence.[68] It seems he is concerned, therefore, with moral and religious epistemology, with how we know ethico-religious truth that is needed in order to exist truthfully, without despair or self-deception.

A straightforward reading takes these two theses to refer to the subjective appropriation of objective truth (i.e. truth that holds independently of the subject's response to it).[69] Truth is then subjective insofar as an individual appropriates (objective) truth,[70] presumably by identifying volitionally with it and by acting upon it. Conversely, subjectivity is untruth insofar as one alienates oneself volitionally from objective truth, thereby failing to act

[63] Cf. Westphal, *Becoming a Self*, 161.

[64] Evans, *Kierkegaard's* Fragments *and* Postscript, 168–73; Westphal, *Becoming a Self*, 158–65.

[65] *SKS* 7, 483–5 / *CUP1*, 532–4; *SKS* 11, 197–213 / *SUD*, 83–101.

[66] *SKS* 7, 186f. / *CUP1*, 204.

[67] *SKS* 7, 189 / *CUP1*, 207.

[68] *SKS* 7, 189 / *CUP1*, 207.

[69] Thanks to Jörg Disse who suggested this interpretation at the August 2017 SKC conference. Thanks are also due to the other participants for comments and discussion of an earlier version of this chapter.

[70] Cf. *SKS* 7, 176, 186, 220f. / *CUP1*, 192, 203, 242.

on it. Both volitional identification and alienation involve second-order volition, since (as we have seen that) inwardness does. The terminology here is similar to Kant's use of subjective and objective principles in ethics. Whereas the moral law is an objective principle, our maxims are subjective principles which we act on. We only exist in truth then if our subjective principles are based on objective ones.

In ethics, Kierkegaard (Climacus) is an anti-consequentialist who thinks that the moral worth of actions lies in the will or intention behind an action, not in its consequences.[71] Ulrich Knappe comments: "The 'how' to which Kierkegaard refers characterizes the subjective or motivational aspect of a moral action and...the how is in truth if it denotes an act from duty."[72] On this Kantian interpretation, the subjective aspect of moral action can only be said to be true if we act from duty, if the motivational reasons are also normative reasons. The "how" then refers to the inwardness of the moral agent. This is not a secular point, but rather an ethico-religious one, since Kierkegaard identifies the good and the divine as the same thing.

"Subjectivity is truth" and "Subjectivity is untruth," then, concerns the subjective, phenomenological aspects of objective ethico-religious truth; that is, they concern how objective, ethico-religious ideals appear in the first-person perspective of an agent. The agent either identifies with these ideals or alienates himself from them. But even the acknowledgement that "Subjectivity is untruth" involves inwardness insofar as one acknowledges personal failure by being conscious of one's state of sin. Indeed, "Subjectivity is untruth" is more inward than "Subjectivity is truth," since inwardness lies not in human perfection without God, but in human sin-consciousness before God.

A subjectivist reading may give a literal account of "Subjectivity is truth," but it is hard to see how it can account for "subjectivity is untruth," and why the latter is described in terms of sin (in the Christian sense). It also overlooks the assumed correspondence between the subjective "how" and the objective "what,"[73] as well as Kierkegaard's (Climacus') denial that he is giving a general account of truth. Both here and elsewhere, Kierkegaard (Climacus) presupposes a notion of truth that is not relativistic. For instance, he presupposes that there is a true God, an eternal happiness, and an ethical task. Take for example this notorious passage:

---

[71] *SKS* 7, 270n / *CUP1*, 296n.

[72] Knappe, *Theory and Practice in Kant and Kierkegaard*, 84n.

[73] *SKS* 22, 414, NB14:121 / *KJN* 6, 420.

> If someone who lives in the midst of Christianity enters, with knowledge of the true idea of God,...the house of the true God, and prays, but prays in untruth, and if someone lives in an idolatrous land but prays with all the passion of infinity, although his eyes are resting upon the image of an idol—where, *then*, is there more truth? The one prays in truth to God although he is worshipping an idol; the other prays in untruth to the true God and is therefore in truth worshipping an idol.[74]

This passage suggests that the best is a Christian who prays sincerely (in truth) to the true God. The second best is a sincere pagan who prays in truth to an idol. The third best is an insincere Christian who prays to the right God wrongly. The worst is an insincere pagan who prays to an idol wrongly. The passage thus distinguishes between subjective and objective aspects of faith. Merold Westphal argues that the subjective "how" here refers to the faith whereby we believe, a faith that can be either sincere or insincere. By contrast, the objective "what" refers to doctrine that is believed. "Subjectivity is truth," therefore, implies that dogmas are less important than the faith whereby we believe.[75] Simple-minded although sincere believers who are confused about religious doctrine are preferable to insincere believers who have got the dogmas right. Having the right inward disposition is more important than holding exactly the right beliefs. The latter would privilege elite theologians, whereas the former is universally available to all humans.

Still, the *Postscript* goes further by connecting subjective truth to a pragmatic argument (or pragmatic reasons) for religious belief. In the middle of the discussion of "Truth is Subjectivity," the *Postscript* sketches a pragmatic argument for postulating God that is reminiscent of Kant's God-postulate.[76] Pragmatic arguments involve subjective, practical justifications for belief that are not warranted by evidence, something that is found in Kant, Kierkegaard, and the American Pragmatists.[77]

---

[74] *SKS* 7, 184 / *CUP1*, 201.

[75] Westphal, *Kierkegaard's Concept of Faith*, 163.

[76] *SKS* 7, 183n / *CUP1*, 200n. See the discussion in Fremstedal, *Kierkegaard and Kant on Radical Evil and the Highest Good*, chapter 6.

[77] This involves a much weaker subjectivism than the relativistic subjectivism discussed previously. For Kierkegaard's pragmatism about religious belief, see C. Stephen Evans, *Subjectivity and Religious Belief: An Historical, Critical Study* (Washington, DC: University Press of America, 1982); Steven Emmanuel, *Kierkegaard and the Concept of Revelation* (Albany: State University of New York Press, 1996).

The *Postscript* describes subjective truth as "*objective uncertainty*" held fast in the "*most passionate inwardness*" of faith.[78] Objective uncertainty implies insufficient evidence from the epistemic perspective. We cannot possibly have sufficient objective knowledge of the existence of God and immortality (eternal happiness), since such knowledge lies beyond the limits of human cognition. Any evidence for God and immortality is therefore insufficient rather than irrelevant.

Still, pragmatists argue that we can have decisive practical reasons for settling the matter, in much the same way that Kant argues that we must postulate God and immortality on moral grounds, since this is an urgent matter that must be decided upon to ensure that our moral motivation does not erode. The *Postscript* defends religious faith as self-defense (*Nødverge*) against despair,[79] something that anticipates the analysis in *The Sickness unto Death*, according to which only genuine religious faith avoids despair consistently.[80] This is a *reductio ad absurdum* of the alternative to faith, but the absurdity does not so much take the form of a formal contradiction (although despair involves two conflicting wills[81]), but is rather an existential absurdity in the form of hopelessness and despair.

The *Postscript* claims that "Christianity is a perfect fit" if "subjectivity is truth," since the Christian "paradox and [human] passion [thereby] fit each other perfectly."[82] Putting it differently, there is a "how" that only fits one object.[83] This correspondence between the "how" and the "what" rules out relativistic subjectivism. The "how" is represented by passion and the maximum of religious inwardness.[84] By contrast, the "what" is represented both by the paradox, in the Christological sense of being both human and divine,[85] and by "eternal happiness,"[86] a synthesis of virtue and happiness

---

[78] *SKS* 7, 186 / *CUP1*, 203.
[79] *SKS* 7, 183n / *CUP1*, 200n.
[80] *SKS* 11, 195f. / *SUD*, 81.
[81] See *SKS* 8, 144 / *UD*, 30.
[82] *SKS* 7, 210 / *CUP1*, 230.
[83] *SKS* 22, 414, NB14:121 / *KJN* 6, 420; *SKS* K22, 528.
[84] *SKS* 7, 210, 554–9 / *CUP1*, 230, 610–6; *SKS* 22, 414, NB14:121 / *KJN* 6, 420.
[85] *SKS* 7, 210 / *CUP1*, 230.
[86] *SKS* 7, 354–9, 388 / *CUP1*, 389–94, 426f.

associated with the kingdom of God.[87] The object of faith, the "what," therefore, represents Christian doctrine, whereas the "how" concerns the faith whereby we believe. Faith is therefore assumed to fit the doctrines of the incarnation and the kingdom of God as the highest good.

Christian doctrine is not based on human needs or natural theology alone, however. Still, belief in Christian revelation is justified on pragmatic grounds as something that fits a natural need by making it possible to overcome despair. Despite the lack of evidence, religious belief is justifiable. Such pragmatism remains controversial, although it is not always clear that beliefs should only be based on sufficient evidence.[88]

IV. CONCLUSION

"Subjectivity is truth" and "hidden inwardness" represent two of Kierkegaard's most controversial contributions to European philosophy and theology. Whereas "Subjectivity is truth" gives the impression of objectionable subjectivism, "hidden inwardness" seem to involve either a private, inner domain or a "negative outwardness" (Mulder). Still, this chapter indicates that these two ideas are not as problematic as they may seem if we employ a charitable, Kantian reading of Kierkegaard. More specifically, "Subjectivity is truth" involves pragmatism about religious belief and the subjective appropriation of objective truth. "Hidden inwardness," by contrast, describes an ethico-religious character that is only indirectly available to us through its expressions in words and deeds.

This chapter does not prove that Kant influences Kierkegaard,[89] but it does indicate that it is possible to make sense of the concept of hidden inwardness and the thesis that "Subjectivity is truth," and that these ideas are largely defensible, if we rely on a Kantian reading of Kierkegaard. This

---

[87] Glenn, "'A Highest Good … An Eternal Happiness,'" 260f.; Fremstedal, *Kierkegaard and Kant on Radical Evil and the Highest Good*, Chapters 5–9.

[88] Cf. Andrew Chignell, "The Ethics of Belief," *The Stanford Encyclopedia of Philosophy*, ed. by Edward Zalta, Spring 2013 ed., http://plato.stanford.edu/archives/spr2013/ entries/ethics-belief; C. Stephen Evans, "Moral Arguments for the Existence of God," *The Stanford Encyclopedia of Philosophy*, ed. by Edward Zalta, Summer 2014 ed., http://plato.stanford.edu/archives/sum2014/entries/moral-arguments-god.

[89] For a recent discussion of Kant's influence on Kierkegaard, see Fremstedal, *Kierkegaard and Kant on Radical Evil and the Highest Good*, chapter 11.

is not to say that Kierkegaard must only be read along Kantian lines, although he does accept pragmatism about religious belief and what amounts to a broadly Kantian view about the limits of human cognition.[90]

[90] This chapter limits itself to key elements that seem necessary in order to reconstruct "hidden inwardness" and "Subjectivity is truth." It does not try to exhaust these two ideas or intend to do full justice to the rich, multifaceted use of them in Kierkegaard's corpus. For a different, less Kantian, approach to "inwardness" in the 1843–46 writings, see Matthias Engmann, *Innerlichkeit. Struktur- und praxistheoretische Perspektiven auf Kierkegaards Existenzdenken* (Berlin: de Gruyter, 2017) (*Kierkegaard Studies. Monograph Series*, vol. 36). See also Christian Tolstrup, "Inwardness/Inward Deepening" in *Kierkegaard's Concepts: Individual to Novel*, ed. by Steven M. Emmanuel, William McDonald and Jon Stewart (Farnham and Burlington: Ashgate, 2014) (*Kierkegaard Research: Sources, Reception and Resources*, vol. 15, tome IV), 33–8.

Nietzsche and the "Refutation" of Christian Theism

Darío González

In the epilogue to *The Case of Wagner*, after reintroducing his concept of a "master morality" as explicitly opposed to "the morality of the Christians," Nietzsche refers to them as two "forms in the optics of value," two "ways of seeing that cannot be approached with reasons and refutations."[1] To say that morality constitutes in each case a "way of seeing" the world or "a view of life" is not in itself an innovative gesture. However, Nietzsche's use of that metaphor is more thoroughgoing, and it would not be wrong to affirm that he actually interprets moral systems as regimes of *sensitivity* to the value of things. On the one hand, the affirmative character of master morality—which here is historically specified as the one corresponding to the "Roman," "heroic," and "classical" periods as much as to the "Renaissance"—consists in the fact that "it transfigures and enhances the world and *makes it rational* [*sie verklärt, sie verschönt, sie* vernünftigt *die Welt*]."[2] On the other hand, Christian morality "impoverishes the value of things and makes them pale and ugly, it negates [*verneint*] the world."[3] This perspective has important consequences for the understanding of Nietzsche's critique of religion. Given that Christian morality is an impoverishing way of perceiving and of educating the senses, Christianity itself becomes rationally *irrefutable*: "You do not refute Christianity, you do not refute an eye disease.... The concepts 'true' and 'not true' do not seem to me to have any meaning in optics."[4] In so far as

[1] Friedrich Nietzsche, *Sämtliche Werke. Kritische Studienausgabe*, vols. 1–15, ed. by Giorgio Colli and Mazzino Montinari (Berlin: de Gruyter, 1999), vol. 6, 51 / *The Anti-Christ, Ecce Homo, Twilight of the Idols, and Other Writings*, ed. by Aaron Ridley and Judith Norman, trans. by Judith Norman (Cambridge: Cambridge University Press, 2007), 261.

[2] Nietzsche, *Sämtliche Werke*, vol. 6, 51 / *The Anti-Christ, Ecce Homo, Twilight of the Idols, and Other Writings*, 261.

[3] Nietzsche, *Sämtliche Werke*, vol. 6, 51 / *The Anti-Christ, Ecce Homo, Twilight of the Idols, and Other Writings*, 261.

[4] Nietzsche, *Sämtliche Werke*, vol. 6, 51 / *The Anti-Christ, Ecce Homo, Twilight of the Idols, and Other Writings*, 261.

an illusion is not just something untrue but, rather, a way of thinking that positively *produces the effect* of truth, a critique of illusion cannot follow the path of logical argumentation. The fact that these remarks concerning Christian morality are made in the context of a critique of Wagner's music has, of course, an explanation. According to Nietzsche, Wagner "wants effects, nothing but effects.... Wagner's music is never true. —But *it is taken to be true*, so everything is fine."[5] Illusions, in other words, constitute themselves beyond the sheer distinction between truth and untruth, in so far as they refer to values rather than to facts. More importantly, illusions cannot be refuted because they are intimately linked to our bodily existence. They are, in a sense, a constitutive dimension of our organic interaction with the world rather than ideas subject to criticism and scrutiny. The impoverishment of values implies at the same time a deterioration of life, the production of a sick organism. It is precisely against this background that Nietzsche interprets Christianity as an "eye disease."

It is interesting to remark that this last expression is used in a text in which Nietzsche tries to make sense of his *own* "diseases." The essay on Wagner is an attempt "to take sides *against* everything sick in myself, including Wagner, including Schopenhauer, including the whole of modern 'humaneness'...Wagner is just one of my sicknesses."[6] Wagner and his view of art had become parts of the moral totality from which and against which Nietzsche elaborates his own self-criticism. As observed above, that moral totality was not just a system of ideas, concepts, dogmas, and beliefs, but also a way of producing a particular kind of organism, a subjectivity-making process that could only be deconstructed from within. Nietzsche's "Attempt at Self-Criticism," written as a preface to a later edition of *The Birth of Tragedy*,[7] had a double significance. It implied on the one side the rejection of the tone and orientation of a work determined by the reading of Schopenhauer—another name for Nietzsche's intellectual disease, symptomatically associated with Wagnerism. On the other side, however, that "attempt" presupposed the need for a new form of critique, a critique addressed not

---

[5] Nietzsche, *Sämtliche Werke*, vol. 6, 31 / *The Anti-Christ, Ecce Homo, Twilight of the Idols, and Other Writings*, 248.

[6] Nietzsche, *Sämtliche Werke*, vol. 6, 12 / *The Anti-Christ, Ecce Homo, Twilight of the Idols, and Other Writings*, 233.

[7] Cf. Nietzsche, *Sämtliche Werke*, vol. 1, 11–22 / *The Birth of Tragedy and Other Writings*, ed. by Raymond Geuss and Ronald Speirs, trans. by Ronald Speirs (Cambridge: Cambridge University Press, 2004), 3–12.

only to the scientific and aesthetic values of Western culture but, more fundamentally, to the moral subject that reproduced those values and resisted their destruction.

The singular position of Wagnerism among Nietzsche's diseases has to do with the fact that it affects the senses—not only the eyes or the ways of seeing the world, but also, and perhaps more importantly, the ways of listening to it, the immediate perception of sounds and words. Wagner is named here as the most extreme symptom of modernity: "*Wagner est une névrose*.... Nothing is more modern than this total sickness [*Gesammterkrankung*], this maturity and over-excitement of the neurological mechanism, which is why Wagner is *the modern artist* par excellence, the Cagliostro of modernity."[8] But the roots of this neurosis are to be sought somewhere else, namely, in Christianity. According to Nietzsche's interpretation, the "problem" of Wagner is the problem of redemption: "...his operas are the operas of redemption. Someone or other is always being redeemed in them: a boy here, a girl there—this is *Wagner's* problem."[9] Brought into the totalizing unity of the work of art, the one who needs to be redeemed is no longer able to interrogate the world; he can only expect to see the world through the eyes of faith. As in the case of *Lohengrin,* he "solemnly prohibits investigation and questioning," guided as he is by "the Christian idea: 'you should and must *believe*.'"[10]

There is a clear parallelism between the view expressed by the Wagnerian *Gesamtkunstwerk*, the *Gesamterkrankung* of modernity, and the totalizing effect of moral asceticism. In each case, they depend on the exclusion of any possible alternative interpretation. We read in the *Genealogy of Morals*,

> The ascetic ideal not only spoilt health and taste, it spoilt a third, fourth, fifth, sixth thing as well—I shall refrain from saying what they all were (I would never reach the end!) ...What does the *power* of this ideal mean, the *monstrosity* of its power? ...The ascetic ideal expresses a will: *where* is the opposing will, in which an *opposing ideal* might express itself?

[8] Cf. Nietzsche, *Sämtliche Werke*, vol. 6, 22f. / *Anti-Christ, Ecce Homo, Twilight of the Idols, and Other Writings*, 242.

[9] Nietzsche, *Sämtliche Werke*, vol. 6, 16 / *The Anti-Christ, Ecce Homo, Twilight of the Idols, and Other Writings*, 237.

[10] Nietzsche, *Sämtliche Werke*, vol. 6, 17 / *The Anti-Christ, Ecce Homo, Twilight of the Idols, and Other Writings*, 238.

> ...Where is the *counterpart* to this closed system of will, goal and interpretation?[11]

The last paragraphs from the third essay of the *Genealogy of Morals* deal with the same difficulty indicated some months later in *The Case of Wagner*, namely, the fact that Christian morality—at least in its modern form—cannot be rationally refuted. Modern science can certainly not do it, insofar as it does not believe in itself as a value-creating power. Understood as a specific form of asceticism, modern science is just a late symptom of that "disease of the eye" that "impoverishes" and "pales" the meaning of things, to the extent that it makes us unable to create new values. Not even the "free spirits" of modernity would be able to go beyond this moral system of interpretation. Their "metaphysical faith" is still the same "Christian faith which was also Plato's faith, that God is truth, that truth is divine...."[12] This remark concerning the survival of metaphysics within the project of modernity is a variation of something Nietzsche had written at the beginning of the fourth section of *Human, All Too Human*:

> How strong the metaphysical need is, and how hard nature makes it to bid it a final farewell, can be seen from the fact that even when the free spirit has divested himself of everything metaphysical the highest effect of art can easily set the metaphysical strings, which have long been silent or indeed snapped apart, vibrating in sympathy; so it can happen, for example, that a passage in Beethoven's Ninth Symphony will make him feel he is hovering above the earth in a dome of stars with the dream of *immortality* in his heart.[13]

This is not just one example among others. The idea of the immortality of human soul is perhaps the last metaphysical idea, the one that survives the "end" of metaphysics. Beethoven's last symphony is certainly not the only work in which this long-silenced or broken string resonates. One of the peculiarities of Wagner's music consists in its ability to infinitely prolong an agonizing sound, in creating the dramatic conditions for its reverberation in space and time. A certain declaration of immortality takes place every time our spirit becomes aware of what seems to be its preeminence or—as it is

[11] Nietzsche, *Sämtliche Werke*, vol. 5, 395f. / *On the Genealogy of Morality*, ed. by Keith Ansell-Pearson, trans. by Carol Diethe (Cambridge: Cambridge University Press, 2006), 109.

[12] Nietzsche, *Sämtliche Werke*, vol. 3, 577 / *The Gay Science*, ed. by Bernard Williams, trans. by Josefine Nauckhoff (Cambridge: Cambridge University Press, 2008), 201.

[13] Nietzsche, *Sämtliche Werke*, vol. 2, 145 / *Human, All Too Human*, trans. by R. J. Hollingdale (Cambridge: Cambridge University Press, 2005), 82.

named in Kant's aesthetics—its own *sublimity* with respect to the threatening powers of nature.[14] It would be necessary to move back from Kant to Burke's "physiological"[15] view of the sublime in order to show to which extent those powers are, at the end, an expression of our own mortality, the mortality of a human organism.

In Nietzsche's perspective, the source of that metaphysical reverberation, the string that has been broken, is the belief in the existence of a living God. Here it is important to stress that the moral system that resists rational refutation—Christian morality—is for Nietzsche a morality that no longer believes in its own values, or, as he also puts it, a morality that does not believe in its own beliefs. That is the formulation he chooses in one of the paragraphs of *The Gay Science* in which is proclaimed the "death of God": "The greatest recent event—that 'God is dead,' that the belief in the Christian God has become unbelievable—is already starting to cast its first shadows over Europe."[16] It is not surprising to find here the same optical metaphor mentioned above:

> To those few at least whose eyes—or the *suspicion* in whose eyes is strong and subtle enough for this spectacle, some kind of sun seems to have set;....But in the main one might say: for many people's power of comprehension, the event is itself far too great, distant, and out of the way even for its tidings to be thought of as having arrived yet. Even less may one suppose many to know at all *what* this event really means—and, now that this faith has been undermined, how much collapse because it was built on this faith, leaned on it, had grown into it—for example, our entire European morality.[17]

As an "event," the death of God can remain unnoticed. It is exactly the kind of optical illusion suggested earlier in the book: "After Buddha was dead, they still showed his shadow in a cave for centuries—a tremendous, gruesome shadow. God is dead; but given the way people are, there may still for millennia be caves in which they show his shadow. —And we—we must still defeat his shadow as well!"[18] A more consistent development of Nietzsche's visual metaphor would lead us to understand that the "shadows" we

---

[14] Cf. Immanuel Kant, *Kritik der Urteilskraft*, ed. by Heiner F. Klemme (Hamburg: Meiner, 2009), 130.

[15] Cf. Ibid., 151.

[16] Nietzsche, *Sämtliche Werke*, vol. 3, 573 / *The Gay Science*, 199.

[17] Nietzsche, *Sämtliche Werke*, vol. 3, 573 / *The Gay Science*, 199.

[18] Nietzsche, *Sämtliche Werke*, vol. 3, 467 / *The Gay Science*, 109.

still observe in the caves of Christianity are not the shadows of the presence of God but, rather, the result of a certain eclipse, a darkening of the divine light. After the first proclamation of the death of God in Book III of *The Gay Science,* the madman who announces the event explicitly compares this absent God with the light of the sun: "'Where is God?' he cried. 'I'll tell you. *We have killed him*—you and I! We are all his murderers. But how did we do this? How were we able to drink up the sea? Who gave us the sponge to wipe away the entire horizon? What were we doing when we unchained this earth from its sun? Where is it moving now? Where are we moving to? Away from all suns?"[19] This is, of course, a traditional motif in metaphysics, and it is not surprising to find an extensive commentary on it in one of Heidegger's essays:

> When he mentions the relation between sun and earth, Nietzsche does not think solely about the Copernican revolution in the modern view of nature. The substantive "sun" evokes at the same time Plato's analogy. Accordingly, the sun and the extent of its light are the sphere in which beings [*das Seiende*] show up in their appearance and in their outlines (ideas)...."Horizon" means the supersensible world as the world that truly is [*die übersinnliche Welt als die wahrhaft seiende*].[20]

The "images" of the sun and the horizon are here, as Heidegger concludes, "probably something other than images."[21] But it is not less important to notice the variations of this metaphor in modern literature, particularly among authors concerned with the destiny of mankind after the decline of religion. Almost eighty years before Nietzsche, Jean Paul could expound in similar terms the consequences of romantic nihilism: "soon after God sets like the sun, the world too enters into darkness."[22] The author of *The Gay Science,* however, does not expect the darkening of the world to be noticed that soon. The madman speaks to a humanity that does not understand him: "Finally he threw his lantern on the ground so that it broke into pieces and went out. 'I come too early,' he then said; 'my time is not yet. This tremendous event is still on its way....Lightning and thunder need time; the light

[19] Nietzsche, *Sämtliche Werke*, vol. 3, 480f / *The Gay Science*, 119f.

[20] Martin Heidegger, *Holzwege*, ed. by Friedrich-Wilhelm von Herrmann (Frankfurt am Main: Klostermann, 1994), 261. My translation.

[21] Ibid.

[22] Jean Paul, *Vorschule der Ästhetik*, ed. by Wolfhart Henckmann (Hamburg: Meiner, 1990), 32. My translation.

of the stars needs time; deeds need time, even after they are done, in order to be seen and heard.'"[23]

The fact that the death of God is presented in *The Gay Science* as a "deed" committed by men, that his death takes the form of a collective murder, the fact that the blood of God is still on the hands of humanity has been pointed out as an essential feature of Nietzsche's critique of religion and morality. René Girard, in particular, has insisted on the difference between what we might call the "natural death" of God, the idea that God—so to speak—dies "of old age," and the violent murder of God indicated in *The Gay Science*:

> The references to the blood, and to the knife, and to the wiping of the blood, forcefully take us back to the first announcement of the madman. God did not die a natural death; he was collectively killed. And the crime is so great that new festivals of atonement, new sacred games will have to be invented. New rituals will undoubtedly appear. The consequences of God's murder are religious, therefore, purely religious. The very deed that seems to put an end to the religious process is really the origin of that process, the sum total of it, really, the religious process par excellence. These new festivals and sacred games will certainly reenact the collective murder of God.[24]

It is Nietzsche himself who, through the voice of the madman, speaks of "festivals of atonement" and "sacred games" to be invented to commemorate the event, although he does it in the form of a series of questions. Girard finds in those references a good argument in favor of an anthropological reflection on the essence of religion. One of Girard's most provocative assumptions is that "God is always the product of his own collective murder."[25] By interpreting the death of God as a collective human act, Nietzsche' *Gay Science* is much closer to Freud's *Totem and Taboo* than to the romantic contemplation of the sunset of religion. Among the consequences of Girard's reading, what most interests us here is his indirect remark on the "historical" dimension of the death of God proclaimed by the madman in *The Gay Science.* The representation of the collective murder itself—Girard

---

[23] Nietzsche, *Sämtliche Werke*, vol. 3, 481 / *The Gay Science*, 120.

[24] René Girard, "Dionysus versus the Crucified," *MLN*, vol. 9, no. 4, French Issue (September 1984), 831.

[25] Ibid.

observes—"is hidden behind the theme of an entirely 'natural' and peaceful death, a radically undramatic death, a death 'sans histoire.'"[26]

In order to comprehend in which sense the death of God *has* a history, however, we should take a step back to Nietzsche's text. The violence of the murder and the specific reference to its human agent is what leads Nietzsche to define the death of God as an *event,* an *Ereignis* that opens a gap in the history of humanity. In a certain sense, the "event" of the death of God is still waiting to become historical. That is why the one who points it out in *The Gay Science,* the madman, is somebody who "came too early."[27] The history of the event is not yet accomplished. Modernity is still situated in the gap that opens itself between an unacknowledged murder and the possibility of its appropriation. Thus, the critique of modernity—the same modernity whose "neurosis" and overexcitement Nietzsche denounces in his essay on Wagner—is first of all the critique of the shadows of God, shadows in which humanity insists on the attempt to recognize its own goodness and its own virtues. The shadows of the dead God are the dark mirror of Christian morality itself. The event of the death of God develops historically insofar as an acknowledgement of the murder would imply the acknowledgement of the death of man as a moral entity—not just because "murder" is supposed to be immoral, but rather because Christian morality depends on the unacknowledged character of that act. More radical than the madman of *The Gay Science,* and yet very close to him, Zarathustra affirms: "*Dead are all Gods: now we want the Overman to live.* Let this be our final will at the great noon."[28] Not by chance Nietzsche formulates this idea as a "will"—the final will—and not as a simple indication of a fact. Fully consistent with that will is the assumption that the human being is only "a bridge" between the animal and the Overman. The "thought" according to which "we have killed God" is *essentially unthinkable for the human beings we are,* unthinkable within the frame of Christian morality or—as Heidegger would prefer to say—within the limits of Western metaphysics. This is also why, according to Heidegger's suggestion, "Nietzsche himself is surprised by this thought" and decides that the sentences "*We have killed him*—you and I! We are all his murderers," are to be immediately followed by the question "But how did we

[26] Ibid., 832.

[27] Nietzsche, *Sämtliche Werke,* vol. 3, 481 / *The Gay Science,* 120. Quoted in full above.

[28] Nietzsche, *Sämtliche Werke,* vol. 4, 102 / *Thus Spoke Zarathustra,* ed. by Adrian del Caro and Robert B. Pippin, trans. by Adrian del Caro (Cambridge: Cambridge University Press, 2006), 59.

do this?" The only two underlined sentences in the aphorism ("*We have killed him*" and "*and yet they have done it themselves*") conceal for Heidegger the secret meaning of the statement "God is dead," a meaning that cannot be reduced to the simple remark "there is no God."[29]

It seems possible to admit that the thought expressed in the words "there is no God," in spite of its provocative power, is at least *thinkable* in metaphysical—human or humanistic—terms. Those words occur explicitly in a text by an author mentioned above, Jean Paul Richter. In 1796—for a number of reasons a crucial year in the history of Idealism—Richter conceives his "Speech of the Dead Christ," a story in which Christ himself appears in the narrator's dream and proclaims "That There is No God." The speech has been said to possess the structure of a Pascalian wager or the mere self-pedagogical function of a deterring image,[30] as is indicated by its conclusion: "My soul wept for joy that I could again worship God."[31] But the content of the dream itself seems to be the expression of a hyperbolic nihilism:

> A Noble, lofty Figure, having the mien of imperishable anguish, now sunk down from on high upon the altar; and all the dead cried out: "Christ! Is there no God? —He answered: "There is none!"..."I descended as far as existence throws its shadows, and gazed into the abyss and called: 'Father, where art Thou?'—but I heard only the eternal storm which no one rules, and the glimmering rainbow stood out of the West over the abyss, without a sun which created it, and fell down in drops. And as I looked up to the immeasurable world for the divine *Eye*, the universe stared upon me with an empty, black, bottomless *Socket*; and the eternity lay upon the chaos, and gnawed it to pieces, and chewed itself again. —Shriek on, dissonances" —burst the shadows with shrieking! —for He is not!"[32]

The very structure of this speech indicates the paradoxical character that atheism necessarily must have had for an author situated at the end of the

---

[29] Heidegger, *Holzwege*, 260.

[30] Cf. Claude Pichois, *L'image de Jean-Paul Richter dans les lettres françaises* (Paris: Corti, 1963), 255; Karl Siegfried Guthke, *Die Mythologie der entgötterten Welt: Ein literarisches Thema von der Aufklärung bis zur Gegenwart* (Göttingen, Vandenhoeck, 1971), 96.

[31] Jean Paul, *Das große Lesebuch*, ed. by Kurt Wölfel (Frankfurt am Main: Fischer, 2013), 230 / A. Kenney, *The Death of an Angel, and Other Pieces Translated from the Works of Jean Paul Friedrich Richter* (London: Black and Armstrong, 1839), 71.

[32] Jean Paul, *Das große Lesebuch*, 228. / A. Kenney, *The Death of an Angel, and Other Pieces Translated from the Works of Jean Paul Friedrich Richter*, 66f.

18th century. Here the words "That There is No God" are pronounced by Christ: suddenly an orphan Son of God who remains eternally suspended between a God who is not and a multitude of dead creatures. The Christ of this story is alone in his eternity. But that is exactly what transforms him into a sort of demonic figure. Very different is the case of the madman in Nietzsche's *Gay Science:* in a sense, he is alone, too, but alone in history, and alone in the midst of the crowd.

Nietzsche is perfectly aware of the fact that something has changed since the time when the sentence "there is no God" was passively received as a message—either a rational truth or a morally inconvenient lie. As he writes in the first book of *Daybreak:*

> In former times, one sought to prove that there is no God—today one indicates how the belief that there is a God could *arise* [*entstehen*] and how this belief acquired its weight and importance: a counter-proof that there is no God thereby becomes superfluous. —When in former times one had refuted the "proofs of the existence of God" put forward, there always remained the doubt whether better proofs might not be adduced than those just refuted: in those days atheists did not know how to make a clean sweep.[33]

The aphorism bears the title "Historical refutation as the definitive refutation." The idea of a *historical* refutation of something that cannot be *rationally* refuted is based on the assumption that the "God" whose existence was supposed to be "proved" is—as mentioned above—not a factual being but the *value* of an ideal that has been historically established as such. The "refutation" of a value—its being put out of circulation in order to be re-evaluated—is only possible in virtue of a critical view of history itself. In later works, that critical view will be specifically qualified as *genealogy*, as the interrogation of the value of values.[34] From the point of view of Nietzsche's critique of Christianity, the shift from the problem of truth to the problem of values implies that the very phenomenon of faith is to be investigated on the level of what he calls "our moral prejudices" rather than through a logical judgment concerning the untruth of a belief.

---

[33] Nietzsche, *Sämtliche Werke*, vol. 3, 86f. / *Daybreak*, ed. by Maudemarie Clark and Brian Leiter, trans. by R. J. Hollingdale (Cambridge: Cambridge University Press, 2003), 54.

[34] Cf. Nietzsche, *Sämtliche Werke*, vol. 5, 250 / *On the Genealogy of Morality*, 5: "...under what conditions did man invent the value judgments good and evil? *and what value do they themselves have?*"

The possibility of a comparison between Kant's refutation of the "proofs of the existence of God" in the *Critique of Pure Reason* and Nietzsche's critique of morality in *The Genealogy of Morals* is already indicated in the aphorism quoted above. This is what Gilles Deleuze had in mind when he tried to outline the correspondences between the three essays of *The Genealogy of Morals* and the three chapters in Book II of Transcendental Dialectics: "Chestov takes pleasure in finding the true *Critique of Pure Reason* in Dostoyevsky, in the *Notes from the Underground.* It is, in fact, primarily a Nietzschean idea to say that Kant's critique failed. But Nietzsche does not rely on anyone but himself to conceive and accomplish the true critique. This project is of great importance for the history of philosophy; for it runs counter not only to Kantianism, with which it competes, but to the whole Kantian inheritance, to which it is violently opposed."[35] If it is true that Kant's critique of "The Ideal of Pure Reason" is accomplished, not by Kant, but by Nietzsche through his interrogation "What do ascetic ideals mean," it is precisely because the ascetic ideal presents itself as a true religious *value.* In a sense, the question concerning the "meaning" of ascetic ideals had already been formulated by Kant. Here again, it is perhaps more fair to say that a certain Romanticism lays down the bridge between the failed critique of reason and Nietzsche's critique of morality. Romanticism itself is that broken bridge. Eric von der Luft observed once that Nietzsche's sentence "God is dead" contained "a literary reference to Heine, who, greatly admired by Nietzsche, at the end of the second book of *Zur Geschichte der Religion und Philosophie in Deutschland*, cited Kant's first *Kritik* as the sacrament brought to a dying God," and that "[i]t is not even too far-fetched to suppose that Nietzsche's Madman in *La Gaya Scienza,* § 125, is a caricature of Heine's Kant."[36] As soon as Kant affirms the exclusively "noumenal" character of God, Heine can certainly interpret the *Critique of Pure Reason* as "the sword with which deism was slain in Germany."[37]

Nietzsche's sentence "God is dead" indicates the death of the *living* God, the God of theism, the God who operates *in history* as the principle of all moral order. This is the reason why the historical refutation is for Nie-

---

[35] Gilles Deleuze, *Nietzsche et la philosophie* (Paris: Presses Universitaires de France, 1962), 100 / *Nietzsche and Philosophie*, trans. by Hugh Tomlinson (London: Continuum, 1983), 88.

[36] Eric von der Luft, "Sources of Nietzsche's 'God is Dead!' and its Meaning for Heidegger," *Journal of the History of Ideas*, vol. 45, no. 2, 1984, 268ff.

[37] Heinrich Heine, *Zur Geschichte der Religion und Philosophie in Deutschland* in *Der Salon*, vols. 1–4, (Hamburg: Hoffman und Campe, 1834), vol. 2, 188. My translation.

tzsche "the definitive refutation." The very notion of a historical refutation presupposes that the God who dies is conceived of as an ideal constituted in history and, thus, immanent to history. Deleuze has remarked on this point:

> the phrase "God is dead"...makes the existence of God depend on a synthesis, it synthesizes the idea of God with time, becoming, history and man....The phrase "God is dead" is not a speculative proposition but a dramatic proposition, *the* dramatic proposition *par excellence.* God cannot be made the object of synthetic knowledge without death entering into him. Existence or non-existence cease to be absolute determinations which derive from the idea of God, but rather life and death become relative determinations which correspond to the forces entering into synthesis with or in the idea of God.[38]

Deleuze's allusion to the "forces" entering in the idea of God is in itself the development of a Nietzschean motif. It implies that the standpoint from which the death of God can be affirmed is not the standpoint of atheism but the position of the "immoralist." Beyond the simple thought of atheism, Nietzsche's critique of Christianity is to be understood as one of the dimensions of a *double* strategy. As he himself explains in *Ecce Homo*:

> My word *immoralist* essentially entails two negations. First, I am negating a type of person who has been considered highest so far: the *good*, the *benevolent*, the *charitable*; second, I am negating a type of morality that has attained dominance and validity in the form of morality as such,—decadence morality or, to put it plainly, *Christian* morality. The second opposition may be considered decisive, since in general I see the overestimation of goodness and benevolence as a consequence of decadence, as a symptom of weakness, as incompatible with an ascending and affirmative life: negation and *destruction* are conditions of affirmation.[39]

Nietzsche knows, however, that the refusal of Christian morality would never have the character of a radical critique of illusion if it did not entail, as its counterpart, the negation of the "type of human being" that secures the reproduction of its de-valuated values—a reproduction that can take place even within a culture dominated by the ideals of modern science. But the reproduction of slave-morality is at the same time what makes possible the survival of the western ideal of *humanity* as such. This has been sufficiently stressed in some of the texts in which Nietzsche outlines his critique of

---

[38] Deleuze, *Nietzsche et la philosophie*, 175 / *Nietzsche and Philosophie*, 152.

[39] Nietzsche, *Sämtliche Werke*, vol. 6, 367f. / *Anti-Christ, Ecce Homo, Twilight of the Idols, and Other Writings*, 145f.

modern culture. In *The Case of Wagner*, the name of the German composer and that of Schopenhauer are mentioned as aspects or symptoms of what Nietzsche calls "modern 'humaneness.'"[40] The sense of Nietzsche's double strategy—the double deconstruction of Christian morality and of the moralist as a *Typ Mensch*—should be taken into account in order to properly understand Foucault's remarks in *The Order of Things*: "Rather than the death of God—or, rather, in the wake of that death and in a profound correlation to it—what Nietzsche's thought heralds is the end of his murderer, it is the explosion of man's face in laughter, and the return of masks."[41]—"God is dead; but given the way people are, there may still for millennia be caves in which they show his shadow."[42] Perhaps our 'humaneness' is that shadow, as much as our morality, our art, and our sciences are the "caves" in which is shown the shadow of a dead God.

---

[40] Nietzsche, *Sämtliche Werke*, vol. 6, 12 / *Anti-Christ, Ecce Homo, Twilight of the Idols, and Other Writings*, 233.

[41] Michel Foucault, *Les mots et les choses* (Paris: Gallimard, 1966), 396f. / *The Order of Things* (London: Routledge, 2002), 420.

[42] Nietzsche, *Sämtliche Werke*, vol. 3, 467 / *The Gay Science*, 109.

The End of Christianity? Remarks about Karl Jaspers' Criticism of Kierkegaard's Concept of Faith

István Czakó

Kierkegaard's German reception was far from homogeneous or free of diverging assessments.[1] One of the most striking contrasts seems to have appeared between the positions of Martin Heidegger and Karl Jaspers. Whereas Heidegger notoriously claimed that Kierkegaard is "not a thinker but a religious writer,"[2] Jaspers considered him explicitly to be "the most important thinker of our post-Kantian age."[3] Jaspers' prominent contribution

[1] See Habib C. Malik, *Receiving Søren Kierkegaard: The Early Impact and Transmission of His Thought* (Washington: The Catholic University of America Press, 1997); Heiko Schulz, "Germany and Austrian: A Modest Head Start: The German Reception of Kierkegaard," in *Kierkegaard's International Reception, Tome I: Northern and Western Europe*, ed. by Jon Stewart (Farnham: Ashgate, 2009) (*Kierkegaard Research: Sources, Reception and Resources*, vol. 8), 307–419. As for the divergent receptions of Kierkegaard's legacy see: Jon Stewart, *Søren Kierkegaard. Subjectivity, Irony, and the Crisis of Modernity* (Oxford: Oxford University Press, 2013), 189ff.

[2] Martin Heidegger, "The Word of Nietzsche: 'God is Dead,'" in *The Question Concerning Technology and Other Essays*, trans. by William Lovitt (New York: Harper and Row, 1977), 53–112; 94. As for Heidegger's view of Kierkegaard as a "religious writer" see Gerhard Thonhauser, *Ein rätselhaftes Zeichen. Zum Verhältnis von Martin Heidegger und Søren Kierkegaard* (Berlin and Boston: Walter de Gruyter, 2016), 426–454 (*Kierkegaard Studies Monograph Series*, vol. 33). See also Vincent McCarthy, "Martin Heidegger: Kierkegaard's Influence Hidden and in Full View," in *Kierkegaard and Existentialism*, ed. by Jon Stewart (Farnham: Ashgate, 2001) (*Kierkegaard Research: Sources, Reception and Resources*, vol. 9), 95–125. According to Caputo's remarkable claim "One wonders how Heidegger can possibly have taken Kierkegaard to be only a 'religious writer' with no ontological concerns. One wonders how he could have written the ontology of 'temporality,' which constitutes the meaning of the Being of Dasein in *Being and Time*, without so much as acknowledging Kierkegaard, when the whole analysis, in my view, derives in its main lines from Kierkegaard!" John Caputo, *Radical Hermeneutics* (Bloomington and Indianapolis: Indiana University Press, 1987), 16.

[3] Karl Jaspers, *The Great Philosophers*, vol. 4, *The Disturbers: Descartes, Pascal, Lessing, Kierkegaard, Nietzsche—Philosophers in Other Realms: Einstein, Weber, Marx*, ed. by Michael Ermath and Leonard H. Ehrlich (New York, San Diego and London: Harcourt Brace, 1994), 191.

to the philosophical interpretation and dissemination of Kierkegaard's thinking at a very early stage of reception is indisputable.[4] The influence of the Danish thinker on him can hardly be overestimated;[5] his entire work can be seen, as Michael Theunissen remarks, "as a unique Kierkegaard commentary."[6] His main philosophical aim fully coincided with that of Kierkegaard; namely, to read "the original text (*Urschrift*) of individual, human existential relations."[7]

The German philosopher, however, did not assimilate Kierkegaard's thought without reserve and ambivalence; he was in fact one of the sharpest critics of some aspects of Kierkegaard's concept of Christianity. He not only claimed that he had never been a "follower" (*Anhänger*) of the Danish thinker, but he also emphasized: "Kierkegaard's Christianity kept me intact….His conception of Christian faith…meant the end of historical Christianity as well as the end of every philosophical life."[8] From this aversion follows in Jaspers *ab initio* not only a negative attitude but also a methodological prin-

[4] The canonization of Kierkegaard's thought in the academic philosophical scene is closely connected with Jaspers' resolute work. As he remarks, the Danish thinker was at the time of his early lectures in effect unknown as a philosopher: "*In meinen Vorlesungen war er [i. e., Kierkegaard] eine der großen Gestalten der Vergangenheit (ich war erstaunt, daß er im Bereich der Universitätsphilosophie nicht existiere, und daß in den Lehrbüchern der Philosophiegeschichte nicht einmal sein Name vorkam.)*" Karl Jaspers, "Nachwort (1955) zu meiner *Philosophie*," in his *Philosophie*, vols. 1–3 (4th ed., Berlin, Heidelberg and New York: Springer, 1973 [1932]), vol. 1, xx.

[5] "The discovery of the concept of *Existenz* itself, and the emphasis and importance Jaspers attributed to it throughout an entire writing life, cannot but be derived from an attentive reading of Kierkegaard, where the concept of existence is foregrounded in so many works." Roger Poole, "The Unknown Kierkegaard: Twentieth-Century Receptions," in *The Cambridge Companion to Kierkegaard*, ed. by Alastair Hannay and Gordon D. Marino (Cambridge: Cambridge University Press, 1999), 51. Jaspers himself claims in his late autobiographical retrospect: "*Kierkegaard verdanke ich den Begriff der 'Existenz', der mir seit 1916 maßgebend wurde, um das zu fassen, worum ich mich bis dahin in Unruhe bemüht hatte.*" Karl Jaspers, *Philosophische Autobiographie* (Erweiterte Neuausgabe, Munich: Piper, 1977), 125.

[6] Michael Theunissen, "Einleitung: Kierkegaards Werk und Wirkung. III. Zur Wirkungsgeschichte. 3. Philosophie. (b) Existenzphilosophie" in *Materialien zur Philosophie Søren Kierkegaards*, ed. by Michael Theunissen and Wilfried Greve (Frankfurt am Main: Suhrkamp, 1979), 62: "*In der Tat kann man das Werk von Jaspers als einen einzigen Kommentar zu Kierkegaard lesen.*" According to Sartre, "*Jaspers, lui, joue cartes sur table: il n'a rien fait d'autre que de commenter son maître, son originalité consiste surtout à mettre certains thèmes en relief et à en masquer d'autres.*" Jean–Paul Sartre, *Critique de la raison dialectique*, vol. 1 (Paris: Gallimard, 1960), 21.

[7] Karl Jaspers, *Vernunft und Existenz. Fünf Vorlesungen gehalten vom 25. bis 29. März* (Groningen and Batavia: J. B. Wolters' Uitgevers—Maatschappij, 1935), 1–27 (8.) (In English as *Reason and Existenz. Five Lectures by Karl Jaspers*, trans. by William Earle (Milwaukee: Marquette University Press, 1997), 19–50 (27). See also *SKS* 7, 573 / *CUP1*, 630.

[8] Karl Jaspers, "Nachwort (1955) zu meiner *Philosophie*," in his *Philosophie*, vol. 1, XX.

ciple, namely, to omit "all 'Christian' matter"[9] from the interpretation of Kierkegaard.

That is to say Jaspers' reception of Kierkegaard was far from being an uncritical assimilation and continuation, but rather it was actually permeated by an essentially ambivalent attitude. In my contribution an attempt will be made to outline a specific religious topic, namely, the issue of the religious negation of the world, which seems to constitute the very core of Jaspers' criticism of Kierkegaard. I wish to argue that although Jaspers' criticism is certainly relevant regarding the late period of Kierkegaard's authorship, it is nonetheless a somewhat simplistic and reductive considering the historical development of Kierkegaard's position.

I. JASPERS' CONCEPT OF THE RELIGIOUS NEGATION OF THE WORLD

Jaspers treats the concept of religious negation of the world (*religiöse Weltverneinung*) in the second volume of his *Philosophy* (*Existenzerhellung*).[10] The context of the discussion is the manifestation of unconditionality (*Unbedingtheit*) of *Existenz* in human activity. Jaspers distinguishes between two forms of unconditional activities: the one is suicide, and the other the religious activity, especially the religious world-negation.

According to Jaspers, the consequence of unconditional religious activities is to grasp the genuine Being (*eigentliches Sein*) exclusively in itself. By grasping the genuine Being in the religious act absolutely the religious person negates everything else which falls outside this act. Whereas in magic, superstition and mythology one tries to constrain the deity by means of sacrifices and asceticism in order to reach world-immanent goals, in the Far Eastern and Western religions appears the phenomenon of total asceticism and world-negation.

Regarding its pure form, world-negation is a negative decision of the individual: one does not identify oneself with either any objectivity of worldly being or with any subjectivity, but one relates oneself exclusively to Transcendence. Thus, one negates everything worldlessly (*weltlos*) for the sake of

---

[9] Karl Jaspers, *Psychologie der Weltanschauungen* (Berlin: Springer, 1919), 370. (In English as "Reading Kierkegaard 1: Becoming Manifest," trans. by Edith Ehrlich, in *Karl Jaspers on Philosophy of History and History of Philosophy*, ed. by Joseph W. Koterski and Raymond J. Langley (Amherst/NY: Humanity Books, 2003), 243–257, 245.)

[10] Karl Jaspers, *Philosophie*, vol. 2: *Existenzerhellung* (4th ed., Berlin, Heidelberg and New York: Springer, 1973), 318–320.

the Transcendence, although this negation is in the world essentially ambivalent, since it is impossible to leave the world within the world itself. Thus, *Existenz* which negates the world is in permanent strife with itself. The individual relates himself to Transcendence in an irresolvable solitude. If this kind of *Existenz* appears as the true one, which is to be followed, then it will be a deceptive will-o'-wisp (*Irrlicht*). If, however, it draws attention to the fundamental questionability of every being, then it will be really true. The fact that there have lived at any given time individuals who sought this worldlessness (*Weltlosigkeit*) is a permanent *memento* for the possibility of *Existenz* in the world.

According to Jaspers, world-negation as a purely negative decision arises from an incomprehensible unconditionality. The world-negating individual is essentially an exception (*Ausnahme*) who can never become an exemplar to be followed. In Jaspers' view it was Kierkegaard who clearly contrasted the individual's positive and negative decisions regarding the world: whereas the positive decision obtains the world, the negative one remains in an existential gliding (*Schweben*). Whereas the positive decision provides security, the negative one remains uncertain and ambiguous. Finally, whereas the positive decision gives stability, the negative one needs to be preserved. The individual making the negative decision wants eternity, but he is unable to grasp it in its hiddenness. This individual can neither stay firmly in the world nor can he be at home in eternity.

The negative decision is an analogue of suicide. However no one may dare to brand this decision to be entirely false. According to Jaspers, the heroes of negativity remain on the border of human possibilities and sacrifice themselves. Their terrible solitude reveals the basic experience of world-negating individuals who undermine the tranquility secured by the world. This negative decision is necessarily self-contradictory since it does not negate a concrete, world-immanent fact, but rather it negates the worldliness (*Weltlichkeit*) of the individual in order to grasp Transcendence directly and absolutely outside the world. Nevertheless Jaspers regards the negative, world-negating attitude as a heroic act by means of which the individual becomes a disturbing exception (*Ausnahme*).

II. THE PROBLEMS OF RELIGIOUS ACOSMISM IN JASPERS' RECEPTION OF KIERKEGAARD

Jaspers, while explicating the problems of religious acosmism in the second volume of his *Philosophy*, directly connects the exposition of the issue with the treatment of Kierkegaard's own conception. It should be pointed out that world-negation is treated here as a heroic act and the world-negating individual is presented as the hero of negativity, as an exception drawing attention to the floating of existence as well as to the original questionableness of it.

With regard to Jaspers' own terminology, it should be noted that the term "religious acosmism" (*religiöser Akosmismus*) does not appear in his published works. Instead, he largely uses the expression "religious negation of world" (*religiöse Weltverneinung*), which entirely corresponds to the former term. On this point, we can refer to a remarkable parallelism between Jaspers' position and Martin Buber's concept of an "acosmic relation to God" (*akosmische Beziehung zu Gott*).[11] This latter concept has a rather critical function in Buber's thinking and plays a decisive role in his interpretation of Kierkegaard.[12] Buber assigns great hermeneutical importance to Kierkegaard's claim: "Everyone should be chary about having to do with 'the others,' and should essentially speak only with God and with himself."[13] According to Buber, "the essential relation to God, which Kierkegaard means, presupposes...a renunciation of every essential relation to anything else, to the world, to community, to the individual man."[14] Due to the absolute exclusivity of the God-relation, intersubjectivity becomes devaluated or even dissolved (e.g., Kierkegaard's relation to marriage and public life). Through the decision of faith the individual becomes isolated and closed in on himself in a solipsistic way. Instead of negating the reality of the world, Kierkegaard's acosmism negates its existential relevance for the individual (*Enkelte*).[15] For the believer everything that falls outside of his absolute relation to

---

[11] Martin Buber, *Die Frage an den Einzelnen*, in his *Dialogisches Leben. Gesammelte philosophische und pädagogische Schriften* (Zurich: Georg Müller, 1947), 208.

[12] As for Buber's critical reception of Kierkegaard see Peter Šajda, "No-One Can So Refute Kierkegaard as Kierkegaard Himself," in *Kierkegaard and Existentialism*, ed. by Jon Stewart (Aldershot: Ashgate, 2011) (*Kierkegaard Research: Sources, Reception and Resources*, vol. 9), 33–62; Peter Šajda, *Buberov spor s Kierkegaardom: O vzťahu náboženstva k etike a politike* (Bratislava: Kalligram, 2013). I am particularly indebted to Peter Šajda for having called my attention to the problems of acosmism in Jaspers' reception of Kierkegaard.

[13] *SKS* 16, 86 / *PV*, 106.

[14] Martin Buber, "What is Man?," in his *Between Man and Man*, trans. by Ronald Gregor-Smith (London and New York: Routledge & Kegan Paul, 2002), 212.

[15] In Kierkegaard's published works appears the term "acosmism" (*Akosmisme*) only in the doctoral dissertation and in the *Postscript*. In the dissertation the term refers to Fichte's idealism: "When Fichte infinitized the *I* in this way, he advanced an idealism beside which any actuality turned pale, an acosmism in which his idealism became actuality even though it was Docetism."

the absolute is ultimately nonexistent. It seems to me that on this point Jaspers' reading and criticism of Kierkegaard fully coincides with that of Buber.

In what follows, I will try to show what significance the problems of acosmism in Jaspers' reception of Kierkegaard have from a historical point of view. As regards the historical arc of Jaspers' thinking, it is remarkable that although he reflects on the problems of acosmism or religious negation of the world very early, this concept did not have any critical or normative function for him in this period. Rather, it had a constative and descriptive role without any pretense of a normative evaluation; moreover, in the second volume of *Philosophy* Jaspers explicitly formulates a methodological demand to abstain from any critical evaluation in this field. In the later works, however, this attitude remarkably changes. In the Basel period (1948–1969), especially in his *Philosophical Faith and Revelation* (1962), the use of the concept "religious world-negation" becomes explicitly critical and Jaspers stresses here the destructive nature of Kierkegaard's conception of faith. Although this change is striking enough, it seems to me that it would be somewhat hasty to conclude from this phenomenon that a deep conceptual shift occurs in Jaspers' position. Changes of this kind are absolutely not characteristic of his intensive reception of Kierkegaard that spanned many decades.[16] It seems to me that instead of a conceptual turn here, there lies a transposition of the thematic emphasis of Jaspers' approach. Although the German philosopher already in his lectures of 1947 in Basel dealt with the problems of philosophical and Christian faith, a systematic exposition of this topic took place only after his resettlement in Basel (1948). Especially in this period he had an intensive experience of the thinking of his colleague, the Swiss theologian Karl Barth (1886–1968), who for his own part was also a

---

SKS 1, 309 / *CI*, 273. In the *Postscript* "acosmism" is mentioned as a possible speculative misunderstanding of the ethical actuality of the subjective individual: "To give thinking supremacy over everything else is Gnosticism; to make the subjective individual's ethical actuality the only actuality could seem to be acosmism." *SKS* 7, 312 / *CUP1*, 341. Later, in one of his journal entries from 1850 Kierkegaard contrasts Mynster's concept of Christianity with that of the Middle Ages: "*Man har beskyldt Middelalderen for Akosmisme—nu Kosmisme er da i ethvert Tilfælde ikke det Christelige.*" *SKS* 24, 89, NB21:143 / *KJN* 8, 85. See also *SKS* 18, 382, KK:11 / *KJN* 2, 348.

[16] Leonard H. Ehrlich, "Jaspers Reading Kierkegaard: An Instance of the Double Helix," in *Karl Jaspers on Philosophy of History and History of Philosophy*, 239.

significant figure in Kierkegaard's reception during his famous early, dialectical period.[17]

Remarkably enough, Jaspers became aware of the acosmic character of Kierkegaard's philosophy already in his early work *Psychologie der Weltanschauungen* (1919). In the context of the analysis of existential limit situations (*Grenzsituationen*) he treats Kierkegaard's concept of guilt or sin (*Sünde*), and he critically claims that Kierkegaard "says nothing about the very experience of world-views themselves. He merely hints that such powers are wholly beyond the world: they are alone with God....It is a reflective, solitary religiosity of thought."[18] Later, in the third volume of his *Philosophy* (1932) Jaspers emphasizes that contrary to Kierkegaard's solipsistic, acosmic faith the very field of our relation to Transcendence is the unity of the world and history: "Worldless love is love of nothing, an unfounded bliss. I really love Transcendence only as my love transfigures the world (*liebende Weltverklärung*)."[19] Also, in his Groningen lectures *Reason and Existenz* (1935), Jaspers highlights the negative acosmic character of Kierkegaard's conception of faith. Jaspers outlines it as "an otherworldly Christianity which is like Nothingness and shows itself only in negation (the absurd, martyrdom) and in negative resolution."[20] "Kierkegaard leaped to a Christianity which was conceived as an absurd paradox, as decision for utter world-negation and martyrdom."[21] It is characteristic that absurdity and martyrdom appear consistently in Jaspers' writings as concrete forms of religious world-negation.

In his Basel lectures *The Philosophical Faith* (1947), Jaspers claims that God is absolutely transcendent; he is a *Deus absconditus*.[22] This position would have been certainly accepted by all of Kierkegaard's pseudonyms. Yet, although the two thinkers wholly agree in the absolute otherness and cognitive incomprehensibility of Transcendence, they totally disagree in the possible forms of the relationship to it. Whereas the worldliness (*Weltlichkeit*) of

---

[17] See Lee C. Barrett, "Karl Barth: The Dialectic of Attraction and Repulsion," in *Kierkegaard's Influence on Theology, Tome I: German Protestant Theology*, ed, by Jon Stewart (Farnham: Ashgate, 2012) (*Kierkegaard Research: Sources, Reception and Resources*, vol. 10), 1–41.

[18] Jaspers, "Reading Kierkegaard: Guilt: The Fundamental Limit Situation," in *Karl Jaspers on Philosophy of History and History of Philosophy*, 256.

[19] Karl Jaspers, *Philosophie*, vol. 3, *Metaphysik* (4th ed., Berlin, Heidelberg, and New York: Springer, 1973), 167.

[20] Jaspers, *Reason and Existenz*, 25.

[21] Ibid., 36.

[22] Jaspers, *Der philosophische Glaube*, 33.

Existenz is, for Jaspers, a *condition of possibility* of this relation, Kierkegaard, on the contrary, conceives the same worldliness as an *obstacle* to relating oneself to the Transcendent. This is the conceptual background of Kierkegaard's concept of absurd faith which is characterized by Jaspers as follows: "no one needs to choose a profession, no one needs to get married, it is only martyrdom in which authentic Christianity consists."[23]

The problem of religious acosmism plays also a central role in Jaspers' late comprehensive work *Philosophical Faith and Revelation* (1962). In this *opus*, however, the critical attitude becomes predominant. Here Jaspers deals with Kierkegaard extensively,[24] but he focuses on only one crucial problem, namely on Kierkegaard's late, serious conflict with the Danish established Church (*Kirchenkampf*, 1854–55). The German philosopher assigns to this conflict a definitive significance, and he believes that the *Kirchenkampf* was an inevitable consequence of Kierkegaard's basic concept of absurd faith. He claims that Kierkegaard's "fight was not a late aberration of his, but the outcome of an irresistibly maturing insight. It resulted from the poetic construction of Christianity he had derived from theological dialectics...."[25] It would be, however, a total miscomprehension to think that the Danish thinker would have been criticizing the established Church from the standpoint of authentic Christianity. What Kierkegaard really wants and demands, is, according to Jaspers, not authentic Christianity but simple and solely "honesty" (*Redlichkeit*).[26] This attitude manifests itself most clearly in one of Kierkegaard's late articles published in the journal *Fædrelandet* with the title of "What Do I Want?," and the first sentence of which reads: "I want—honesty."[27] Later on he formulates it even more strongly: "I am neither leniency nor stringency—I am human honesty."[28] The significance of this sentence can be hardly overestimated. The demand for honesty was namely the leading tone of the philosophical tendencies appearing in the period of the dissolution of German Idealism. Whereas Schopenhauer apostrophizes the German Idealists as dishonest inane charlatans, and Nietzsche

[23] Ibid., 128.

[24] Karl Jaspers, *Philosophical Faith and Revelation*, trans. by E. B. Ashton (London: Collins, 1967), 346–356.

[25] Jaspers, *Philosophical Faith and Revelation*, 346.

[26] Ibid. 347: "Kierkegaard is not fighting here as a Christian, for Christianity, but as a human being, for veracity. 'Quite simply: I want honesty. I am neither clemency nor rigour—I am human honesty.'"

[27] *SKS* 14, 179 / *M*, 46.

[28] Ibid.

announces the demand of intellectual honesty, Kierkegaard reveals the fundamental inauthenticity of the established Christianity. The radicality of Kierkegaard's criticism is based even on the principle of honesty with which he identifies himself. According to Jaspers, the truth of Kierkegaard lies in the unconditionality of his will to honesty which can be certainly compared to Nietzsche's famous word: "I am no man—I am dynamite."[29]

Nevertheless, Jaspers apparently here formulates his sharpest criticism of Kierkegaard's conception of Christianity: "Having made my choice, I may express my opinion that the way shown by Kierkegaard under the pseudonyms of Climacus and Anticlimacus—the way to a faith on the strength of absurdity, by an ingenious and seductively conceived categorial edifice and a construction of following Christ in the unequivocal sense of total world denial—would lead astray."[30] In his *Nachlass* Jaspers describes the paradox of faith as a "world-less transcendence of the isolated soul with God."[31]

The negativity of the religious acosmism destroys also interpersonal relations and also the religious community itself. According to Jaspers, if Kierkegaard "were right, it would mean the end of Christianity in the world. If the Christian faith is what he construed it to be, probably no one can believe it any more—and Kierkegaard, though passionately eager to believe, never claimed to be doing so in person."[32] That is, if Kierkegaard were right, Christianity could not exist at all. In the *Nachlass* Jaspers explicitly claims: "If Kierkegaard's Christianity is the one and only one, then his thinking would spell the end of Christianity brought about by Christian thinking itself."[33] As a result of this we do not have to follow the Danish religious writer but to take his plea for honesty seriously. For Jaspers, Kierkegaard does not represent a standpoint but rather a "way of thinking"[34] which cannot be surpassed. Still, the negativity of this way of thinking implies that "a Christian faith that uses Kierkegaard's theological construct to comprehend itself as incomprehensible, as necessarily absurd—thus justifying itself, so to speak,

---

[29] Friedrich Nietzsche, *Ecce homo*, trans. by Anthony M. Ludovici, in *The Complete Works of Friedrich Nietzsche*, vols. 1–18, ed. by Oscar Levy (New York: MacMillan, 1911), vol. 17, 131.

[30] Jaspers, *Philosophical Faith and Revelation*, 348.

[31] Karl Jaspers, *Die grossen Philosophen. Nachlass*, vols. 1–2, ed. by Hans Saner (Munich and Zurich: Piper, 1981), vol. 2, 817.

[32] Jaspers, *Philosophical Faith and Revelation*, 349.

[33] Jaspers, *The Great Philosophers*, vol. 4, 285.

[34] Jaspers, *Philosophical Faith and Revelation*, 351.

in a modern world—would be as apt to mean the end of this Christianity and this church as would Kierkegaard's exposure of ecclesiasticism."[35]

Jaspers' criticism of Kierkegaard's acosmic conception is apparently based on a *reductio ad absurdum*: namely, as we have seen, if Kierkegaard were right, then Christianity could not exist. Since, however, the existence of Christianity is an undeniable historical fact, Kierkegaard's position is in itself quite dubious. But Kierkegaard, however, could simply reply that Jaspers' conclusion does not follow from his premises because Christianity does not exist at all: what namely exists is only an appearance, or what is even worse, a travesty, a distortion and betrayal of Christianity. This contradiction, however, is only apparent: namely, whereas Jaspers stresses the factical and historical existence of Christianity, Kierkegaard's criticism lies on his fundamental and polemical distinction between authentic Christianity (*Christendom*) and its alienated, watered-down form (*Christenhed*). Thus Jaspers considers the existence of Christianity evident, and he sharply criticizes Kierkegaard's acosmic conception. Even though this conception has genuine Christian origins, paradoxically enough it is the negation of the religion itself, and it is constructed in the final analysis on a faith in God—without religion.

Despite all of these sharp polemics, Jaspers by no means concludes that Kierkegaard's position is entirely erroneous. According to Jaspers, the Danish thinker is an "exception" (*Ausnahme*), a "great awakener" (*großer Erwecker*), a dialectician of negativity, a prophet of negativity indispensable for any existential self-understanding, even though to follow him is neither necessary nor possible for us. It is certainly not surprising that on Jaspers' view the best element in Kierkegaard's thinking in not the world-negating Christianity which is based on the negative decision of the individual: "Kierkegaard's greatness can hardly be derived from his interpretation of Christian faith, which on the contrary he formulates in a manner that strikes us as the self-destruction of this faith. It is an artful dialectic of unsolved contradictions that discovers in them the truth of God's actuality."[36]

III. REMARKS ON JASPERS' CRITICISM OF KIERKEGAARD

In conclusion let me make some short remarks about Jaspers' critical reception of Kierkegaard with special regard to the problems of religion, especial-

[35] Ibid., 350.

[36] Jaspers, *Die grossen Philosophen*, vol. 2, 845.

ly Christianity. As we have seen, Jaspers' criticism refers primarily to the negativity of Kierkegaard's conception of Christianity and faith which can be defined as a kind of "acosmism;" moreover, he also sharply criticizes in this context the existential category of the "absurd" as a pure negation of reason.

First of all, it should be pointed out that Jaspers read Kierkegaard "backwards" in the sense that he first became acquainted with the late, polemical writings of the Danish thinker from the period of the controversy with the Danish Church. Moreover, Jaspers assigned a decisive significance to these writings with respect to the interpretation of the whole textual *corpus*. The German philosopher considered these texts to be the proper hermeneutical keys to Kierkegaard's *oeuvre*. Jaspers' basic argument here is that Kierkegaard's late conflict with the Danish Church was not a casual incident but a necessary consequence of his concept of absurd faith.[37] No doubt, in the early period of the German reception, the late polemical writings were strongly present, and they had a significant effect. It is similarly certain that the basic conception of these writings can be correctly explained by means of negative concepts such as acosmism and religious world-negation: authentic Christian existence constitutes itself in the negative choice, and it culminates in martyrdom. Still, it seems to me by no means evident that this short characterization would be entirely appropriate for Kierkegaard's thinking as a whole. I believe that Jaspers' methodology, to expand Kierkegaard's late conception of religion to the whole *oeuvre* is rather dubious. In the following I would like to highlight just a few examples to show that Kierkegaard's own position itself was far from historically immutable but instead underwent significant changes; therefore, it cannot be described in a reductionist and simplified way. At the same time, I wish to argue that the question dealt with here is not only a particular and isolated problem in the history of reception, but it is also relevant as a genuine form of reconsidering the fundamental problems of religion and Christianity.

---

[37] Jaspers, *Philosophical Faith and Revelation*, 346: "This fight was not a late aberration of his [i.e. Kierkegaard's], but the outcome of an irresistibly maturing insight. It resulted from the poetic construction of Christianity he had derived from theological dialectics and communicated mainly under the pseudonyms of 'Climacus' and 'Anti-Climacus'. Hardly ever has an entrance into the public arena been so slowly, so thoughtfully, so hesitantly prepared for as was this step of Kierkegaard's. Once his mind was made up, however, he followed through with matchless vehemence, in supreme consciousness, in line with the situation and with the historic moment."

A brief glance at Kierkegaard's writings is enough to see a significant turn in his concept of religion. Whereas in the early writings the category of hidden "inwardness" (*Inderlighed*) played a central role in his understanding of religion and faith, later after his work *Practice in Christianity* (1850) the open break with the established Church and "the world" became predominant as well as the concept of martyrdom. In the early, famous work *Fear and Trembling* (1843), Abraham, the father of faith, fulfills the movement of "infinite resignation,"[38] which is undoubtedly a negative decision, yet this negativity is at the same time "sublated" in his movement of faith (*Tro*), which is essentially repeating, regaining, turning back to finite reality, to the "world." According to Johannes de silentio, "By faith Abraham did not renounce Isaac, but by faith Abraham received Isaac."[39] Abraham's faith is in no way a one-sided world-negation, but, on the contrary, it is an affirmation and regaining of finitude. Similarly, in *Repetition* (1843) Constantin Constantius describes Job's faith as a regaining of and a returning to the finite world:

> [T]he Lord and Job have come to an understanding, they are reconciled, "the confidence of the Lord dwells again in the tents of Job as in former days"—men have come to understand Job. *Now* they come to him and eat bread with him and are sorry for him and console him; his brothers and sisters, each one of them, give him a farthing and a gold ring—Job is blessed and has received everything *double.* —This is called a *repetition.*"[40]

Further, if we recall Johannes Climacus' criticism of the monastic movement of the Middle Ages in the *Concluding Unscientific Postscript* (1846), we can find that he criticizes this movement (rightly or wrongly) just because of the inadequacy of its world-negation. According to Kierkegaard/Climacus, the monastic movement expresses the world-negation as an external moment of the absolute and pathetic relation of the individual to the absolute *telos*, whereas this relation must be essentially an inner one.[41] The relation of the individual to the absolute *telos* is in the *Postscript* far from

---

[38] *SKS* 4, 132 / *FT*, 37: "This is the peak on which Abraham stands. The last stage to pass from his view is the stage of infinite resignation. He actually goes further and comes to faith."

[39] *SKS* 4, 143 / *FT*, 49.

[40] *SKS* 4, 79 / *R*, 212.

[41] *SKS* 7, 372 / *CUP1*, 409: "The monastic movement wants to express interiority by an outwardness that is supposed to be interiority. Herein lies the contradiction, because to be a monk is just as much something outward as being a councilor of justice. Mediation abolishes the absolute τέλος."

being an acosmic negation of the external, objective, material relations; rather, it is not an exodus from the empirical world, but it is substantially an incognito, a becoming inward and subjective on the part of the existing individual.

Consequently, although Jaspers' claim that Kierkegaard's concept of religion in its integrity would be acosmic and world-negating is not entirely groundless, it is undoubtedly simplistic and one-sided. Jaspers' effort in his main work *Philosophy* to distinguish between religion and philosophy on the grounds of world-negation seems to be also questionable, since there could hardly be a more acosmic philosophical position than that of Schopenhauer. As it is well known, in the fourth, ethical part of his *magnum opus* Schopenhauer explains that the mortification of the will to live (*Lebenswille*) in the ethical action of asceticism is at the same time also a pure negation of the world as a will-in-itself and also as a phenomenon: "to those in whom the will has turned and has denied itself, this our world, which is so real, with all its suns and milky-ways—is nothing."[42] Even though it is indisputable that this conception was strongly influenced by Indian thinking in particular by Buddhism, the genuine philosophical character and relevance of Schopenhauer's metaphysic of will is clearly beyond question.

Jaspers' interpretation of the category of the absurd in the context of negative decision and world-negation is not less simplistic than his criticism of Kierkegaard's conception of religion and Christianity. The absurd is by no means a mere negation of reason although some of Kierkegaard's well-known texts certainly could give this impression. In fact, however, in his main work, the *Concluding Unscientific Postscript*, he clearly distinguishes between nonsense and the absurd;[43] moreover, in one of his notebooks he characterizes the relation between faith and reason similarly to Leibniz:

> What I usually express by saying that Christianity consists of paradox, philosophy in mediation, Leibniz expresses by distinguishing what is above reason and what is against reason. Faith is above reason. By reason he understands, as he says in many places, a linking together of truths, a conclusion from causes. Faith therefore cannot be *proved, demonstrated, comprehended,* for the link which makes a linking together possible is missing, and what else does this say than that it is a paradox. This, precisely, is the irregularity in the paradox, continuity is lacking, or at any

---

[42] Arthur Schopenhauer, *The World as Will and Idea*, trans. by Richard Burdon Haldane and John Kemp, 7th ed. (London: Keagan Paul, Trench, Trübner, 1909), 532.

[43] *SKS* 7, 505–518 / *CUP1*, 555–570.

rate it has continuity only in reverse, that is, at the beginning it does not manifest itself as continuity.[44]

In those texts of Kierkegaard in which the author approaches faith from the position of a nonbeliever, faith manifests itself as paradox and absurd; but in the late, Christian texts this problems entirely vanishes. In one of his later notebook entries Kierkegaard explicitly claims: "When the believer has faith, the absurd is not the absurd—faith transforms it, but in every weak moment it is again more or less absurd to him. The passion of faith is the only thing that masters the absurd—if not, then faith is not faith in the strictest sense, but a kind of knowledge."[45] Of course, this claim does not confute Jaspers' interpretation of Kierkegaard's concept of religion; however, it reveals the one-sidedness and selectivity of his methodology. Anyway, notwithstanding all these critical remarks, it must be emphasized that Jaspers has been the leading figure of German philosophical reception of Kierkegaard for many decades, and for this reason the Danish thinker owes much to him.

Does Kierkegaard's concept of faith actually mean the end of historical Christianity? There can be no doubt that form of Christianity which is represented by the established Church (*Christenhed*) cannot be justified at all in the mirror of any of his writings. We have to take into consideration, however, that the existential categories of subjectivity (*Subjektivitet*), incognito (*Incognito*), inwardness (*Inderlighed*) and even more repetition (*Gjentagelse*), which were for a long time key concepts of his interpretation of faith, cannot be simply explained as different forms of existential or religious acosmism. Rather it seems to me that Kierkegaard, the dialectician of negativity, has grasped and explored one of the constitutive moments of genuine Christianity (*Christendom*), which can be expressed by the biblical phrase: "My kingdom is not of this world."[46] It is no surprise that his pseudonym Anti-Climacus considers this statement "eternally valid," which clearly expresses the position of Christianity "in this world"—without being "of this world."[47] In this context we can state that Jaspers' criticism of Kierkegaard's concept of faith is undoubtedly relevant, even though it is not less one-sided than Kierkegaard's own position especially in his late polemical writings. Their

[44] *SKS* 19, 390f.; Not13: 23. / *KJN* 3, 388.
[45] *Pap.* X–6 B 79, 86 / *JP* 1, 10.
[46] John 18:36.
[47] *SKS* 12, 207 / *PC*, 211.

dialogue, however, in spite of all these conceptual differences, is not in the least unproductive, but, on the contrary, it is part and parcel of a millennial striving to comprehend Christianity—or at least its incomprehensibility.

Ambiguity, Indecision, Nonexceptionality: Kierkegaard in Carl Schmitt's *Political Theology*

Peter Šajda

I. CARL SCHMITT AND THE GERMAN KIERKEGAARD RENAISSANCE

Carl Schmitt's productive reception of Kierkegaard's thought took place to a large extent in the interwar period. During this period the German-speaking intellectual world experienced a phenomenon that some contemporary authors referred to as the *Kierkegaard Renaissance*.[1] Kierkegaard's intellectual

The paper was produced at the Institute of Philosophy of the Slovak Academy of Sciences as part of the grant project VEGA 2/0110/18.

[1] I treat the phenomenon in more detail in my monograph *Kierkegaardovská renesancia. Filozofia, náboženstvo, politika* [*The Kierkegaard Renaissance: Philosophy, Religion, Politics*] (Bratislava: Premedia, 2016). Unlike Gerhard Thonhauser and Keisuke Yoshida I do not limit the timespan of the Kierkegaard Renaissance to the interwar period. Instead, I propose that it lasted from 1909 to 1945. Its *symbolic* beginning is connected to the publication of the first volumes of the influential Jena edition of Kierkegaard's *Collected Works* (1909–1922) and the subsequent popularization of Kierkegaard in the journal *Der Brenner*, especially by Theodor Haecker. Its *symbolic* end is connected to the death of its two key figures, Christoph Schrempf and Haecker, and the beginning of the new *research*-oriented period of the German Kierkegaard reception after World War II. For more detail on the German reception and its periodization see Heiko Schulz, "Germany and Austrian: A Modest Head Start: The German Reception of Kierkegaard," in *Kierkegaard's International Reception*, Tome I, *Northern and Western Europe*, ed. by Jon Stewart (Farnham: Ashgate, 2009) (*Kierkegaard Research: Sources, Reception and Resources*, vol. 8), 307–419. For Thonhauser's and Yoshida's comments on the Kierkegaard Renaissance see Gerhard Thonhauser, *Ein rätselhaftes Zeichen. Zum Verhältnis von Martin Heidegger und Søren Kierkegaard*, (Berlin and Boston: Walter de Gruyter, 2016) (*Kierkegaard Studies. Monograph Series*, vol. 33), 105, 119–126; Keisuke Yoshida, "Der Schatten der Kierkegaard-Renaissance: Eine rezeptionsgeschichtliche Studie über die dezisionistisch-irrationalistischen Kierkegaard-Interpretationen zwischen den Weltkriegen in Deutschland," *Kierkegaard Studies Yearbook*, 2015, 272–275. For contemporary reactions to the Kierkegaard Renaissace see Werner Elert, *Der Kampf um das Christentum. Geschichte der Beziehungen zwischen dem evangelischen Christentum in Deutschland und dem allgemeinen Denken seit Schleiermacher und Hegel* (Munich: Beck, 1921), 430–434; Hermann Diem: "Zur Psychologie der Kierkegaard-Renaissance," *Zwischen*

legacy became a source of inspiration for a broad and diverse range of philosophers, theologians, psychologists and writers. This phenomenon did not, however, appear like a bolt from the blue. On the contrary, it was a result of a growing number of intellectual initiatives that had become increasingly intertwined and reacted to each other.

The first German reactions to Kierkegaard appeared already during his life and in the second half of the nineteenth century two dozen translations of his writings as well as a number of interpretations of his philosophy were published.[2] The German discourse on Kierkegaard gained momentum also due to the fact that his thought became an object of a debate which in some respects resembled the older debate about Hegel's philosophy. In Kierkegaard's case, too, the debate concerned to a large extent his philosophy of religion. In the early stage of the German reception the most active representative of the "right" side of the debate was Albert Bärthold (1804–1892) while the "left" side was most prominently represented by Christoph Schrempf (1860–1944).[3] The "right" side was later joined by Theodor

den Zeiten, vol. 10, 1932, no. 3, 216–248; Franz Josef Brecht, "Die Kierkegaardforschung im letzten Jahrfünft," *Literarische Berichte aus dem Gebiete der Philosophie*, vol. 25, 1931, 5–35; Martin Heidegger, *Gesamtausgabe* (Frankfurt: Klostermann, 1975ff.), vol. 1, 56; vols. 29/30, 225; vol. 49, 19; Yves Congar, "Kierkegaard," *Revue des sciences philosophiques et théologiques*, vol. 22, no. 3, 1933, 551–2.

[2] The most detailed overview of German translations of Kierkegaard as well as other German Kierkegaard literature can be found in Eva Kaminski, Gerhard Schreiber and Heiko Schulz, "German," in *Kierkegaard Bibliography*, Tome III, *Estonian to Hebrew*, ed. by Peter Šajda and Jon Stewart (London and New York: Routledge 2017) (*Kierkegaard Research: Sources, Reception and Resources*, vol. 19), 59–212.

[3] Both sides included German authors as well as Scandinavian authors, whose works had been translated into German. The foundational figure of the "left" side was Georg Brandes who formulated three basic insights that shaped the "left" spectrum: 1) Kierkegaard's thought is characterized by religious dogmatism, which constrains it. 2) Kierkegaard's life and *oeuvre* include moments that are antagonistic to dogmatism and can facilitate its overcoming. 3) The *dogmatic Kierkegaard* must be "corrected" with the *critical Kierkegaard*, the antidogmatic lines of his thought must be followed to their ultimate consequences. Brandes' *Sören Kierkegaard. Ein literarisches Charakterbild* appeared in 1879. His works were translated and popularized by Adolf Strodtmann who also adopted his view of Kierkegaard. This view was supported also by Harald Høffding and Christoph Schrempf. The "right" side—which read Kierkegaard through the prism of a self-critical renewal of Christianity—included Albert Bärthold, Olaf Peder Monrad, and Theodor Haecker. For Bärthold's and Schrempf's critical reactions to each other see Christoph Schrempf, "Vorrede des Übersetzers," in *Zur Psychologie der Sünde, der Bekehrung und des Glaubens. Zwei Schriften Sören Kierkegaards*, trans. and ed. by Christoph Schrempf (Leipzig: Richter, 1890), VII–X; Albert Bärthold, *Geleitbrief für Sören Kierkegaards: „Ein Bißchen Philosophie!"* (Leipzig: Richter, 1890).

Haecker (1879–1945), who, like Bärthold and Schrempf, was an important translator of Kierkegaard's *oeuvre*. Haecker played a key role in Schmitt's becoming acquainted with Kierkegaard.

Both sides of the debate contributed substantially to the dynamic of the Kierkegaard Renaissance. Schrempf was a co-editor of the twelve-volume edition of Kierkegaard's *Gesammelte Werke* (1909–1922),[4] which popularized the Danish thinker among the broader literary public and was used by influential contemporary thinkers, such as T. W. Adorno, Karl Barth, Martin Buber, Rudolf Bultmann, Karl Jaspers, and Martin Heidegger. Schrempf's early translations were published already in the 1890s. A characteristic feature of his translations was that they contained polemical forewords and afterwords in which he promoted his view of Kierkegaard and attacked opposing views. In the foreword to the 1907 edition of Kierkegaard's late writings Schrempf stirred the debate with the following claim: "Kierkegaard, who only intended to restore the authority of Christianity, in fact leads everyone who not only reads his work, but also studies it, not only studies it, but also lives it, to reject Christianity as the decisive religious authority."[5] Schrempf, who was a suspended Lutheran pastor, presented himself as such an existential reader of Kierkegaard.

Schrempf's controversial reading of Kierkegaard *against* Kierkegaard was categorically rejected by Haecker. Haecker was originally a Protestant but converted to Catholicism in 1921. In the following years he contributed substantially to the increase of interest in Kierkegaard in the Catholic literary milieu. In 1925 he encouraged the readers of the prominent Catholic periodical *Hochland* to read Kierkegaard both critically and open-mindedly and expressed also his view of Kierkegaard's philosophy of religion. He suggested that the opponents of Christianity misuse Kierkegaard's late polemic with the Danish state church for the advancement of their own agenda and intentionally ignore much of Kierkegaard's earlier authorship. He rejected such a selective approach and insisted on an integrative interpretation of Kierkegaard's entire authorship. Such an interpretation necessarily takes into account also the revealed truth of Christianity: "Kierkegaard's great and

---

[4] Søren Kierkegaard, *Gesammelte Werke*, vols. 1–12, trans. and ed. by Hermann Gottsched and Christoph Schrempf (Jena: Diederichs, 1909–22).

[5] Christoph Schrempf, *Sören Kierkegaard. Ein unfreier Pionier der Freiheit* (Frankfurt a. M.: Neuer Frankfurter Verlag, 1907), 5–6. If not stated otherwise translations from foreign languages are my own.

valuable insights...clearly presuppose belief in dogmatic Christianity; they require dogmatic Christianity and develop it."[6]

Haecker joined the discourse on Kierkegaard in 1913 when he published his monograph *Sören Kierkegaard und die Philosophie der Innerlichkeit*, which received wide acclaim. From 1914 onward he continuously popularized Kierkegaard in the Innsbruck-based journal *Der Brenner*, which had a substantial impact on German and Austrian intellectual life. In this period Haecker published his translations of Kierkegaard's works and *Nachlass* both in the journal and as separate books. Similar to Schrempf, Haecker used the translations for the promotion of his own intellectual program and in his forewords and afterwords commented on the controversial issues of the time. The translation which attracted probably the greatest attention was *Kritik der Gegenwart* (1914),[7] which was the first German translation of a fragment of *A Literary Review*. In the afterward Haecker harshly criticized the contemporary liberal press while drawing inspiration from Kierkegaard's critique of the existential-social processes of the nineteenth century. The combination of Kierkegaard's analysis of the turbulent mid-nineteenth century with Haecker's polemical commentary on the German *status quo* on the eve of World War I provoked a lively debate on Kierkegaard's contribution to the understanding of the processes of modernity.[8] Haecker's largest translation project was the 850-page edition of Kierkegaard's journals which appeared in 1923.[9]

Schmitt's contact with Kierkegaard was influenced by both Schrempf and Haecker, but the latter's influence was much more intensive. Schmitt owned Schrempf's early translations from the nineteenth century as well as

[6] Theodor Haecker, "Sören Kierkegaard," *Hochland*, vol. 22, no. 2, 1925, 191.

[7] Søren Kierkegaard, *Kritik der Gegenwart*, trans. and ed. by Theodor Haecker (Innsbruck: Brenner–Verlag, 1914). The translation was also published in *Der Brenner*, vol. 4, 1914, no. 19, 815–849; no. 20, 869–908.

[8] Theodor Haecker, "Nachwort," in Kierkegaard, *Kritik der Gegenwart*, 62–87. I provide a more detailed analysis of Haecker's commentary and his influence on other thinkers in Peter Šajda, "Haeckerova kritika liberálnej tlače inšpirovaná Kierkegaardom," *Filozofia*, vol. 69, no. 5, 2014, 378–387. A more complex evaluation of Haecker's place in the German reception of Kierkegaard's thought can be found in Markus Kleinert, "Theodor Haecker. The Mobilization of a Total Author," in *Kierkegaard's Influence on Literature, Criticism and Art*, Tome I: *The Germanophone World* ed. by Jon Stewart (Farnham: Ashgate, 2013) (*Kierkegaard Research: Sources, Reception, Resources*, vol. 12), 91–114.

[9] Søren Kierkegaard, *Die Tagebücher*, trans. and ed. by Theodor Haecker (Innsbruck: Brenner-Verlag, 1923), vols. 1–2.

his later *Gesammelte Werke* edition.[10] When Schmitt learned in October 1914 of the death of his best friend Fritz Eisler on the French front he found solace in Schrempf's translation of *The Concept of Anxiety*.[11] Schmitt became acquainted with Haecker through translations and commentaries on Kierkegaard, but later met him in person and befriended him.[12] The deep impression Haecker's translations left on the young Schmitt can be seen from his journal entry from May 11, 1915. At that time Schmitt was a soldier in the German army:

> Went down the street, when the Captain had been gone for an hour, accidentally saw a book by Kierkegaard in a shop and bought it: *Kritik der Gegenwart*. Was excited with joy (the translator is Theodor Haecker and lives in Munich), delved inside the book and didn't get any other work done.[13]

Two weeks later Schmitt began reading Haecker's translation of Kierkegaard's upbuilding discourse "The Thorn in the Flesh" and noted in his journal: "Haecker, the publisher, is just my kind of person."[14]

---

[10] Bartholomew Ryan, "Carl Schmitt. Zones of Exception and Appropriation," in *Kierkegaard's Influence on Social-Political Thought*, ed. by Jon Stewart (Farnham: Ashgate, 2011) (*Kierkegaard Research: Sources, Reception, Resources*, vol. 14), 183, 207.

[11] Carl Schmitt, *Tagebücher: Oktober 1912 bis Februar 1915*, ed. by Ernst Hüsmert, 2nd revised edition (Berlin: Akademie Verlag, 2005), 222.

[12] Reinhard Mehring points out that through Haecker, Schmitt came into contact with a broader literary movement which sought to combine Catholic intellectuality with literary "Moderne." In this movement, which included Haecker, Franz Blei and Konrad Weiß, there was a lively debate about Kierkegaard. Cf. Reinhard Mehring, *Carl Schmitt. Aufstieg und Fall* (Munich: C. H. Beck, 2009), 143. On other aspects of Schmitt's relationship with Haecker see Ibid., 97, 181, 182, 194, 455. During the Third Reich Schmitt and Haecker stood on the opposite sides of the barricade. Haecker was prevented from publishing and public speaking and provided intellectual support for the dissident group *The White Rose*, whose main representatives—including Hans Scholl (1918–1943) and Sophie Scholl (1921–1943)—were executed in 1943. Other Catholic authors of the Kierkegaard Renaissance, such as Romano Guardini and Alois Dempf, were persecuted, too. Schmitt's tragic involvement with the Nazi regime is well-known.

[13] Carl Schmitt, *Die Militärzeit 1915 bis 1919*, ed. by Ernst Hüsmert and Gerd Giesler (Berlin: Akademie Verlag, 2005), 66. I use Bartholomew Ryan's English translation which I have slightly modified. Ryan also pointed out—quoting Ellen Kennedy's *Constitutional Failure*—that in 1918 Haecker gave Schmitt another translation of Kierkegaard (the anthology entitled *Der Begriff des Auserwählten*), in which Schmitt made a number of annotations. Cf. Ryan, "Carl Schmitt. Zones of Exception and Appropriation," 183–184, 190.

[14] Schmitt, *Die Militärzeit 1915 bis 1919*, 74. Haecker's translation *Pfahl im Fleisch* (Innsbruck: Brenner, 1914) comprises the second discourse of the *Four Upbuilding Discourses* published in 1844.

Thus Schmitt came into contact with Haecker's translations and interpretations of Kierkegaard even before the main wave of the Kierkegaard Renaissance swept across Germany. This happened after World War I when the interest in Kierkegaard increased dramatically and his thought inspired new intellectual initiatives such as the philosophy of existence, dialectical theology, dialogical philosophy, Neo-Marxism, and the Catholic Hochland Circle. After his conversion Haecker joined the last of these movements.

Haecker's reception of Kierkegaard's critique of modernity and his use of Kierkegaard's insights for the description of the trends of German society in the early twentieth century appealed to Schmitt. He drew inspiration from Haecker's line of reception in his analysis of the liberal leveling in the first half of the nineteenth century as well as in his confrontations with later forms of liberalism. The "echo" of Kierkegaardian-Haeckerian motifs is particularly strong in Schmitt's *Political Theology* (1922). Similar to many other authors of the Kierkegaard Renaissance, Schmitt often adopted impulses from Kierkegaard without explicitly identifying the source of inspiration. Günter Maschke states that "the Catholic critique of modernity is in Schmitt markedly 'enriched' by Kierkegaard's arguments, which was quite usual at that time."[15] The fact that such an "enrichment" was "quite usual" should first and foremost be credited to Haecker's influence.

Schmitt's first references to Kierkegaard appear in *The Visibility of the Church: A Scholastic Consideration* (1917) and *Political Romanticism* (1919).[16] He makes more intensive use of Kierkegaardian motifs in *Political Theology* in which he elaborates on the concepts of *exception* and *decision* and develops a critique of bourgeois liberalism along Kierkegaardian lines. He draws on Kierkegaard's works *A Literary Review*, *Repetition* and *Fear and Trembling*. In the following sections I will first outline Kierkegaard's critique of the self-paralyzing tendencies of modernity in *A Literary Review*. Then I will elucidate the broad scope of Schmitt's reception of Kierkegaard's ideas in *Political*

---

[15] Günter Maschke, "Drei Motive im Anti-Liberalismus Carl Schmitts," in *Carl Schmitt und die Liberalismuskritik*, ed. by Klaus Hansen and Hans Lietzmann (Opladen: Leske & Budrich, 1988), 74.

[16] An overview of references to Kierkegaard in Schmitt's writings can be found in Ryan, "Carl Schmitt. Zones of Exception and Appropriation," 206–207. Some of the data in the overview are incorrect, therefore I include the corrected bibliographical references: Carl Schmitt-Dorotić, *Politische Romantik* (Munich and Leipzig: Duncker & Humblot, 1919), 58; Carl Schmitt, *Politische Theologie. Vier Kapitel zur Lehre von der Souveränität* (Munich and Leipzig: Duncker & Humblot, 1922), 15.

Theology and the originality of his "continuation" of the Kierkegaardian-Haeckerian critique of modernity.

II. KIERKEGAARD'S CRITIQUE OF THE PRESENT AGE: FROM AMBIGUITY TO INDECISION

In 1915 Schmitt read Haecker's translation of a fragment of Kierkegaard's *A Literary Review* (1846) which appeared under the title *Kritik der Gegenwart*.[17] It comprised the final part of *A Literary Review*, the original title of which is *The Present Age*. In this text Kierkegaard examines the connection between the changes in individuals' existential stances and the development of society in *the present age*. Although he does not identify *the present age* with a concrete historical epoch—just as he does not historically situate its counterpart *the age of revolution*—Haecker identified *the present age* with the age in which the text was written. According to this interpretation the text is a diagnosis of the *status quo* of European modernity on the eve of the revolutionary year 1848.

Kierkegaard's most fundamental observation is that *the present age* is a *hostage* of reflection. While he does not doubt the importance and usefulness of reflection, he depicts *the present age* as an age paralyzed by reflection. Reflection has become so pervasive that it has obliterated inwardness, passion and resoluteness in individuals' lives. Extreme reflection enables only short flarings up of enthusiasm that promptly result in rationalized apathy.[18] Reflection thrives best in an environment dominated by *ambiguity*, which it finds much more stimulating than the unambiguous choice of a single option.[19] Ambiguity spreads together with reflection, because reflection not only seeks it out, but also creates it in contexts that were previously considered unambiguous. This process takes place both at the theoretical and the practical level. At the theoretical level the increase of ambiguity supported by reflection leads to the questioning of qualitative differences. At the practical level ambiguity weakens the individuals' motivation to adopt decisions in the form of a qualitative disjunction, either/or. Unambiguous differentiation of positions, roles and hierarchies is called into question and individuals

---

[17] Schmitt recalls his reading of Kierkegaard's "amazing" book with Haecker's "equally amazing" afterword in his essay "Donoso Cortés in gesamteuropäischer Interpretation," in his *Donoso Cortés in gesamteuropäischer Interpretation. Vier Aufsätze* (Cologne: Greven Verlag, 1950), 101.

[18] *SKS* 8, 66 / *TA*, 68; *SKS* 8, 70–1 / *TA*, 73.

[19] *SKS* 8, 75 / *TA*, 78.

become reluctant to adopt unambiguous existential commitments. The life of the individual is increasingly characterized by "existential equivocation."[20]

This development affects a broad spectrum of relations which determine the life of society. Ambiguity pervades the relations between individuals, between the individual and God, between individuals and institutions, between human collectives, and it also affects people's relations to values. The weakening of qualitative differences and the unwillingness or even inability to adopt a qualitatively unambiguous and binding decision transforms the relations between man and woman, parent and child, teacher and student, believer and church, citizen and state. Kierkegaard notes that "[t]he coiled springs of life-relationships, which are what they are only because of qualitatively distinguishing passion, lose their resilience."[21]

A characteristic feature of ambiguity supported by reflection is that while it weakens qualitative differences, it does not abolish them. Externally, the structure of relations is not subject to dramatic changes, but the internal dynamic of relations diminishes: "The relations do manifest themselves as present, and yet as absent, but not completely, rather in a sort of slouching, semi-somnolent non-cessation."[22] Passionless reflection is incapable of initiating an eruption of radicality that would annihilate or completely transform relational structures. The existing order of relations remains valid, but reflection does not support unambiguous attitudes: it dissuades individuals from making passionate decisions that would entail serious personal commitment. Kierkegaard calls the emptying-out of qualitative differences and the spread of relational ambiguity at the level of society *leveling*.

The social effect of the expansion of ambiguity can be illustrated by the attitude of *the present age* to secular and religious authorities. The leveled society constructs half-hearted solutions that correspond to its passionlessness:

> The established order continues to stand, but since it is equivocal and ambiguous, passionless reflection is reassured. We do not want to abolish the monarchy, by no means, but if little by little we could get it transformed into make-believe, we would gladly shout "Hurrah for the King!" We do not want to topple eminence, by no means, but if simultaneously we could spread the notion that it is all make-believe, we would approve and admire. In the same way we are willing to keep Christian terminolo-

[20] Ibid. See also *SKS* 8, 75–77 / *TA*, 78–80.
[21] *SKS* 8, 75 / *TA*, 78.
[22] *SKS* 8, 77 / *TA*, 80.

> gy but privately know that nothing decisive is supposed to be meant by it....We do not want a powerful king any more than we want a liberator or a religious authority. No, quite harmlessly and inoffensively we allow the established order to go on, but in a reflective knowledge we are more or less aware of its non-existence.[23]

The crisis of relationships, commitments and loyalty in a leveled society is accompanied by extensive *communication*, which constitutes an attempt to compensate for the weakening of existential relations. This communication takes place to a large extent in the anonymous collective of *the public*.[24] This is not a community based on personal relationships rooted in qualitatively distinguishing passion; on the contrary, the public is created in a situation characterized by the decline of the sense of community. The key promoter of the public and its main medium of communication is *the press*. Through this medium the amorphous collective of the public supports and spreads *leveling*, which is "abstraction's victory over individuals."[25] *The present age* is "an age of publicity"[26] and of fast dissemination of information which is aimed at extensive presentation of the results of reflection, not at the support of intensive personal decision-making. Chattering and conversation without commitment are the preferred modes of communication among individuals who are "experienced in indecisiveness and evasions."[27] What happens *in the form of reflection and observation* does not have continuation *in the form of action*,[28] and the sphere of discourse is separated from the sphere of existence. *In dicto* one can be everything, but *in existentia* one does not have to be anything.

The result of the interplay of ambiguity, reflection and discourse without existential demand is *indecision*. Individuals experience a reduction of the internal tension that prompts them to make a decision:

> [T]he urge to decision is precisely what reflection dispels or wants to dispel, and as a result the individual suffers from dyspeptic, abnormal common sense. Decisiveness in life tries in vain to snare the individual, but

[23] *SKS* 8, 77–78 / *TA*, 80–81.

[24] *SKS* 8, 86 / *TA*, 90. For more detail on the concept of the public see *SKS* 8, 86–91 / *TA*, 90–96.

[25] *SKS* 8, 81 / *TA*, 84.

[26] *SKS* 8, 68 / *TA*, 70.

[27] *SKS* 8, 100 / *TA*, 105. See also *SKS* 8, 95 / *TA*, 100.

[28] *SKS* 8, 71 / *TA*, 74.

> the benediction upon the moment of decision waits in vain: although we deceive ourselves, we know clever ways of avoiding decision.[29]

Even if the individual in the end makes a decision, it lacks vigor and determination due to procrastination. It is a slack decision of someone who perhaps no longer has predispositions for what he has decided for. The postponing of existential decisions, if possible *ad infinitum*, has become a technique that *the present generation* continually perfects. This generation is an expert in prolonging the period of indecision: "its competence, its sensibleness, its technical skill consist in never letting matters reach a verdict and decision through action."[30] Reflection and communication without inwardness and passionateness form a vicious circle of stagnation. The principle of the *qualitative disjunction either/or* has been replaced with the principle of *not embracing anything wholeheartedly*. Even if the leveled generation pretends to accomplish something of importance, its activities are not dynamic enough to provoke a political revolution, religious renewal or scientific breakthrough. Exceptionality—which is the opposite of leveling—cannot be born without the risk of a passionate decision. In *the present age* "[a]ction and decision are just as scarce…as is the fun of swimming dangerously for those who swim in shallow water."[31]

III. SCHMITT'S CRITIQUE OF LIBERALISM: FROM AMBIGUITY TO DECISION

Schmitt's reception of Kierkegaard's ideas in *Political Theology* is both explicit and implicit. The explicit reception—which I will deal with in the next section—is important especially from the strategic perspective. Schmitt quotes Kierkegaard directly only once, but it is the second longest quotation in the whole work and is located in a crucial passage at the end of the first chapter.[32] In the quoted text Kierkegaard discusses the concept of *exception*, which is at the heart of *Political Theology*. Schmitt introduces the concept in

---

[29] *SKS* 8, 73 / *TA*, 76.

[30] *SKS* 8, 66–67 / *TA*, 69. Translation modified.

[31] *SKS* 8, 69 / *TA*, 71.

[32] Schmitt, *Politische Theologie*, 15 (English translation: *Political Theology: Four Chapters on the Concept of Sovereignty*, trans. by George Schwab [Chicago and London: The University of Chicago Press, 2005], 15).

the very first sentence of his work. The Kierkegaard quotation stems from *Repetition*, which Schmitt owned in Gottsched's translation.[33]

Kierkegaard's implicit presence is much more extensive than the explicit one and is visible in instances where Schmitt makes use of motifs that he knew from Kierkegaard's works. Schmitt uses them in new thematic contexts and enriches them with impetuses from other thinkers. The structural constellation of the motifs, however, reflects Kierkegaard's original structure, which was a guiding line for Schmitt.[34] The implicit reception is particularly strong in the final chapter of Schmitt's work. Here he examines the intellectual developments of the late eighteenth century and the nineteenth century with an emphasis on the transformations that took place in the years 1789–1848. His diagnosis of this period of European modernity clearly echoes three fundamental themes of Kierkegaard's critique of the present age: *ambiguity*, *nonbinding communication*, and *indecision*. Similar to Haecker—who drew on Kierkegaard's critique in his polemic with liberalism—Schmitt makes use of the Kierkegaardian motifs in his confrontation with liberal positions.

Kierkegaard described the ambiguous attitude of the present age to secular and religious authorities as an interplay of affirmation and non-affirmation, preservation and emptying-out. He illustrated it with the attitude of the present generation to the authority of the king and Christianity. Schmitt adopts this description and applies it to the liberal bourgeoisie of the July Monarchy (1830–1848). Thus, he comments on the epoch in which Kierkegaard wrote his critique:

> The insecurity and immaturity of the liberal bourgeoisie of the July Monarchy can be recognized everywhere. Its liberal constitutionalism attempted to paralyze the king through parliament but permitted him to remain on the throne, an inconsistency committed by deism when it excluded God from the world but held onto his existence....Although the liberal bourgeoisie wanted a god, its god could not become active; it wanted a monarch, but he had to be powerless.[35]

[33] A complete reference to the German, Danish and English editions of *Repetition* is found in note no. 55.

[34] For an insightful analysis of Schmitt's reflections on Kierkegaard's concepts, categories, diagnoses and modes of inquiry see Rüdiger Kramme, *Helmuth Plessner und Carl Schmitt. Eine historische Fallstudie zum Verhältnis von Anthropologie und Politik in der deutschen Philosophie der zwanziger Jahre* (Berlin: Duncker & Humblot, 1989), 161–178.

[35] Schmitt, *Politische Theologie*, 52. (*Political Theology*, 59.)

In continuity with Kierkegaard, Schmitt highlights the fact that the propagator of an ambiguous approach to secular and religious authority is a group that is proud of its rationalism.[36]

When Schmitt examines liberalism's ambiguous approach to authority he draws inspiration from philosophers of state and law, who were Kierkegaard's contemporaries. When discussing the liberal view of the king, he quotes the German thinkers Lorenz von Stein (1815–1890) and Friedrich Julius Stahl (1802–1861). The former identifies two kinds of tension that characterize the position of the king in the system proposed by the liberals:

> They wanted a king who would be above parties, who would thus also have to be above the people's assembly; and simultaneously they insisted that the king could not do anything but execute the will of this people's assembly. They declared the person of the king to be inviolable but had him take an oath on the constitution, so that a violation of the constitution became possible but could not be pursued.[37]

Stahl highlights the fact that liberals oscillate between two positions while not fully identifying with either of them. Resentment of the king and aristocracy pulls them to the left, but fear of the nationalization of property by the socialists and radical democrats forces them to find refuge in the power of the monarchy.[38]

Schmitt explains the liberal position on the authority of Christianity with reference to the conflict between Catholicism and atheist-anarchist socialism envisaged by the Spanish counterrevolutionary philosopher Juan Donoso Cortés (1809–1853). Donoso lived in almost the same years as Kierkegaard, and Schmitt explicitly compares him with Kierkegaard in the essay *A Pan-European Interpretation of Donoso Cortés*.[39] Donoso describes the late eighteenth century and the first half of the nineteenth century as the era in which a "bloody decisive battle…flared up between Catholicism and atheist socialism."[40] This conflict, which is in the final analysis a conflict between authority and anarchy—between the claim of a decision and the faith in the spontaneous production of correct forms—is perceived by both sides as absolute. Schmitt illustrates the radical nature of the contradiction between

---

36 Schmitt, *Politische Theologie*, 53. (*Political Theology*, 60.)

37 Ibid.

38 Schmitt, *Politische Theologie*, 53. (*Political Theology*, 61.)

39 Cf. Schmitt, "Donoso Cortés in gesamteuropäischer Interpretation," 106–108.

40 Schmitt, *Politische Theologie*, 52. (*Political Theology*, 59). See also Kramme, *Helmuth Plessner und Carl Schmitt*, 162–167.

these two convictions with the claims by key representatives of the involved parties. Cardinal John Henry Newman insists that "[n]o medium exists...between catholicity and atheism," and Friedrich Engels proposes in an uncompromising way that the "[t]he essence of the state, as that of religion, is mankind's fear of itself."[41] The Kierkegaardian theme of ambiguity is echoed in the thesis advocated by both Donoso and Schmitt that the strategy of liberalism is "not to decide in this battle."[42] Interestingly, both conflicting parties agree on the criticism of this ambiguous stance, and while they latently respect each other, they view with disrespect the hesitation of liberalism.[43] Schmitt remarks that in the era of great ideological struggles, when the situation requires a firm decision, the ambiguous attitude of the liberals is in no way constructive. It is merely an effort to postpone the decision by means of a nonbinding discussion.

Schmitt considers the Kierkegaardian moment of nonbinding communication, which downplays the importance of unambiguous attitudes, a basic characteristic of the liberal bourgeoisie. He borrows from Donoso the description of the liberal bourgeoisie as a "discussing class"[44] and suggests that liberalism's response to the question "Christ or Barabbas?" is a proposal to defer the case or appoint an investigative commission.[45] Ambiguity combined with extensive communication prompts the liberals to see the discussion forums of the parliament and the press as their favorite spaces. The "religion" of the liberal bourgeoisie is the freedom of speech and the press.[46] A connected idea is the "everlasting conversation"[47] popularized in Germany by Romantic authors. Schmitt considers it a variation of the liberal idea of a continuous discussion and deems it incompatible with decisionist philosophy.

---

[41] Schmitt, *Politische Theologie*, 55–56, 49, 45. (*Political Theology*, 64–66, 53, 51.)

[42] Schmitt, *Politische Theologie*, 52. (*Political Theology*, 59).

[43] Schmitt, *Politische Theologie*, 53, 55. (*Political Theology*, 60, 63.) Schmitt was aware of the existence of liberal Catholicism, whose representatives included Alexis de Tocqueville (1805–1859), Charles de Montalembert (1810–1870) and Henri-Dominique Lacordaire (1802–1861). For this reason he described the Catholic Church as a complex of opposites (*complexio oppositorum*). Cf. Carl Schmitt, *Roman Catholicism and Political Form*, trans. by G. L. Ulmen (Westport, CT and London: Greenwood Press, 1996), 4, 7–9, 11, 14, 23, 38.

[44] Schmitt, *Politische Theologie*, 52. (*Political Theology*, 59.)

[45] Schmitt, *Politische Theologie*, 54. (*Political Theology*, 62.)

[46] Ibid.

[47] Schmitt, *Politische Theologie*, 49. (*Political Theology*, 53.)

Connected to ambiguity and nonbinding communication is the third problem of liberalism: indecision. This problem is for Schmitt the point of contrast to his key concept of decision. Kierkegaard characterized the present age as an essentially indecisive age, which, due to excessive reflection and ambiguity, became a "virtuoso" in rendering decision impossible. Schmitt uses this diagnosis when describing bourgeois liberalism as an intellectual paradigm based on the paralysis of decision. In order to strengthen its ambiguous position, liberalism develops an efficient mechanism for the negation of decision: "To suspend the decision at the crucial point by denying that there was at all something to be decided upon."[48] For Schmitt the counterpoint to liberalism's principled indecision is the approach of the counterrevolutionary thinkers Joseph de Maistre (1753–1821), Louis de Bonald (1754–1840) and Donoso Cortés, whose importance lies "in the consistency with which they decide."[49] Their primary contribution to the philosophy of the state is the emphasis on the moment of decision, which Kierkegaard pointed out as a key lacuna of the present age. The counterrevolutionary philosophers' assessment of the situation of the society of the first half of the nineteenth century corresponds to Kierkegaard's assessment: if the present age is to overcome the marasmus of indecision, the individuals' ability to make passionate decisions must be renewed. Kierkegaard's key concept in this context is the *qualitative disjunction, either/or*, which is a form of decision based on an unreserved choice of a single existential option. Schmitt uses both Kierkegaardian diction and logic when he explains the decisionist doctrine of the counterrevolutionary philosophers. Their point of departure was the awareness that "their times needed a decision. And with an energy that rose to an extreme between the two revolutions of 1789 and 1848, they thrust the notion of the decision to the center of their thinking."[50] These philosophers "formulated a big either/or"[51] and regarded the moral-existential opposites that they described as disjunctive and nonunifiable in a higher synthesis. Schmitt calls attention to the contradiction between the counterrevolutionary thinkers' approach and Schelling's and Hegel's synthetizing efforts which seek to bridge the disjunction by means of a dialectical movement.[52] Schmitt subscribes also to Kierkegaard's princi-

---

[48] Schmitt, *Politische Theologie*, 54. (*Political Theology*, 61.)
[49] Schmitt, *Politische Theologie*, 56. (*Political Theology*, 65.)
[50] Schmitt, *Politische Theologie*, 49. (*Political Theology*, 53.)
[51] Ibid.
[52] Schmitt, *Politische Theologie*, 49–50, 53. (*Political Theology*, 54–55, 61.)

ple that the realization of a decision is more important than its form. When analyzing De Maistre's thought, he affirms that "as far as the most essential issues are concerned, making a decision is more important than how a decision is made."[53]

Schmitt's implicit reception of Kierkegaard's intellectual structures is most obvious in the passages where he describes the problems of modernity. He draws less on Kierkegaard when discussing potential solutions to the problems. This corresponds to the nature of Kierkegaard's analysis of the present age, which is a critical, rather than a constructive philosophical project. Despite this fact some concepts highlighted by Kierkegaard—especially decision and exception—play a crucial role in Schmitt's constructive theory of the state and law. He uses them in an innovative way when defending his theory of sovereignty against contemporary legal theoreticians.

IV. SCHMITT'S CONCEPTION OF THE UNAMBIGUOUS DECISION ON THE EXCEPTION

Schmitt's explicit reception of Kierkegaard is limited to the first chapter of *Political Theology*, in which he discusses the issue of exception. This issue is closely linked to the issue of decision which he clearly expresses in the claim that "[t]he decision on the exception is a decision in the true sense of the word."[54] Schmitt uses Kierkegaard's reflections in *Repetition* to emphasize the importance of exception.

Schmitt's basic insight is that the philosophical systems of the eighteenth and nineteenth century marginalized the issue of the exception, which also affected adversely the legal theory of that time. The dominance of the discourse on *the general* led to a radical decrease of the relevance of exceptional cases for legal thought. Although the early twentieth century experienced a certain renaissance of the interest in the concept of the exception, the marginalization of exceptionality remained common in trend-setting philosophical-legal systems, especially of the Neo-Kantian provenance. Schmitt values Kierkegaard as a thinker who did not succumb to the trends of the nineteenth century and insisted on the constitutive importance of the exception for the understanding of the general. Schmitt follows his example and regards *the exceptional* as the point of departure for the explication of *the general*, *the normal*, *the repeated*. He cites from *Repetition* a longer passage,

[53] Schmitt, *Politische Theologie*, 50. (*Political Theology*, 55–56.)

[54] Schmitt, *Politische Theologie*, 9. (*Political Theology*, 6.)

which describes the relation between the exception and the general with an emphasis on the importance of the former:

> The exception explains the general and itself. And if one wants to study the general correctly, one only needs to look around for a true exception. It reveals everything more clearly than does the general. Endless talk about the general becomes boring; there are exceptions. If they cannot be explained, then the general also cannot be explained. The difficulty is usually not noticed because the general is not thought about with passion but with a comfortable superficiality. The exception, on the other hand, thinks the general with intense passion.[55]

Schmitt regards this approach as an example of philosophical thinking that is not detached from concrete life and confronts the issue of the exception not out of logical caprice but with the view to its practical relevance. He considers the shift of emphasis from the general to the exception as a step in the right direction: "The exception is more interesting than the rule. The rule proves nothing; the exception proves everything: It confirms not only the rule but also its existence, which derives only from the exception."[56]

Although Schmitt explicitly quotes only from *Repetition*, it is almost certain that *Fear and Trembling* was another source of inspiration for his reflections on the decision and the exception. He was familiar with this work,[57] which discusses the relation between the exception and the general against the background of the Biblical story of Abraham's binding of Isaac. The key question the work aims to answer is whether an individual can on the basis of a teleological justification legitimately suspend a valid ethical order that he affirms.[58] Ethical normativity would be overruled during the exceptional action but subsequently it would be restored. Thus, the exception would ultimately not eliminate normativity, but rather confirm it.

---

[55] Schmitt, *Politische Theologie*, 15. (*Political Theology*, 15.) Schmitt quotes this edition: Søren Kierkegaard, *Wiederholung*, trans. by Hermann Gottsched (Jena: Diederichs, 1909) (*Gesammelte Werke*, 1909–1922, vol. 3), 200–201. Schmitt slightly modified the quotation. In the Danish and English editions the quotation is found in *SKS* 4, 93 / *R*, 227.

[56] Schmitt, *Politische Theologie*, 15. (*Political Theology*, 15.)

[57] Cf. Ryan, "Carl Schmitt. Zones of Exception and Appropriation," 183.

[58] See especially the chapter "Problema I: Is there a Teleological Suspension of the Ethical?" Cf. *SKS* 4, 148–159 / *FT*, 54–67. See, for example, Schmitt's claim: "What characterizes an exception is principally unlimited authority, which means the suspension of the entire existing order." Schmitt, *Politische Theologie*, 13. (*Political Theology*, 12.)

Schmitt's philosophical-legal reflections focus primarily on *the decision on the state of exception*.[59] He is concerned with the authority that adopts such a decision and claims that it has a personal nature, that is, it is *the sovereign*: "[s]overeign is he who decides on the exception [*Ausnahmezustand*]."[60] Schmitt highlights the benefits of this practical and unambiguous definition and contrasts it to abstract and ambiguous definitions of sovereignty that fail to solve concrete contentious cases. A characteristic feature of the proposed definition is the decisive importance of the state or case that is exceptional, critical, extreme or *extremus necessitatis casus*.[61] The authority of the sovereign lies in the fact that he passes the definitive verdict on the crucial either/or issue: does society find itself in a *normal* or *exceptional* state? If the former is true, the existing legal order is valid and the life of the state is governed by accepted norms. If, however, the latter is true, the sovereign is justified to suspend the validity of the existing norms. These are meaningful and useful in the state of order but become meaningless and useless when the order has collapsed.[62] The position of the sovereign is characterized by a tension: on the one hand, he is part of the normally valid legal order, but, on the other hand, he is outside of it because he can adopt a decision that leads to its suspension. When the sovereign declares the state of exception, he also determines the procedure of dealing with it and restoring normality. He can make such a decision responsibly only in the critical moment, since in the state of normality it is impossible to anticipate exhaustively the possibilities of the state of exception and to determine adequately the means of overcoming it. Such an anticipation is possible only in an approximative way, but not "factually."[63] The state of exception can neither be "derived" from the valid legal order, nor can it be solved on the basis of it. A crucial feature of Schmitt's theory is that the response to the state of exception does not follow from impersonal legal norms, but from the personal decision of the sovereign. On the basis of this decision the state of normality can be restored and legal order can be established anew:

---

[59] On Schmitt's usage of the expressions *Ausnahmezustand*, *Ausnahmefall*, *Notfall*, *Notstand* see Tracy B. Strong, "Foreword," in Schmitt, *Political Theology*, xiii–xiv.

[60] Schmitt, *Politische Theologie*, 9. (*Political Theology*, 5.)

[61] Schmitt, *Politische Theologie*, 9, 10, 12, 13. (*Political Theology*, 5, 8, 10, 12.) For more detail on the connection between Schmitt's reflections on sovereignty and the domestic political development of the Weimar Republic see George Schwab, "Introduction," in Schmitt, *Political Theology*, xliv–lii.

[62] Schmitt, *Politische Theologie*, 13. (*Political Theology*, 13.)

[63] Schmitt, *Politische Theologie*, 9. (*Political Theology*, 6.)

> The exception is that which cannot be subsumed; it defies general codification, but it simultaneously reveals a specifically juristic element—the decision in absolute purity. The exception appears in its absolute form when a situation in which legal prescriptions can be valid must first be brought about.[64]

According to Schmitt, modern theories of the state and law have sought to eliminate the concept of the sovereign as a personal authority that is justified to suspend the existing legal normativity. As a result, modern theoreticians of the state and law systematically "[do] not know what to do with the exception."[65] Schmitt points to Hans Kelsen (1881–1973) and Hugo Krabbe (1857–1936), who advocate the idea that the highest legal authority is an impersonal system of norms. Both thinkers seek to replace personal instances of decision-making with a hierarchical set of abstract legal norms. *Rule of persons* is to be replaced with the *rule of norms*, which is based on "men's feeling or sense of right."[66] Krabbe suggests that this would lead to a liberation from the oppression by personal state authority.

The attempt to eliminate the personal element from the concept of the state runs up against the problem that legal ideas are never realized by themselves and in pure form but are always subject to a decision by a personal entity: the application of a legal principle involves *auctoritatis interpositio*.[67] The meaningfulness of the personalist and decisionist moment in the theory of the state and law is manifested most clearly in the state of exception. If legal deliberation is not to be limited to everyday normality and exceptionality is not to be excluded as meaningless "disturbance,"[68] it is necessary to integrate the mentioned moments in the overall conception of the state and law. Then the crucial importance of the exception for the understanding of normality and its rules—which was emphatically pointed out by Kierkegaard—becomes apparent.

V. CONCLUSION

Both Schmitt's explicit and implicit reception of Kierkegaard constitutes an integral part of key positions and structures of *Political Theology*. The concepts of decision, exception, qualitative disjunction or either/or, suspension

[64] Schmitt, *Politische Theologie*, 13. (*Political Theology*, 13.)

[65] Schmitt, *Politische Theologie*, 14; see also 10. (*Political Theology*, 14; see also 7.)

[66] Schmitt, *Politische Theologie*, 23. (*Political Theology*, 22.)

[67] Schmitt, *Politische Theologie*, 31. (*Political Theology*, 31.)

[68] Schmitt, *Politische Theologie*, 13. (*Political Theology*, 12.)

of normative order, as well as the critique of the present age—of its ambiguity, nonbinding communication and indecision—all these are motifs that were first emphasized by Kierkegaard and later by Schmitt. The fact that Schmitt read *A Literary Review*, *Repetition*, and *Fear and Trembling* is evidence that the parallels between the two thinkers are not merely accidental analogies. Schmitt became familiar with some of Kierkegaard's concepts and positions already during World War I, and thus at the time of writing of *Political Theology* he had internalized them to a large extent. He drew on Kierkegaard in his analysis of the existential-social processes of the first half of the nineteenth century, which were of great interest to Kierkegaard. He drew on Kierkegaard, however, also in his discussion of the nature of the state and law, which was beyond Kierkegaard's intellectual scope. In both cases Schmitt combined Kierkegaardian structures and motifs with elements from other authors. The fact that Schmitt's implicit reception of Kierkegaard is much more extensive than the explicit one is nothing unusual in the context of the Kierkegaard Renaissance. Schmitt's reception of Haecker—who inspired him to use Kierkegaard in the polemic with liberalism—was also mainly implicit. It is precisely the integration of Kierkegaard's ideas into the philosophical polemics of the early twentieth century that constitutes one of the most interesting aspects of Schmitt's reception.

Kierkegaard, Facticity, and Selfhood

K. Brian Söderquist

No doubt one of the most groundbreaking and consequential of Jon Stewart's contributions to Kierkegaard studies is his rethinking of Kierkegaard's relationship to Hegel. As much as any single monograph in the last two decades, Stewart's *Kierkegaard's Relations to Hegel Reconsidered* has changed the way scholars approach this issue. With its thorough treatment of the historical and intellectual context in which Kierkegaard reacted to Hegel and Danish Hegelian thinkers, Stewart's text was able to show how complicated and nuanced Kierkegaard's own appropriation of Hegelian thought was.[1] Equally important in my mind, however, is his work on the way Kierkegaard's thought has been appropriated by later thinkers. Stewart has retained a steady interest in many of the issues that exercised him at the outset of his career, especially issues raised by French phenomenologists and existentialists,[2] and his studies in this field have helped show how complicated and nuanced their appropriation of Kierkegaard has been.

In this article, I will visit one of the themes Stewart has raised on several occasions: the existential importance of what Kierkegaard calls "actuality."[3] In particular, I will focus on Kierkegaard's insistence in *The Sickness unto Death* that the self is dependent both upon its factical placement, as

---

[1] See, for example, Jon Stewart, *Kierkegaard's Relations to Hegel Reconsidered* (Cambridge: Cambridge University Press, 2003), 32–44.

[2] See Jon Stewart, "Introduction" and "Philosophy and Political Engagement: Letters from the Quarrel between Sartre and Merleau-Ponty," in *The Debate between Sartre and Merleau-Ponty*, ed. by J. Stewart (Evanston: Northwestern University Press, 1998), xiii–xl, 327–354; Jon Stewart, *Idealism and Existentialism* (London: Continuum International Publishing Group, 2010); Jon Stewart, *The Unity of Form and Content in Philosophical Writing* (London: Bloomsbury, 2013).

[3] See, for example, Stewart, *Idealism and Existentialism,* 79–82. Perhaps even more than Stewart's publications, this study is motivated by countless conversations with him at work and on walks throughout the streets and parks of Frederiksberg and Nørrebro. There, themes raised by existentialist thinkers were almost always central. I would like to thank Jon for his constant and absolutely loyal support both professionally and personally.

well as the fact that is was "placed by" or "established by"[4] something other than itself. On this interpretation, Anti-Climacus' discussion of dependence begins to resemble later thinkers, particularly Sartre, and I conclude with some brief thoughts about the possible similarities.

I. "IF THE HUMAN SELF WERE SELF-ESTABLISHED"

In the famously tricky opening passage of *The Sickness unto Death*, Kierkegaard's pseudonym Anti-Climacus describes the self as a self-conscious relationship of qualities of soul (infinitude, eternity, and freedom) and qualities of embodiment (finitude, temporality, and necessity), a definition that already gives us enough to think about. But he concludes this passage with the assertion that this understanding of the self is incomplete: "Looked at in this way," he writes, "a human being is still not a self."[5] But before he supplies the reader with the missing information about what it is the self lacks, he offers two ways of thinking about the ultimate status of this relational self. He writes: "This kind of relation, which relates to itself—that is, a self—must either have established itself, or have been established by something else."[6] And he thinks the way that this disjunction is resolved matters. For *if* the human self is established by something else, he continues, a consciousness of that something else must accompany a consciousness of self in order to find the proper equilibrium. But what might it mean to relate to or be conscious of this something else? Conversely, what might it mean to be self-established or self-placed as opposed to established by something else? What would this autonomous self look like? In short, how might we understand this ultimate dependence—or independence—implied in *The Sickness unto Death*?

---

[4] *SKS* 11, 129 / *SUDP*, 43. The English translations in this article have been slightly modified.

[5] *SKS* 11, 129 / *SUDP*, 43.

[6] *SKS* 11, 129 / *SUDP*, 43. The Danish term *sat* is here translated by Hannay (and the Hongs) as "established." In Danish, the word *sat* is the past participle of the verb *at sætte*, which can mean "to place," "to set," or "to posit." The key is to note the Danish term has to do with placement or position, and thus suggests an emphasis on finding oneself in a factical context. See Rasmus Rosenberg Larsen, "The Posited Self: The Non-Theistic Foundations in Kierkegaard's Writings," *Kierkegaard Studies Yearbook*, 2015, 31–54.

II. TO BE GROUNDED TRANSPARENTLY IN THE POWER THE ESTABLISHED IT

Anti-Climacus provides a kind of answer to his own implicit question about whether the self has "established itself," or has been "established by something else."[7] He writes: "the human self *is* this derived, established relation, a relation that relates to itself and, as it relates to itself, relates to something else."[8] But immediately afterward he makes an interesting, somewhat cryptic, claim:

> This is why there can be two forms of authentic despair. If the human self were self-established, there could only be a question of one form: not to want to be itself, to want to be rid of itself. But there could be no question of the second form: in despair, to want to be itself. This formula is the expression of the *dependence* of the entire relationship (the self), the expression of the fact that the self cannot independently find balance and equilibrium, but can only do so by relating to that which established the entire relationship as it relates to itself.[9]

There are two themes I would like to focus on here: first, Anti-Climacus' suggestion that there are two general forms of despair: a despair that does not want to be itself—i.e., a vague unwillingness to take *responsibility* for oneself as a self-directed subject. And then a despair that in despair, wants to be itself—later called defiant despair[10]—which is described as a conscious decision to autonomously take *control* of oneself and one's own self-interpretation. And he suggests that the latter form of despair, defiant despair, wouldn't be despair at all *if* the human self were its own foundation. It seems rather, that if we were self-established, the so-called defiant despairer might actually be a model of selfhood: in that case, if I am strong enough to want to be a self—i.e., to take control of myself, my destiny, my convictions, my choices, my auto-biographical narrative, my own interpretation of myself—then I would indeed *be* that self; I would be myself.

Before I take a closer look at these two forms of despair in order to tease out the essential differences between them, let us consider the concluding paragraph of this rich first section of *The Sickness unto Death*: "This then is the formula that describes the state of the self in which despair is com-

---

[7] *SKS* 11, 129 / *SUDP*, 43.

[8] *SKS* 11, 130 / *SUDP*, 43.

[9] *SKS* 11, 130 / *SUDP*, 43–44.

[10] *SKS* 11, 181–187 / *SUDP*, 98–105.

pletely eradicated: while relating to itself and with a will to be itself, the self is grounded transparently in the power that established it."[11] This formula of health, which places emphasis on the fact that self is founded in something other than its own will, is repeated in various forms throughout the book, but elsewhere it is slightly modified. Just a few pages after the introduction, for example, we see that the term "the power that established it" is replaced with the simple designation "God."[12] And shortly afterwards again, the complicated discussion in the opening section is summed up in a single sentence: "The self is the conscious synthesis of infinitude and finitude, which relates to itself, whose project is to become itself, which can only be done in the relationship to God."[13]

With these reformulations in mind, I don't think it is a misinterpretation to return to the opening paragraphs and read "God" *as* that "something else" upon which the self is dependent. But I think there's a reason Anti-Climacus doesn't immediately use the term "God." By speaking of a "*ground*," and "the *dependence* of the self," he calls attention to that very aspect of the God-relationship that is critical here, namely *dependence*. At this point, we have been told nothing else about this divine power except that, without it, we remain ill with the sickness unto spiritual death. But how should we interpret this grounding—or lack of it? And what might this tell us about God, this "something else?" A closer look at weak and defiant forms of despair indicates some possible interpretations.

III. WEAK DESPAIR

The first general category of despair, weak despair, is marked by passivity and is generally summed up as lost life: the individual is lost, and often at a loss to explain why. This passive imbalance takes several forms but in none of them is there enough self-direction or control to guide the individual toward any determinate project. Life gets lived through the individual, passively, in a way reminiscent of Heidegger's "they-self."[14]

It is important that for Anti-Climacus this passive mode of living would be deadly even if we didn't assume that the human self were "established by something else." Subjectively viewed, there is not enough of a sus-

[11] *SKS* 11, 130 / *SUDP*, 44.

[12] *SKS* 11, 132 / *SUDP*, 46.

[13] *SKS* 11, 146 / *SUDP*, 59.

[14] Martin Heidegger, *Being and Time*, trans. by John Macquarrie and Edward Robinson (Oxford: Blackwell Press, 1962), 163–168.

tained inner life or enough wilfulness to choose a guiding existential project. The consciousness of self that must accompany any genuine project is missing and thus, regardless of whether or not one considers the question of the self's dependence on a God, this life is lost. The situation is different in a defiant mode of despair.

IV. DEFIANT DESPAIR

Defiant despair—in despair, to want to be oneself—is first and foremost characterized by a consciousness of the infinite, i.e., the defiant self knows what it means to reflect beyond finitude and views itself as more than a passive object in a world outside its control. With that kind of reflection comes wilfulness. As Anti-Climacus writes, "The more consciousness, the more will; the more will, the more self.[15] Intelligent and creative enough to understand that she is free to direct her life projects, the defiant person cultivates her natural capacities of mind in order to maintain control over herself. Or at least she cultivates those aspects of self that seem to be within her control: the freedom to determine her own directions and values and the interpretation of herself that follows. This individual knows that she has the capacity to decide what self-conception she likes and what self she would like to be. And this is accompanied by a certain kind of wilful tenacity, not driven by commitment to any one sustained goal or project, but certainly by a commitment to retain control over what matters to her and what doesn't. Anti-Climacus writes that the defiant self wants to be itself, wants "to savour the full satisfaction of making itself into itself, of developing itself, of being itself; it wants to take credit for this fictional, masterly project: its own way of understanding itself."[16]

Despite the strength of purpose, Anti-Climacus is suspicious of this kind of autonomy. The problem has to do with what this self is founded in. He writes that the defiant individual is ultimately grounded in itself, in its own will, its own natural capacities, its own power of imagination: And he concludes that despite "such self-discipline, such imperturbability, such composure….it is grounded in nothing."[17]

We know, of course, that for Anti-Climacus, the self free of despair makes the opposite movement: it is grounded in something else, i.e., it is

---

[15] *SKS* 11, 145 / *SUDP*, 59.
[16] *SKS* 11, 183 / *SUDP*, 101.
[17] *SKS* 11, 183 / *SUDP*, 101.

grounded in God. Its groundedness in God is ultimately the reason why the defiant self—even though it is reflective, intelligent, wilful, artistic, and independent—is said to be in despair rather than simply declared to be authentic. Indeed, as noted earlier, Anti-Climacus admits that if the self were self-established, this would hardly be despair at all. This would be the formula for selfhood.

But his analysis does not stop here, as if mentioning the proper grounding in God were enough. A closer examination of defiant despair provides details about what he means when he says that the defiant self is grounded in nothing. In a rich passage describing the despairing self's attraction to its own autonomous power of self-interpretation, Anti-Climacus adds some important detail to his understanding of what it means *not* to be grounded in God. Note especially the emphasis on a lack of *concretion*, *context*, and *embodiment*. He writes, the despairing self gets rid of

> any relation to the power that established it, severing it from the conception that there is such a power....The self wants to rule over himself, create himself, make this the self he wants to be, determine what he will have and what he won't have in his concrete self. His concrete self, his concreteness, indeed has necessity and limits, is quite this definite thing, with these aptitudes, predispositions, etc., in this concrete set of circumstances, etc.....He doesn't want to take his own self upon himself, doesn't want to see his project in his given self; he wants...to construct it himself.[18]

With this focus on concretion, we see that this particular form of despair is a defiant denial of the self's facticity and its groundedness in the given. Here and elsewhere in the discussion, he alludes to bodily dispositions and drives, the cultural environment, and personal history. And this dependence upon given situatedness is explicitly tied to the "power that established it," to "God."

The same emphasis on embodiment is again apparent in the most extreme form of defiant despair, defiant demonic despair, where we are told that the individual stumbles upon some "flaw" in the composition of self. In demonic rage against the God who seems to be responsible for placing him in this particular and peculiar body, he holds his embodied self up to God as proof that God is a second-rate creator. Indeed, in these examples of defi-

[18] *SKS* 11, 182 / *SUDP*, 99.

ance, the implication seems to be that one's relation to *God* is *grounded* in one's relation to *the given*.

V. ON THE GIVEN AND GOD

This tie here in *The Sickness unto Death* between the divine and the given, between God and embodied consciousness, is consistent with what we find elsewhere in Kierkegaard's authorship, even if it seems initially counterintuitive when we consider Kierkegaard's reputation. He has traditionally been introduced in philosophical circles as an epistemological and ethical *subjectivist*, concerned first and foremost with the private interior space where truth claims must be evaluated. In theological circles, Kierkegaard is often viewed as a theologian of *transcendence*, primarily concerned with freeing religious life of images of divinity that are all too human by calling for a confrontation with a transcendent God we cannot know or fully relate to. One of my aims here, however, is a reformulation of Kierkegaard's basic thinking about human existence by underscoring the issue of the embodied self. This might be described as a shift from a focus on Kierkegaard's philosophy of transcendence to a focus on his philosophy of immanence. And in doing so, I hope to reaffirm the radical nature of his focus on facticity, in the name of both philosophy and theology.

We find a good example of this focus on facticity in his dissertation at the University of Copenhagen, *On the Concept of Irony,* where he writes that "the divine element in a human being" is bound up with "actuality" or "the particularity of individuality."[19] Kierkegaard argues that the Romantic attempt to sever the self's dependence on actuality is at the same time an attempt to sever the self from something divine.[20] In fact, his general critique of the German Romantics is centered on their "irreligious" dismissal of the limitations imposed by actuality.[21] By contrast, the religious soul accepts that one's given context is "in part a gift that refuses rejection and in part an assigned project that must be actualized."[22]

In *Either/Or*, which is a literary investigation of the same themes treated academically in his dissertation, Wilhelm, writing to A, (a Danish Romantic rather than German Romantic), takes the bond between facticity and

---

[19] *SKS* 1, 316 / *CI*, 280.
[20] *SKS* 1, 316 / *CI*, 280.
[21] *SKS* 1, 330 / *CI*, 297.
[22] *SKS* 1, 312 / *CI*, 276.

divinity even further. He writes that an inner appropriation of the given is the only way to "understand" God:

> The enviable thing about a human life is that a person can come to the aid of the divine, can understand Him; put differently, the only way of understanding the divine worthy of human being is to freely appropriate everything that's been given to [*tilkommet*] him, both the joyful and the sorrowful.[23]

The passage continues with an emphasis on the same factical elements named in *The Sickness unto Death*. Note the emphasis on embodiment and everything that it implies:

> [A] person who chooses himself ethically chooses himself concretely as this definite individual...with these aptitudes, these tendencies, these instincts, these passions, influenced by these definite surroundings, as this definite product of this definite environment. But in becoming self aware in this way, he assumes responsibility for it all.[24]

I've taken these examples from Kierkegaard's early works, but I could just as well take a work written at the same time as *The Sickness unto Death*, namely, the devotional literature about *The Lilies and the Birds*. In this text, Kierkegaard asks how we ought to understand Jesus' words about learning from lilies and birds, given the fact that plants and animals obviously lack that which sets us apart from most other living things: our complicated language, our human mind, our ability to transcend the factical. His answer is that we should learn by focusing on precisely that which we share with these forms of life: our situatedness in time and place, our embodiment. To learn to be silent in the face of embodied suffering, to learn to be obedient to the place we find ourselves rooted, to learn to be happy about the here and now are all lessons about the self being willing to appropriate its given factical context.[25]

On the reading I have been pushing here, one might say that to be grounded in God comes very close to being grounded in God's gift of situatedness. If we return to the discussion about defiant despair in *The Sickness unto Death*, we see that defiance is not a problem merely because of its wilful refusal of religious life or because it impiously severs itself from the idea of a

---

[23] *SKS* 3, 239 / *EO2*, 250.

[24] *SKS* 3, 239 / *EO2*, 250.

[25] See Kierkegaard, "The Lily in the Field and the Bird of the Air" in *WA*, 1–45 / *SKS* 11, 7–48.

God. It is not just that one *ought not* to autonomously construct one's own self-definition Anti-Climacus' point rather is that the autonomous defiant self *cannot* be constructed at all. Given the human condition, it is simply impossible for imagination to control the self by explaining away or ignoring the facticity that it is grounded in. Whether I like it or not, my peculiar existence is necessarily limited by this brain in this body, the only one I will ever have, and my existence is limited by own utterly unique time, place, and social setting. And to be grounded in all this is intimately related to being grounded in that something else that Anti-Climacus calls God.

VI. ON FACTICITY AND SITUATION

As Stewart has argued persuasively, this reading can be supported by source work research, especially research into Kierkegaard's critique of the autonomy of the poetic mindset that he saw in the German Romantics and which continued in his authorship as a critique of the aesthetic or poetic mindset in general.[26] In addition to this evidence, I would like to briefly suggest, with Stewart, that by looking forward to Kierkegaard's reception in the twentieth century, we find thinkers whom we can read alongside Kierkegaard who are equally sensitive to factical situatedness.[27] My use of the term "facticity" to describe "the given" already indicates that I have made some moves in this direction. One might argue, for example, that we find something similar in Sartre's discussion of the dialectical relationship of facticity and transcendence, in which we are also granted a structural outline of self that resembles the one sketched in *The Sickness unto Death*. I can give no more than a cursory indication now, but in *Being and Nothingness*, Sartre claims that although there is no essential self, we can speak of the dualistic "metastable structure of selfhood"[28] within which the consciousness of self operates. At one pole is embodiment and everything associated with it, i.e., what he calls "facticity,"[29] and at the other pole is the capacity of mind and imagination to

---

[26] Jon Stewart, *Søren Kierkegaard: Subjectivity, Irony, and the Crisis of Modernity* (Oxford: Oxford University Press, 2015), 87–110.

[27] Stewart, *Idealism and Existentialism*, 186–190.

[28] Jean-Paul Sartre, *Being and Nothingness*, trans. by Hazel E. Barnes (New York: Washington Square Press, 1993), 81.

[29] Sartre, *Being and Nothingness*, 78–83, 503–517; Stewart, *Idealism and Existentialism*, 188.

transcend that embodiment, i.e., "transcendence."[30] Like Anti-Climacus, Sartre claims that "these two aspects of human reality are, and ought to be, capable of a valid coordination," which he even calls a "synthesis."[31] And for Sartre, the tendency toward imbalance is just as strong as it is in Anti-Climacus, perhaps even stronger, and there are all sorts of ways he thinks a person can lean to a despairing interpretation of herself. She can deny her freedom of self-determination by interpreting herself in factical terms where the key line is "I had no choice" or "I couldn't help it" (not unlike Anti-Climacus' mode of weak despair, in which the individual is too passive to recognize that she need not be a slave to her own habits but has the power to choose new projects). Or a person can deny facticity as she interprets herself in terms of her intentions, her selective autobiography, and her own self-fashioned self-image. It is especially the latter form of bad faith that would lend itself to a comparison with Anti-Climacus' defiant despair, and the results could be fruitful. If we push Anti-Climacus a bit and argue that to be grounded in God comes very close to meaning to be grounded in facticity, Anti-Climacus and Sartre come to resemble each other on precisely that issue that is traditionally said to separate them: namely the idea of being grounded in God. Perhaps this opens possibilities for reexamining the relationship between the two thinkers again, this time concerning themes that were overlooked earlier.

VII. A REGULATIVE PRINCIPLE: FACTICITY "AS IF" IT WERE A GIFT

Even if a comparison with Sartre, or other less theologically inclined thinkers might prove fruitful, it is important to admit that Anti-Climacus' assertion that the self is dependent upon God seems to point to more than a dependence upon facticity. Obviously, the entire discussion in Part Two of *The Sickness unto Death*, with its emphasis on Jesus Christ as a divine figure, forgiveness, etc., is presented in theological language that leads beyond Sartrean discourse about existential situatedness. I would like to suggest in closing that there are plenty of ways that Anti-Climacus' understanding of a ground differs from that of Sartre.

---

[30] Sartre, *Being and Nothingness*, 78–83, 503–517; Stewart, *Idealism and Existentialism*, 188–189.

[31] Sartre, *Being and Nothingness*, 79.

First of all, if defiant despair could be reduced to a refusal to accept our existential groundedness in facticity, one might rightly ask why Anti-Climacus uses theological language rather than simply pointing out the impossibility of outrunning our factical limits, as does Sartre. It strikes me that there is an important difference in perspective: it is one thing to view one's situatedness as something one simply cannot escape, and another to view it as a divine gift that *ought* to be cared for. Following George Pattison's line of thinking,[32] I think it's fair to say that Anti-Climacus' God can be interpreted as a kind of regulative principle that allows the individual to see the world *as if* it were created and to see one's own particularity *as if* it were more than coincidence. It is a matter of seeing the self, myself, *as if* it were placed in this particular time and positioned at this particular place, and *as if* the way I care for my space has implications that I cannot see or imagine.

Secondly, though both thinkers insist that self-directed activity must take place within the limits of the given, I think we find different evaluations about how open-ended that activity ought to be or about how many directions are possible within those limits. Perhaps the differences become most apparent if we use a distinction made by Ingolf Dalferth.[33] He has suggested that in *The Sickness unto Death*, Anti-Climacus differentiates between 1) choosing to exist "in one way or another" (given our context, of course), and 2) choosing to exist in the "true way." Even if we don't go as far as Dalferth when he speaks of the "true way," there's no question that in *The Sickness unto Death* we sense a desire, or better yet, a longing, for the ideal integration of the multiple selves that are open to an individual within factical limits. We sense a longing for a ground that gathers the undeniable natural disunity of self into continuity. While Sartre might say that the attempt to live in good faith is more or less a "true way," a way that seeks to act on belief, and believe in one's actions, he probably couldn't agree with Anti-Climacus' claim that "every human being is primitively organized as a self, characteristically determined to become himself."[34] As Sartre writes in *Being and Nothingness*, there is no self "to *receive* or *accept*."[35]

---

[32] See George Pattison, "'Before God' as a Regulative Concept," *Kierkegaard Studies Yearbook*, 1997, 70–84.

[33] Ingolf U. Dalferth, "Selfless Passion: Kierkegaard on True Love," *Kierkegaard Studies Yearbook*, 2013, 177–180.

[34] *SKS* 11, 149 / *SUDP*, 63.

[35] Sartre, *Being and Nothingness*, 463, 490–491.

Finally, it is important to admit that Anti-Climacus not only alludes to a self grounded in a divinely given finitude; the self is also grounded in a divine infinitude. And this is where a tension in a Sartrean interpretation becomes most apparent. Anti-Climacus' ambiguous description of a consciousness of God also seems to point inward, toward space where the self could meet a God, a space for divine worship, gratitude, meditation, etc. That meeting is not possible for Sartre.

Thinking's Regeneration in the Valley of the Shadow of Death: Kierkegaard's Systematic Unsaying of Apophaticism's Unsaying

Curtis L. Thompson

There are enough nuances within the Kierkegaard research program to occupy the full attention of Kierkegaard scholars. Like other religious writers of his time, he shares his thinking about self, world, and God. However, of these three notions, the middle one—the world—usually receives the least attention in Kierkegaard studies. Because of this under-emphasis on the world, the sense that meaning only transpires in relation to the whole, and the awareness that the world is bigger than Søren Kierkegaard, a scholar might yield to the temptation to cast the net more widely and query into Kierkegaard under the horizon of a more comprehensive and expansive range of concerns. I plead guilty on this count as in this essay my reflections on Kierkegaard and death are framed by considerations of the worldly reality of sociality—the social dimension of the evolutionary development of human thinking and morality and the social character of intercarnational entanglements. My intent is for those reflections to set the stage for delving into Kierkegaard's apophatic thinking about death.

I. THE SOCIALITY OF THINKING AND MORALITY

Human thinking is a complex operative capacity that requires fundamental features to be in play for it to function appropriately. Like healthy plants, the thinking of humans needs certain conditions and nutrients to assume a healthy form that enables human beings to live well. Research on great apes and children by Michael Tomasello and his colleagues is helping the researchers construct an evolutionary history of human thinking in which social coordination is seen as contributing essential elements to thinking's development.[1] This coordination that sponsored the emergence of unique kinds of thinking within the human species points as well to a high level of human cooperation that facilitated the development of a species-unique morality.[2] In his parallel books on human thinking and human morality, Tomasello argues that the same two-step evolutionary development of human social life was at work: the first step is "new forms of collaborative activity," and this is followed by the second step of "new forms of cultural activity."[3] The respective emergence of collaboration and culture carried with them possibilities for advancement. Although precisely when these steps happened are not all that important for his argument, Tomasello suggests that the first step of collaboration likely began to take place roughly 2 million years ago after the emergence of the genus *Homo* and culminated in hominins of about 400,000 years ago, namely, the mysterious *Homo heidelbergensis* that was "the common ancestor to Neanderthals and modern humans."[4] The second step, "the first clear signs of distinct human culture," likely appeared "with *Homo sapiens sapiens*, that is, modern humans, beginning at the earliest some 200,000 years ago."[5] During these creative periods, new external circumstances forced adaptations that led to new ways of thinking and closely related novel forms of moral psychology.

So how is the evolutionary emergence of collaborative activity and cultural activity that occasioned momentous developments in human thinking and human morality relevant to making sense of Kierkegaard? Tomasello's claims affirm sociality rather than individuality as the crucial feature of humanity's advancement, and Kierkegaard's focus fell instead primarily on the single individual. Also, Tomasello depicts thinking and morality as coevolving, reciprocally-affecting realities, whereas Kierkegaard stressed the divergence of thinking from morality or, for him, we had best say from the broader ethico-religious arena. And yet, when Kierkegaard's person and writings are investigated from a perspective that recognizes his creativity as having been empowered by a rich interdependency with the cultural milieu of Golden Age Denmark that was produced and sustained by complex social

---

[1] Michael Tomasello, *A Natural History of Human Thinking* (Cambridge, MA: Harvard University Press, 2014).

[2] Michael Tomasello, *A Natural History of Human Morality* (Cambridge, MA: Harvard University Press, 2016).

[3] Tomasello, *A Natural History of Human Morality*, ix.

[4] Tomasello, *A Natural History of Human Thinking*, 36.

[5] Ibid., 84.

collaboration and cooperation, then the relevance of the evolutionary narrative becomes more apparent. Quietly at work behind Søren's strident differentiating between thinking and the morality-religion complex or between reason and faith was the tacitly functioning process of a more cooperative rationality. Kierkegaard believed that it was possible for thinking to be regenerated and that, while God was the ultimate origin of such regeneration, ideas and actions of an ethico-religious nature regnant in his social milieu were its penultimate source. I engage here in an experiment of digging into worldly entanglements that influenced Kierkegaard's view of thinking's regeneration. The concept or image or paradigm of death, in particular, will receive primary consideration in this experiment.

II. FROM INCARNATION TO INTERCARNATIONAL PARADIGMS

The Christian doctrine of the Incarnation or the intimate entanglement of divine and human in a single person plays a central role in the thinking of Søren Kierkegaard. The incarnation of God in Jesus the Christ constitutes the absolute paradox that constrains reason's autonomy and calls for the response of passionate faith. Without the constricting presence of the paradoxical Christ, Kierkegaard's thinking would not possess the distinctive character that it does.

In this essay I surely do not propose deleting this central Christian dogma from Kierkegaard's thought. I do suggest, though, to attempt an experiment, an imaginative thought experiment in the spirit of Kierkegaard himself, in which we play with the notion of incarnation centered in the historical figure of Jesus to find broader relevance and application more generally in the world and more particularly in the work carried forth by Kierkegaard's person and writings.

Martin Luther claimed that the incarnation of the Word in Christ makes manifest God's glory, and so does the incarnate Word as preached. Commenting on the biblical book of Zechariah, Luther waxes eloquent about Christ's kingdom, which "has no other elegance than the preaching of the Word of the Gospel," which adorns the Christ with his "most splendid glory."[6] The incarnation of the Word, then, does not for him come to a full

---

[6] Martin Luther, *Lectures on the Minor Prophets III, Zechariah*, vol. 20 in *Luther's Works*, vols. 1–55, ed. by Jaroslav Pelikan and Helmut T. Lehman, American Edition (Philadelphia: Muehlenberg and Fortress, and St. Louis: Concordia, 1855–86), Zec 6:13–14, where Luther

stop with its enfleshment in Jesus of Nazareth. For the presence of this one proclaimed in the Gospel becomes incarnate in the lives of hearers of the Word.[7] Incarnation is extended by the Reformation's maverick theologian to include preaching that brings the Word all the way into the worldly, carnal arena of those embodied beings listening to sermons. Kierkegaard does not own being a genuine preacher of the Gospel. He insists on not labeling his discourses as sermons because, without having been ordained, he does not regard himself as operating with authority, so we cannot technically speak of his preaching as including him within the extended incarnation Luther suggests. However, there is little doubt that Kierkegaard's authorship has functioned to bring the incarnate Word with vigor, freshness, and power into the lives of those who have invested themselves in his texts and the thoughts and practices they present. We could say, somewhat irreverently (because of his disdain for the notion of "mediation" as Hegel's key concept), that Kierkegaard "mediated" the incarnate Word.

A contemporary Lutheran theologian, Niels Henrik Gregersen, has extended the incarnation in a different way with his notion of "deep incarnation." He and various colleagues are reconsidering the import of Jesus as interpreted through the lenses of biological, ecological, and evolutionary understandings of human personhood. Gregersen explains that the phrase "deep incarnation"—which he coined in 2001 and sees as resonating with earlier Christian theology, especially the "logos-sarx Christology" of Athanasius and Gregory of Nyssa—is the view that

---

writes: "That is the great adornment and praise of Christ. Kings of this world are purple-clad, clothed and bedecked with gold and jewelry. But Christ wears the light. Through the Gospel are preached His gentleness, sweetness, righteousness, holiness, and kindness. When He is preached 'full of grace and truth' (John 1:14), then He is adorned with His finest jewelry and most splendid glory. In this priesthood and kingdom there is nothing external....Here all things are spiritual....So also God is adorned when we preach Him in Word and faith. In this way the earth becomes filled with the glory of the majesty of the Lord."

[7] Thus in Martin Luther, *Sermons on the Gospel of St. John, Chapter 6–8*, in *Luther's Works*, 23, we find Luther having the Christ say: "'My words are spiritual,' they are 'the highest wisdom and the life; they have life and spirit, and they also give life. But they must be believed.' "Then Luther counsels his listener-reader: "Now if you, too, want to have life for yourself, you must become a new, spiritual person who is not swayed by his reason like any man born of woman but who begins to believe these words. Otherwise you will never acquire life. But if you do this, it will prove to be your life." And then he offers a concrete suggestion: "This is the way to become spiritual and a new man, when by faith you make these words your own; for they are spirit and life. This Word calls for a Teacher different from your reason." All three quotations in this footnote are from *Luther's Works* 23:165.

> the Logos of God (the eternal Son) "became flesh" in Jesus, assumed a particular body and mind in him, and hereby also conjoined the material, living, and mental conditions of being a creature in any epoch. God thus became a human being (not only a man), a social being who lived with and for others in a sinful world (not an autistic individual), a living being vulnerable like sparrows and foxes (not just a member of *homo sapiens*), a material being made out of stardust and earth (not bringing with him a heavenly flesh), thus susceptible to death and disintegration. Likewise, the divine Logos in Jesus assumed an ensouled human person with human mind, will, and passions (not an omniscient superhuman being). "Assumption" here means not only tolerating all of this but embracing it as part of the condition for being a creature in God's own world of creation—despite all sin and evil.[8]

The full entanglement of Jesus as flesh and blood reality entirely enmeshed in the cosmos establishes an intimate relation between God and the world in the incarnation. Gregersen's mention here of "birds" (and elsewhere "lilies") overlaps with the content reflected upon in three of Kierkegaard's discourses but suggests little connection between the two Danes on the specific notion of "deep incarnation;" however, one can see a similarity in their Lutheran striving to relate themselves to their contemporary culture in a serious way, although Kierkegaard stood primarily in a critical relation to secular culture and its shaping of Christendom while Gregersen seems to be endeavoring to identify positive points of contact between the post-secular world and religion, including Christianity, more in the tradition of the Scandinavian Creation Theology of Knud Løgstrup, Regin Prenter, and Gustaf Wingren, as inspired by N. F. S. Grundtvig (1783–1872).

If incarnation is all about embodied entanglements, then it is not difficult to entertain Kierkegaard as a worthy incarnational agent. One does not have to contend with Kierkegaard for half a century to gain a sense for the multifarious entanglements that were embodied in the creative Danish thinker. The potent religious hurricane named Kierkegaard that hit Copenhagen in the mid-nineteenth century devastated Denmark for less than two decades; however, though Søren's life was not long, he accomplished much in his 42 years. He did a lot, and to do is to embody. Relationally, his life

[8] Niels Henrik Gregersen (ed.), *Incarnation: On the Scope and Depth of Christology* (Minneapolis: Fortress Press, 2015), 7 of the Introduction. See also Gregersen's essays, "Deep Incarnation: Why Evolutionary Continuity Matters in Christology," *Toronto Journal of Theology*, vol. 26, no. 2, 2010, 173–87, and "The Cross of Christ in an Evolutionary World," *Dialog*, vol. 40, 2011, 192–207.

was intensely entangled in numerous areas. He was intimately engaged in relating to his whole world, including relating to God, to people, to texts, to ideas, and to practices. Incarnation is evinced in all of these areas because of Kierkegaard's passionate actualizing by which bodily enactment or inscribing took place.

In moving ahead on our experiment we can be assisted by two thinkers who have made creative use of the notion of incarnation. The first is Nancy Bradley Warren, author of *Embodied Word*.[9] In studying English religious cultures of the fourteenth through the sixteenth centuries, Warren deliberates on "the tight, complex relationships among bodies and texts, pasts and presents, selves and others, that run through the writings and devotional practices of the women" she considers, and in so doing she employs "a set of foundational concepts that cast long shadows simultaneously forward and backward through medieval and early modern religious cultures Catholic and Protestant, orthodox and heterodox": "These concepts are incarnational piety, incarnational epistemology, incarnational textuality, and incarnational politics."[10] Warren utilizes these four "incarnational paradigms" to study "the ways in which women conceive of relationships among gendered selves, God, and human others," for it is through these "incarnational paradigms that such relationships are socially formed, historically categorized, and textually mediated."[11] Explicating "the modes of incarnationality" enables Warren to build bridges between pasts and presents, selves and others.[12] Warren clearly defines the meaning of the four incarnational paradigms. For her, incarnational piety means "devotional practices and forms of spirituality focused on holy interactions with holy bodies;" incarnational epistemology "refers to processes of knowledge production and acquisition grounded in corporeal, sensual, and affective experiences;" incarnational textuality points to "porous boundaries" that "obtain between embodied writers and readers and the textual *corpus*;" and incarnational politics describes "visions and revisions of bodies politic shaped or legitimated by holy bodies, and particularly by the sufferings of holy bodies."[13] Warren's employment of these paradigms works for a number of reasons, not least being the fact that women receiving

---

[9] Nancy Bradley Warren, *Embodied Word: Female Spiritualities, Contested Orthodoxies, and English Religious Cultures, 1350–1700* (Notre Dame, IN: Notre Dame University Press, 2010).

[10] Ibid., 7.

[11] Ibid., 20.

[12] Ibid., 11.

[13] Ibid., 7.

significant attention—St. Birgitta of Sweden, St. Catherine of Siena, and Julian of Norwich—were "closely contemporary holy women who produced substantial bodies of written work, much of it grounded in experiences of divine revelation."[14] Building on Warren's methodological approach, we can identify appropriate incarnational paradigms to use in analyzing Kierkegaard's thinking.

The second resource for advancing our imaginative experiment of relating the world-affirming notion of incarnation to Kierkegaard is Catherine Keller, author of *Intercarnations*, and one of the most creative theologians of our time.[15] Keller creates the word "intercarnation" that can prove useful for our experiment. The word emphasizes the entanglements or relationships by which a given reality is constituted. Keller operates as a scholar who usually has the process philosophy of Alfred North Whitehead not far in the background, and "intercarnation" gives expression to what Whitehead speaks of as the mutual immanence of occasions, each in the other. Particulars are constituted by their relations to other particulars. As Keller puts it: "Their particularity is nothing but their mode of participation in one another."[16] If all bodies exist in and through the relationships connecting them, we can see why the inter-bodily or intercarnational dimension comes to be significant for this thinker. Her word underscores the importance of worldly, fleshy, messy, material entanglements to which theology must be attuned: "Intercarnation highlights the intermittencies, the intervals and interdependencies, of *world* relations....Only in the twists and tangles of creaturely becoming, which is always becoming bodily, does the subject matter of theology matter now."[17] This term pushes the analysis away from a reality's singularity out to the multiplicity of its enriching associates and entanglements; these connections are to different particulars, and theology disregards reality in its relational fullness if it does not focus on the dynamic movement taking place

---

[14] Ibid., 20.

[15] Catherine Keller, *Intercarnatons: Exercises in Theological Possibility* (New York: Fordham University Press, 2017). See also the rather closely related notion of "sacred interconnections" dealt with in the much earlier book, *Sacred Interconnections: Postmodern Spirituality, Political Economy, and Art*, ed. by David Ray Griffin (Albany: State University of New York Press, 1990). In the introduction to that work, Griffin writes, 1, that no feature of postmodern spirituality is emphasized more than that of "internal relations," and "the central thread running through all" the essays in *Sacred Interconnections* is "the idea that all things are interconnected, and that these interconnections are internal to the very essence of things themselves."

[16] Keller, *Intercarnations*, 6–7.

[17] Ibid., 2.

between embodiment (of particulars) and multiplicity (of entanglements), for such movement makes possible that relationality.[18] Keller recognizes that any individual functions as immersed in sociality: "We actualize our possibilities only in enmeshed networks of asymmetrical reciprocity. Our bodies are networks of networks within larger networking fields. This boundless multiplicity of interdependent socialities" is a supplemental consideration that needs to be taken into account in grasping the import of any singular event.[19] If embodiment is the basis of a particular that is irreducibly "different" from other particulars, and if multiplicity covers the wide spectrum of a particular's "entanglements," then we can understand why Keller thinks that the phrase *entangled difference* "may be considered a paraphrase of intercarnation."[20] Intercarnation is the interplay of embodiment (creating difference) and multiplicity (of entanglements).

On Keller's view, any particular body, upon being opened up for closer scrutiny, quickly breaks into a multitude of all that composes it, nourishes and enlivens it.[21] That is surely the case when one thinks of Søren Kierkegaard as a particular. From a Kierkegaardian perspective one can certainly view him as having made good on his goal of becoming a genuinely single individual. From an intercarnational perspective, however, the view becomes more complex. Kierkegaard was entangled in myriad ways with thinkers and their ideas that came before him, he embodied endless entanglements in his own creative work, and he came to be connected to many who, coming after him, found rich resources in his writings. Delving into the figure of Kierkegaard, then, we are given three interrelated loci of intercarnationality for learning more about him: 1) the entanglements running to him in his inheritance from the past, 2) the innumerable relational connections of his creative life and labors, and 3) the lines of enmeshment running from him to figures who later appropriated his legacy.

Each of these loci of intercarnation could be dealt with in many ways. My interest in this essay is in the second locus of the many relational connections functioning in Kierkegaard's creativity. In delving into this rich intercarnational network of multiplicity, one could examine, for instance, Kierkegaard's pseudonymous writings, the signed works, or the journals, for

[18] Keller writes: "So theology must, *can*, help to keep more honestly in view the movement between multiplicity and embodiment that is relationality itself" (Ibid., 6).

[19] Ibid., 31–32.

[20] Ibid., 6.

[21] Ibid., 1.

each of these complex literary wholes could disclose much about Kierkegaard's entanglements. One could investigate the stages of existence as these are delineated in Kierkegaard's writings. One could scrutinize the theory of communication that Kierkegaard employs in his authorship. The approaches to unpacking the entanglements one finds in Kierkegaard's life and work are many. I have chosen a conceptual approach. I identify four central concepts of Kierkegaard's authorship to see what can be brought to light through them concerning Kierkegaard's systematic thinking. Here we can combine Warren's "incarnational paradigms" with Keller's "intercarnation" and come up with the category of "intercarnational paradigms." In my case it should maybe become "intercarnational concepts;" however, since the four central concepts I'm using are large concepts that each identify a cluster of many other interrelated concepts, they can bear the label of paradigm. These four large concepts or paradigms are dialectic, desire, decision, and death. The first three of these closely related intercarnational paradigms cover respectively the fields of cognition, affection, and volition or the faculties of thinking, feeling, and willing in the old faculty psychology.[22] Dialectic, desire, and decision concern themselves with the routine activities of life's projects, plans, and purposes, with, as the psalmist would say, the life of green pastures, still waters, and paths of righteousness. Death, the fourth intercarnational paradigm, occupies a privileged status in relation to the first three paradigms; it functions at a different, deeper level and functions critically over against the other three.[23] It stands opposed to life in its routineness and ordinariness in order to make space for a higher, regenerated form of life. In the psalmist's valley of the shadow of death one is opened to a new existence structured around the human's relation to a comforting God. Death's resulting rebirth regenerates dialectic, redirects desire, and potentiates decision. These four paradigms, therefore, work together to bring human beings full-

---

[22] It is an untidy task to place certain concepts under a given paradigm when their presence is obviously required in more than one paradigm. So the following placements are imprecise at best and often somewhat misleading. Even with these shortcomings, it is beneficial to identify concepts that fit best under a given paradigm. With that said, other important concepts in the intercarnational paradigm of dialectic are: duplicity, language, constraint, logic, contradiction, consciousness, reflection, doubt, laws, necessity, possibility, paradox. Desire's intercarnational paradigm subsumes the concepts of passion, longing, need, lack, emotion, feeling. The intercarnational paradigm of decision includes the concepts of freedom, responsibility, conscience, anxiety, despair, recollection, guilt, venture, repetition, temporality, moment.

[23] Concepts falling most naturally under this death-paradigm are faith, love, hope, eternity, instant, apophasis, releasement, annihilation, nothingness, unsaying, and redoubling.

ness of life. We can say: *Rational dialectic shaped by measured desire empowered through steadfast decision is all made possible with death's regeneration.* The remainder of this essay will scrutinize the importance of this intercarnational paradigm of death for Kierkegaard's thinking.

III. THE INTERCARNATIONAL PARADIGM OF DEATH

Within Kierkegaard's writings the notion of death is entangled with many different meanings. Patrick Stokes and Adam Buben note that Kierkegaard's "remarkable, lifelong preoccupation with death, dying, and the dead" and emphasize that "the themes of death and morality haunt Kierkegaard's signed and pseudonymous works" as "a constant presence appearing in a variety of guises and concerns."[24] There is death as the finality that awaits us all at life's end. We can label this as death^{F}. This understanding of death as final is to be differentiated from death as a symbol referring to the dying that can characterize living as a form of profound spiritual miserableness, despair, dying to the world, or recognition of self-vacuity or emptiness in relation to the divine. We can label this symbolic or spiritual use of the word death as death^{S}. These two understandings of death are quite separable, although the ever-awaiting, pervasively penetrating reality of death^{F} funds to a certain extent the meaning of death^{S}, as the metaphorical death^{S} "carries over" the significance of death^{F} into a different context. The intercarnational paradigmatic quality of death being pursued here concerns death^{S}, the representational or figurative or metaphorical meanings of death, and especially its meaning as the self-recognition of being nothing before God. Death^{S} is essentially spiritual or religious in character. The concept of death^{S}, then, functions as a figure or metaphor for the ending that can bring the beginning, for the closure in whose wake can occur a generative event. Such death happens at the depth of reality, within life's ground. This death thereby is linked to the abyss. The dynamics of death occur subterranean to the more routine, regular, normal dynamics of dialectic, desire, and decision. The death situated at the heart of this conceptual model is the annihilation that results as the end-point of religion marked by earnestness. If it is the end-point, this death is also the beginning-point. Death is the crucifixion of consciousness that liberates the ego's bondage to autonomy and self-

---

[24] Patrick Stokes and Adam Buben, *Kierkegaard and Death* (Bloomington: Indiana University Press, 2011), 1–2. This book contains a number of fine essays that shed significant light on different ways Kierkegaard employs the notion of death in his authorship.

sufficiency. Death opens out onto a theonomic relation to God.[25] Such death is the termination of the self that opens up new possibilities for it to become a regenerate reality. This death is the annihilation of the human that creates space for the divine. Death^{S} is the creative work of God that brings into being a new creation. This death brings the event of an origin that, appropriately grasped, is an expression of grace that brings joy. Death^{S} is the releasement as that letting be by which faith as gift comes into being. This death makes possible the moment's union with the eternal. Death^{S} involves dying from the world in each new moment. Death^{S} is an ongoing reality for the self that is healthy.

These many thoughts are the result of Kierkegaard's complex entanglements with different literary sources but especially with intuitions and ideas streaming from the apophatic tradition of mysticism. Michael Sells clarifies that apophatic language is a "discourse on the transcendent" that "contains both saying and unsaying": the *apophasis* of "un-saying or speaking-away…is commonly paired with *kataphasis*" that involves affirmation or saying, for any saying demands a corrective unsaying, just as the correcting "proposition which unsays the previous proposition is in itself a 'saying' that must be 'unsaid' in turn."[26] Insisting that the transcendent cannot be named, apophatic discourse unsays what has been said and then unsays the unsaying. Kierkegaard came to appreciate this distinctive type of discourse and his entanglements in it shaped his conceptualizing and discourse of death.

The network of this intercarnational paradigm has been mined by a few devoted scholars. My entrance into Kierkegaard's entanglements will be at second-hand, since the focus will be on the world of scholars and their literary work done on Kierkegaard's apophaticism. The concept of redoubling (*Fordoblelse*) plays a very important role in Kierkegaard's thinking on death^{S} and its closely related concepts. Therefore the extended explanatory notes of Howard and Edna Hong on the terms of "redoubling" and "reduplication"

---

[25] I, therefore, with Kierkegaard, want to advocate "in praise of theonomy," rather than "in praise of heteronomy" as Merold Westphal advocates in his provocative book, *In Praise of Heteronomy: Making Room for Revelation*, (Bloomington: Indiana University Press, 2017). Singing the praise of theonomy can incorporate most all of Westphal's critique of the autonomy of human reason in Kant, Hegel, and Spinoza that effectively closes the door to divine revelation. With its affirmation of human autonomy as grounded in dependence on God, theonomy softens heteronomy's insistence on the severity of God while maintaining persistent criticism and constraint of human autarchy and self-sufficiency.

[26] Michael A. Sells, *Mystical Languages of Unsaying* (Chicago: The University of Chicago Press, 1994), 2–3.

should be highlighted as helpful contributions to unpacking the intercarnational paradigm of death.[27] Marie Mikulová Thulstrup attended to Kierkegaard's connections to asceticism, pietism, and mysticism.[28] Jeremy Walker inquired seriously into the non-pseudonymous or edifying writings because he understood Kierkegaard's authorship to be directed toward the self-edification that results from placing self-examination at the heart of ethical existence: as the self through humility undergoes the process of becoming nothing it enters ever more fully into love that is also the divine.[29] David Law, who examined the strain of apophatic theology within the tradition of Christian mysticism that was a significant entanglement of Kierkegaard, did not find much explicitly apophatic language in Kierkegaard's writings but identified instances of what he terms "apophaticism," or those elements in Kierkegaard's thought that stress the human's incapacity for grasping the divine.[30]

Another scholar, George Pattison, needs to be included in this trajectory of thinkers who focus on themes in Kierkegaard that are more at the margins of the traditional musical melodies and refrains pouring from Kierkegaard's pen. Many of Pattison's books on Kierkegaard have journeyed into less traversed terrain and shed intercarnational light on interesting entanglements of aesthetics, the void, and the upbuilding or edifying discourses.[31]

---

[27] See the explanatory notes on redoubling and reduplication of the Hongs, *JP*, 3, 908–911.

[28] See, for instance, Marie Mikulová Thulstrup's essays in *Bibliotheca Kierkegaardiana*, ed. by Niels Thulstrup and Marie Mikulová Thulstrup, "Studies of Pietists, Mystics, and Church Fathers," in vol. 1, *Kierkegaard's View of Christianity* (Copenhagen: C. A. Reitzel, 1978), 60–80; "The Role of Asceticism" and "The Significance of Mortification and Dying away (to)" in vol. 2, *The Sources and Depths of Faith in Kierkegaard* (Copenhagen: C. A. Reitzel, 1978), 153–159 and 160–167; "Pietism," in vol. 6, *Kierkegaard and Great Traditions* (Copenhagen: C. A. Reitzel, 1981), 173–222; and "Suffering," in vol. 7, *Kierkegaard and Human Values* (Copenhagen: C. A. Reitzel, 1980), 135–162. See also her *Kierkegaard og Pietismen* (Copenhagen: Munksgaard, 1967).

[29] Jeremy Walker, *Kierkegaard: The Descent into God* (Kingston and Montreal: McGill-Queen's University Press, 1985).

[30] David R. Law, *Kierkegaard as Negative Theologian* (Oxford: Clarendon Press, 1993). Law concluded that Kierkegaard is more negative than most negative theologians in that he does not allow his pursuit of the way of negation to lead to affirming the human's mystical union with God. He described the nature of negative theology by considering three negative theologians: Clement of Alexandria, Dionysius the Areopagite, and Meister Eckhart.

[31] See, for example, his *Kierkegaard: The Aesthetic and the Religious: From the Magic Theatre to the Crucifixion of the Image, Studies in Literature and Religion* (London: Palgrave Macmillan, 1992; 2014). George Pattison, *Agnosis: Theology in the Void* (London: Macmillan Press, 1996).

Pattison substantially advanced the inquiry into Kierkegaard's signed discourses in his book on *Kierkegaard's Upbuilding Discourses*.[32] Pattison contends that Socrates, Kierkegaard's mentor, often begins his investigations in life's peripheral "infinitely interconnected and variegated motley,"[33] and Pattison situates such intercarnational entanglements at the heart of Kierkegaard's understanding of language.[34] For Kierkegaard, language is open-ended and this open-endedness of our social linguistic system rules out final closure of meaning: thus, "Kierkegaard connects the impossibility of closure with the relational, social character of language."[35] If intercarnationality describes the way things are in life's situation where language's sociality connects us so deeply with other bearers of meaning, it also is a normative goal for the labor of edification or building up: we are, even in the face of death's constant threat, to commit "ourselves to a process of unfinalisable striving for unity, meaning and purpose," which "gives us an inner consistency" and "provides the basis for building up the bonds of common life—of mutual respect, trust, and, ultimately, love."[36] But morality cannot be separated from mortality. The central theme of the upbuilding discourses Pattison identifies as the self's death, annihilation, becoming as nothing.[37] This moment (of death^{S}) marks the high point of spirituality or religiosity, for it leads to God shining through the centered nothingness with transfiguration, transparency, self-revelation resulting as the divine image sinks into the nothingness.[38]

Søren Kierkegaard, *Spiritual Writings: Gift, Creation, Love*, Selected, translated, and with an introduction by George Pattison (New York: Harper Perennial Modern Thought, 2010).

[32] George Pattison, *Kierkegaard's Upbuilding Discourses: Philosophy, Literature, Theology* (London and New York: Routledge, 2002).

[33] Ibid., 4.

[34] Ibid., 132. Here he summarizes the way, for Kierkegaard, Spirit supervenes on the sensuous-soulish, such that as it is "taken over" by Spirit "it becomes the trans-ferred (i.e. the 'metaphorical')": "The phenomenon of human language relies upon its material embeddedness in the sensuous. The time, space, audibility and visibility of language belong to this sensuous dimension, without which it just does not exist. But this means that it is possible to use language in a purely sensuous way, without understanding its spiritual meaning. The sensuous person and the spiritual person can both say the same thing—but mean quite different things by it." These comments on what I would call the intercarnationality of language are referring to the passage that begins Kierkegaard's first discourse in the second part of *Works of Love* (*SKS* 9, 212 / *WL*, 209).

[35] Pattison, *Kierkegaard's Upbuilding Discourses*, 134.

[36] Ibid., 115.

[37] Ibid., 26, 47, 73 30, 50–56, 62, 83, 86, 88, 90, 93, 94, 95–96, 103–4, 106, 114–15, 130–31

[38] Ibid., p 53; 97.

Death[S] brings life, the regeneration of new birth that comes from being in the proper posture to relate appropriately to God. Pattison makes a noble case for making regulative use (that involves accessing direction for living the moral and religious life), as over against constitutive use (that involves affirming an objective truth), of "what Kierkegaard says about the God-relation."[39] That is, he understands Kierkegaard's religious ideas and ideals presented in the discourses "as functioning in a manner analogous to Kant's regulative ideals of reason: as moral and religious principles that serve to give measure and direction to living but that do not presuppose any general ontology or any particular world-view."[40]

A most significant voice reporting on Kierkegaard research done by way of this intercarnational paradigm of death has come from David J. Kangas. He translated Hans L. Martensen's 1840 writing on medieval mysticism from which Kierkegaard likely learned much.[41] He also wrote his Ph.D. dissertation on Kierkegaard's apophatic thought, investigating Kierkegaard's thinking in relation most specifically to German Idealism and Neoplatonic apophatic theology, arguing that his interpretation of the latter's radical, non-mediatable form of negation leads to the ruination of the conceptual edifice of the former.[42] In arguing for a connection between Kierkegaard and negative or apophatic theology, Kangas had been drawn to enigmatic passages in Kierkegaard's writings exemplified by the following 1850 undated entry from the *Papirer*: "But to become involved with God in any other way than being wounded is impossible, for God himself is this: how one involves himself with him…In respect to God, the *how* is the *what*."[43] In dealing with such difficult passages, Kangas found it helpful to distinguish Kierkegaard's understanding of "concept" from that of Hegel. For Hegel, "the concept provides an encompassing framework of rationality in which individual

[39] Ibid., 118; 97.

[40] Ibid., 9. See also 97–100, 104–106, 113, 204.

[41] Hans Martensen, *Between Hegel and Kierkegaard: Hans L. Martensen's Philosophy of Religion,* translations by Curtis L. Thompson and David J. Kangas (Atlanta: Scholars Press, 1997). The second writing included in this book is *Mester Eckart. Et Bidrag til at oplyse Middeladerens Mystik* (Copenhagen: Reitzels, 1840): English translation, *Meister Eckhart: A Study in Speculative Theology*, 148–243. For a thoughtful account of the likelihood of Kierkegaard's dependence on this Martensen writing, see George Pattison, "Kierkegaard, Martensen, and the Meaning of Medieval Mysticism," *Estudios Kierkegaardianos: Revista de Filosofía*, no. 3, 2017, 65–80.

[42] David John Kangas, "The Draw of the Absolute: Kierkegaard's Apophatic Thought," Ph.D. dissertation, Yale University, 1999.

[43] *Papirer* X^2 A 644 n.d., 1850 / *JP* 2, 1405, in Kangas, "The Draw of the Absolute," 7. This corresponds to *SKS* 23, 215, NB17:70 / *KJN* 7. 219.

aspects gain meaning by their relation to the whole. The concept has the form of 'totality.' Because of its total scope, there is really only *one* concept in Hegel."[44] For Kierkegaard, on the other hand, concepts are plural; "a concept is not a locus of intelligibility or explainability;" in fact, instead of explaining things, a concept such as anxiety or irony is "that which itself has to be explained;" therefore, "a concept is always involved with the presentation of a limit to intelligibility," with the notion of limit being understood "as that which prevents closure;" consequently, "this is why in the *Papirer* Kierkegaard sometimes speaks about 'negative concepts.'"[45] It is apparent that Kierkegaard's view of the concept functions in the service of apophaticism. This dissertation concentrated on Kierkegaard's edifying writings rather than the pseudonymous writings.

In his book on *Kierkegaard's Instant*[46] Kangas turned to mostly pseudonymous texts written between 1841 and 1844 (*The Concept of Irony*, *Either/Or*, *Johannes Climacus* or *De omnibus dubitandum est*, *Repetition*, *Fear and Trembling*, and *The Concept of Anxiety*). He argues that Kierkegaard tears down the foundation of human self-consciousness that German Idealism's major figures of Kant, Fichte, the early Schelling, and Hegel had established in human self-consciousness. In the apophatic reading Kangas gives of Kierkegaard, the strong ego of Idealism's subjectivity is reduced to nothing by way of a view of beginning that has no end. Making his case by arguing for a specific interpretation of Kierkegaard on temporality, he juxtaposes Kierkegaard to Hegel and Plato. For the latter two thinkers, recollection and mediation respectively are key and human subjective consciousness is the locus for time's shaping. The result is a view of temporality as continuous, with human subjectivity providing the basis or ground for this continuity. Human autonomy prevails as the divine is relegated to the margins. Hegel's logic in particular makes the case for rational thinking or the ideality of consciousness as determining what is reality: the real is what secures a meaningful place within the rational functioning of consciousness. Kierkegaard's understanding of temporality is very different. Placing the narrative's analytical focus on existence rather than the more typical stages of existence, Kangas emphasizes that existence is an event of the coming into existence and that this event, relentlessly repeating itself, is ever bringing a beginning

---

[44] Kangas, "The Draw of the Absolute," 11.

[45] Ibid., 11–12.

[46] David J. Kangas, *Kierkegaard's Instant: On Beginnings* (Bloomington: Indiana University Press, 2007).

or newness that precedes and precludes a representing of existence.[47] This moment of beginning is Kierkegaard's instant, which means that self-consciousness is never able to catch up to it, never able to achieve a coincidence of the instant with itself. As a result of this infinite or ever-repeating beginning, existence is never stable and possesses no ground or goal. Having drawn the link from the ego "to a beginning prior to presence," Kierkegaard's thinking in his early works involves him in critically "recalling the originary condition of the ego's involvement with itself."[48] Kierkegaard's temporality, therefore, is marked by rupture, by discontinuity. This is not the case, of course, if human subjectivity is time's ground; but if each moment is given to us by God as a new instant to respond to as yet another beginning, then one has at hand a view of time that is much more discontinuous, momentary, episodic. Kangas regards everything that *is* as existence out of grace, sheer gratuity, pure goodness. The call is to think "the simultaneity of life and death," that is, "letting go of pure life and pure meaning, allowing death to be," for this is what constitutes the religious movement, and it means "allowing the death of the conception of the self as an origin of meaning, or allowing the metaphysics of the subject to founder."[49] This provocative apophatic reading of the Dane draws numerous links back to Meister Eckhart and especially to his notion of *Gelassenheit* or releasement for grasping the true nature of faith. Our discussion will be enriched by returning to Kangas one more time in this section and again in the next section.[50]

---

[47] It seems that the clue to the interpretation being offered in this book by Kangas lies in the thought of the second coming into existence expressed so clearly by Kierkegaard's Johannes Climacus in the Interlude of *Philosophical Fragments*, *SKS* 4, 273–276 / *PF*, 73–76, and especially in the following passage, *SKS* 4, 276 / *PF*, 76: "Yet coming into existence can contain within itself a redoubling [*Fordobling*], that is, a possibility of coming into existence within its own coming into existence. Here in the stricter sense, is the historical, which is dialectical with respect to time. The coming into existence that is here shared with the coming into existence of nature is a possibility, a possibility that for nature is its whole actuality. But this distinctively historical coming into existence is nevertheless within a coming into existence—this must be grasped securely at all times. The more special historical coming into existence comes into existence by way of a relatively freely acting cause, which in turn definitively points to an absolutely freely acting cause." The "relatively freely acting cause," of course, is a reference to the free human being, and the "absolutely freely acting cause" is a reference to God.

[48] Kangas, *Kierkegaard's Instant*, 195.

[49] Ibid., 114.

[50] Here can be mentioned a few other contributions to this trajectory that cannot be delved into in this essay. Two essays by Peter Šajda focusing on Hans Lassen Martensen advance the discussion. See his "Meister Eckhart: The Patriarch of German Speculation who was a *Lebemeister*: Meister Eckhart's Silent Way into Kierkegaard's Corpus" in *Kierkegaard and the*

But first two other fascinating books need to be mentioned. Significant entanglements of Kierkegaard's existential thinking are uncovered by Noreen Khawaja's study of asceticism in philosophy.[51] She argues that philosophy's encounter with Protestant forms of piety leads to a new form of asceticism, and Kierkegaard is the major representative of such Pietism, which she understands as "the dimension of Protestant theology concerned with the experiential and devotional structure of an individual Christian life."[52] Khawaja interprets Kierkegaard's question of what it means to become a Christian "as a thinly veiled psychological reformulation of Pietistic notions of conscious, ongoing conversion," even though he decided against using the language of conversion.[53] The author underscores the insight of *Sickness* that death connects one to eternity, for death is that *unto* which or toward which the self moves but does not reach because to be in despair is to be dying while living: the self's "inalienable alienness" or "inexhaustible alienation" is what *Sickness* calls "the eternal," which is the self's "*inalienable relationality*, the fact that the self *i ethvert Øieblik*—"at every moment"—is invested in the existence in which it finds itself, and the fact that it is responsible, if not for existing, for the continued investment existing implies."[54] The ongoing task is to continually come before God as nothing, while at the same time being infinitely, unconditionally engaged.[55] Such sustained annihilation provides the regenerative, saving principle of limitation for the self: death, producing a scarcity of time, becomes the means

---

Patristic and Medieval Traditions, ed. by Jon Stewart (Farnham: Ashgate, 2008) (*Kierkegaard Research: Sources, Reception and Resources*, vol. 4), 237–53; and "Martensen's Treatise *Mester Eckart* and the Contemporary Philosophical–Theological Debate on Speculative Mysticism in Germany," in *Hans Lassen Martensen. Theologian, Philosopher and Social Critic*, ed. by Jon Stewart (Copenhagen: Museum Tusculanum, 2012), 47–72. See also my discussion of Kierkegaard's use of Martensen in Chapter 3 of *Following the Cultured Public's Chosen One: Why Martensen Mattered to Kierkegaard* (Copenhagen: Museum Tusculanum, 2008). Finally to be mentioned is Randall G. Colton, *Repetition and the Fullness of Time: Gift, Task, and Narrative in Kierkegaard's Upbuilding Ethics* (Macon, GA: Mercer University Press, 2013).

[51] Noreen Khawaja, *The Religion of Existence: Asceticism in Philosophy from Kierkegaard to Sartre* (Chicago: The University of Chicago Press, 2016).

[52] Khawaja, *The Religion of Existence*, 22, 46.

[53] Ibid., 26, 70. She sees Kierkegaard being influenced by the pietistic movement in which "conversion is transformed from one moment in the process of justification into an encompassing devotional ideal" (p. 73).

[54] Ibid., 90–91.

[55] Ibid., 91, and cited is Kierkegaard's *For Self- Examination/Judge for Yourself!*, 104 (that is, *SKS* 16, 160 / *JFY*, 104).

within the logic of rational constraint by which dialectic or thinking is harnessed for serving life's well-being.[56]

Another important contribution to our theme is provided by Peter Kline in his book *Passion for Nothing*.[57] Kline acknowledges a deep dependence on the work of David Kangas,[58] but from many entanglements he creatively pulls together diverse insights into Kierkegaard's apophatic theology and brings significant clarity to this subject-matter often left shrouded in obfuscation. Kline suggests that "Kierkegaard's theology can be read as a creative repetition of Eckhartian apophaticism."[59] The light-hearted, free-wheeling quality of this lucidly-writing author who—as he says, wants to play with Kierkegaard rather than master him—manages to render appealing Kierkegaard's thinking that recognizes that its saying needs to be unsaid. His claim is that "Christ incites a desire, a passion, for nothing," and in that passion "*God is*" and God works: in this "gift of a liberating nothingness" there is a letting go of the lesser self that is suffocated and determined, as, in becoming nothing, a genuinely free self emerges that has the power to "rise up against a world overrun by violence, exploitation, and an economy of misery and shame."[60] If apophaticism is situated at the heart of what Kierkegaard has to offer, then on Kline's view "infinite reduplication expresses the apophatic core of Kierkegaard's thought."[61] On thinking of God, Kline differentiates Kierkegaard's view from that of Hegel. They both think of God as differentiating Godself, as a subjectivity that doubles itself: "However, for Kierkegaard, such doubling does not place the divine life in opposition to itself as the possibility of its self-knowledge. What is double in God is not a necessary moment of objectivity and self-othering through which God's essence mediates itself. The double of divine subjectivity is simply subjectivi-

---

[56] Khawaja, *The Religion of Existence*, 100–101. The formulation of this summary of the logic of rational constraint maybe reflects more my own perspective than that of the author, but it was inspired by Khawaja's account.

[57] Peter Kline, *Passion for Nothing: Kierkegaard's Apophatic Theology* (Minneapolis: Fortress Press, 2017).

[58] Ibid., 5, n. 25.

[59] Ibid., 5, 84–7.

[60] Ibid., xvii.

[61] Ibid., 64. For Kline (63–64) the notion of *Fordoblelse* or redoubling is quite ubiquitous in Kierkegaard's thought, for he sees it as "a concept that Kierkegaard deploys unsystematically across an extraordinary range of problematics: God, Christ, writing, communication, suffering, joy, patience, faith, hope, love, inwardness, hiddenness—each of these has *Fordoblelse* at its heart."

ty again, subjectivity a second time."[62] The God of pure, reduplicating subjectivity is "an infinitely active withdrawing from objectivity," for "pure subjectivity is a self-relation without any mediation at all": and this means that "God does not have a determinate nature, essence, or subject-hood. God is nothing."[63] God's *how* is God's *what*, we might say. This divine nothingness is not static, and so Kline creates the verb "nothin-*ing*" to underscore that God even negates "its own nothingness as static accomplishment," for the divine pure subjectivity and infinite reduplication indicates "simply relation itself—limitless, bottomless relation" and the incessant movement of this relating means that "the possibility of a static and centered subjectivity is always, already, eternally abandoned in favor of [a] wildly open and hospitable field of relationality that offers itself without reserve as the possibility of multiple and singular others."[64] While God's nothing excludes determinacy, it includes "an infinite intimacy with its own nothingness,"[65] for the subjectivity of God is possibility that ever gives itself in love. The abyss of God's nothingness consists of possibilities that are brought into relation to singular, unique others: "God relates to God as the abyssal possibility of singular selves who each enact an absolutely unique and unrepeatable relation to God and point of view on existence. God is the gift and happening of singularity....God is the whence of such irreducible multiplicity that opens an apophatic relationality."[66] Kline concludes this endorsement of intercarnationality's entanglements with the aphophatic affirmation: "God is the wholly otherness of every other that will never, not now, not in all eternity, be mediated into a determinate and objective totality."[67] The open-endedness of both God and human selves translates into a whylessness for both, since the asking of why implies an exercising of intentionality that requires "a delimited subject, a relation of subjectivity to its objective nature

[62] Ibid., 16. Kline points out (78–80) that for Hegel, the Absolute is the result and this result is the Totality that is an immanent "in-and-for-itself" after having begun with nothing, while Kierkegaard, with the mystics, ends with nothing as the opening of a fresh beginning that is absolutely always taking place in relation to the pure subjectivity that is God.

[63] Ibid., 85.

[64] Ibid., 85–86. Kline winsomely states (28) that for Kierkegaard, "to live before God as nothing, which is to live 'in' God, is to undergo the joyful liquidation of objective identity and purpose and become the joy of coming into existence upon an open sea of possibility."

[65] Ibid., 21.

[66] Ibid., 88.

[67] Ibid., 88.

through which subjectivity can put itself in relation objectively, aiming itself at delimited objects, ends, or goals":

> God's relation to the self is not an intentional relation to an object but an infinite relation to the self's non-objectivity, to what is eternal and infinite in the self, the self's subjectivity or soul. This relation of subjectivity to subjectivity...is an apophatic relationality that shows itself only through an undoing of teleological discourse. God relates only to reduplicate subjectivity in the self, only to birth God in the soul. God relates only to edify, only to grant the freedom to work without end or goal, never to exercise objective intention.[68]

Of course, this moment of birth is the moment of death[S]. It is the birth of nothing that is Eckhart's birth of God in the soul, *Gottesburt*, that is repeated in Kierkegaard's *Øieblikket*, the instant; and appropriating the death of this birth or instant "is the movement of releasement or letting-go: *Gelassenheit*, in Eckhartian terms, and "faith," in Kierkegaardian terms."[69] For Kierkegaard, "faith is the repetition of the self's giftedness, a letting-be of God's letting-be."[70] With God understood as pure subjectivity and infinite reduplication, the human is called in faith to "an infinite that holds itself in and repeats the instant of opening or birth while abandoning all forms of closure and totality.[71] Being a self, then, is a reduplication [*Fordoblelse*]: "Religious subjectivity, which is a 'repetition' or 'reduplication'—a 'reduplicating repetition' [*fordoblende Gjentagelse*]—of the infinity of divine subjectivity, is a movement of limitless relation and bottomless openness. Faith brings regeneration as it avails the self of "the gift of time ceaselessly repeated and renewed, opened forward before the eternal." He continues, "Faith gives the self over to...a new kind of relationality, one in which the self is absolutely immersed in existence, in its determinate and finite responsibilities, tasks, and pleasures, but with a difference, a qualitative difference, without any need to secure or ground itself there, without any need for results or finality."[72] He summarizes, "What is always at issue 'before God,' then, is a negation that opens existence absolutely: the 'wound of negativity' that, by virtue

---

[68] Ibid., 93–94.

[69] Ibid., 26, 76.

[70] Ibid., 24.

[71] Ibid., 1–2.

[72] Ibid., 71.

of 'the absolute's own resistance,' is held open without closure."[73] This continual "gaping open of time before the eternal" sponsors an unrelenting "passion of existence" that prevents any cognitive self-possession of oneself.[74] The self's genuine self as subjectivity can no more be known than can the subjectivity of God be known by God.[75]

Before the premature death[F] of our cherished colleague David Kangas (1964–2016). he wrote another book on Kierkegaard's apophaticism, this time with the focus on the religious discourses.[76] The philosophical payoff of a close reading of these discourses, he contends (it seems with no little influence coming from the later thought of Heidegger), is that one can gain a "glimpse of an experience of being" through them, although grasping fully this experience requires a patient reading that tends to the edifying.[77] Kangas might not mind my saying in this context that these "superfluous" discourses are not for the regeneration of reason, although they regenerate the reader, including her reason. They are superfluous, as he says, because "they are not *for anything*—not even for edification! They are edifying in their superfluity, their 'uselessness.'"[78] The edifying discourse "expands and marks out this prior attunement of the reader to the surplus of being; it elicits it, brings this forward against the dominant reading of surplus as lack," which lack is traditionally regarded as providing the condition of the project as well as the condition of a desire "that orients existence around a transcendent absolute, a first principle or final-goal."[79] In place of surplus as lack, the edifying discovers surplus as affirmation: "The edifying discourse, rejecting lack, brings the surplus of being forward as the *measure of human existence*."[80] One who recognizes surplus as surplus or as gift is already being edified; to have recognized life's giftedness is to have begun being "built up," which is not the process of self-constitution through projects but rather the work of patience and faith, "modes expressive of an unconditional affirmation of

[73] Ibid., 3. See Kline's excellent deliberation on reduplication in his Chapter 3 on "Infinite Reduplication."

[74] Ibid., 11.

[75] On the discussion of God's unknowability to God, see Kline, *Passion for Nothing*, 86–92.

[76] David J. Kangas, *Errant Affirmations: On the Philosophical Meaning of Kierkegaard's Religious Discourses* (London: Bloomsbury Academic, 2018).

[77] Ibid., 2–3.

[78] Ibid., 4.

[79] Ibid., 4–5.

[80] Ibid., 5.

reality," that exposes one to "the nothing" and to existing "for nothing," by taking the measure of one's being "from the gratuity of being itself," which is "an affirmation of reality itself."[81] Kierkegaard's discourses endorse an affirmation not grounded or founded by principles or structures of a moral or theological nature; the affirmation thereby possesses the quality of an "errant affirmation" that functions to dismantle "representational modes of thought that are rooted in the human power of imagination" and demystify "the human project of 'self-overcoming.' "[82] These "edifying discourses bring thinking back to an origin that cannot be mastered and to an ultimate situation of in-capability that defines human reality."[83] They do not fall victim to Heidegger's critique of onto-theology that strives to give an account of the being of all things by means of a highest being serving as the ultimate principle or origin: instead, their "logic" avoids positing a conditioning highest being because such positing involves the introducing of "belief" together with its counter-effect of "doubt," and this correlative twosome would fund "an infinite dialectic of belief and doubt—a 'bad' infinity in Hegel's sense."[84] Kierkegaard's discourses, therefore, replace this belief-and-doubt structure with "the attunement" that operates at the deeper level he calls "faith (*Troen*)."[85] Kangas sees what I am designating as death^{S} or the death of becoming nothing as being integral to knowing God, which is "inseparable from grasping [or being grasped by] the being of the human being, its fundamental ontological constitution": he insists that this being is not a closed reality but an open one because of including the always-originating event by which its being is experienced and by which that being must be acknowledged as a gift.[86] Kangas considers particular discourses, providing analysis of concrete instantiations of recurring themes and identifying Meister Eckhart as a frequent resource for Kierkegaard's reflections. For instance, we read that the human being is "the being capable of undergoing its own nihilation [*Tilintetgjørelse*]," for it is in this destruction that the human has its truth, with the proviso that the capability is not that "*by which*" one undergoes the annihilation but rather that it is "in the annihilation [or death^{S}] itself that the human

---

[81] Ibid., 5.
[82] Ibid., 6–7.
[83] Ibid., 7.
[84] Ibid., 8–9.
[85] Ibid., 9.
[86] Ibid., 10.

being is invested with capability."[87] Regeneration comes to the human, but it comes not by self-overcoming but "in the encounter with an absolute incapacity it undergoes with respect to its own being." Relevant here is Kierkegaard's dialogical encounter between the "first self" and the "deeper self," with "their differing relation to human capability": "The first self is oriented in the direction of discovering and elaborating its own capabilities, its power to economize, adapt, establish its continuity in being," always taking the initiative on its "project of being," guided by the ideals of self-transparency and self-determination; the deeper self, on the other hand, "endorses the first self's projects," though it offers opposition "when the project structure is allowed to occlude the decisive issue, the fundamental need of the human being," which is its highest perfection, that is, to recognize "the non-ultimacy of the world of project," that "it is capable of nothing, nothing at all," and that only in the anguish of such incapacity, such nihilation, does the self discover "the power by which it exists, the very power of being," which power Kierkegaard indicates as being "God."[88] The book's pattern of analysis effectively demonstrates how such themes as expectancy, gift, patience, need, confession, death, patience, silence, care, spirit, glory, and obedience leads, each in its own way, to "giving time and space to the gift of being" and, in so doing, dilating "the cramped attunement of the human being as informed by care," or by investment in life's project structure, with such dilatation creating "the room to breathe, the very breath of affirmation."[89] The highest glory of the human being, the being who is capable of becoming, is "to be nothing through the act of worship," for "becoming nothing is the way of human becoming."[90] Worship recognizes the incapability of human capability.

IV. UNSAYING APOPHATICISM'S UNSAYING

This section of the essay carries out the last task of the experiment: to show the need to unsay Kierkegaard's unsaying. Meister Eckhart's most famous line is "Therefore pray God that we may be free of God." This poignantly expresses what Hans Lassen Martensen in his book on Meister Eckhart identified as the oscillation between the Godhead of mystery and the God of

[87] Ibid., 70.
[88] Ibid., 74–76.
[89] Ibid., x.
[90] Ibid., 127–128.

revelation in which mysticism becomes ultimately entrapped.[91] Kataphatic claims about God can get lost amidst apophatic claims about the Godhead if mysticism's cool enthusiasm is given free reign of the theological terrain. Bright, revelatory insights into God and God's actions in the world can become diminished when the mystic's movement into the dark, abyssal nothingness of the divine depths ends in silence. Solid scholarship has shown us that Kierkegaard was significantly influenced by his entanglements in the traditions of mysticism and pietism. Themes central to those traditions found their way into his thinking and therefore are present in his pseudonymous works and edifying discourses alike. Without including an account of these entanglements in the narrative of Kierkegaard's thinking the story would be left incomplete: they clearly are an important, indispensable part of that fascinating story. Intercarnational relationships, with the mystics especially, need to be ascertained and sorted out. This does not mean, though, that the delineation of aphophatic entanglements should take the form of a meta-narrative characterizing the first and last word and all that is important within Kierkegaard's thinking and writing.

I stated earlier that in Kierkegaard's authorship: *Rational dialectic shaped by measured desire empowered through steadfast decision is all made possible with death's regeneration.* A logic is at work in Kierkegaard's apophatic thinking, and that logic might well include the critique of rational thinking, measured desire, and steadfast deciding, and have its power of regeneration metaphorically expressed by death[S]. But this does not rule out that there being many other dialectics or logics at play in the Kierkegaardian literary *corpus.* At one point Kierkegaard states that each passion has its own dialectic. Each "whole" within the authorship, be it a book, a chapter, a discourse, a journal entry, a pseudonym's works, a stage of existence—has a dialectic, style, and point of view characterizing it. And these can vary greatly, each one from the other, or overlap at times as well. But Kierkegaard is doing more in his authorship than simply giving expression to an apophatic system. He might well in many instances be engaged in systematically setting forth an aphophatic perspective. However, at many other points he is seriously articulating points of view that cannot be neatly summed up under the category of the negative.

[91] See Šajda, "Martensen's Treatise *Mester Eckart*," in *Hans Lassen Martensen: Theologian, Philosopher and Social Critic*, 52.

This essay can be considered on its own, independent terms, but it is also entangled in the larger project of making a case for Kierkegaard as a systematic thinker. Kierkegaard fought against the system, to be sure. The existence of a human being is a temporal process of becoming that precludes the fanciful adopting of a perspective from eternity required to grasp reality in its fullness as a totality or as a system. Kierkegaard's thinking is securely anti-system. However, there is a systematic quality to his anti-system thinking. The commitment he makes to apophaticism constitutes a key contribution to his systematic thinking and it ought to be acknowledged as the important accent that it is. But care should be taken not to allow Kierkegaard's apophatic commitment and pronouncements to become all-dominating and thereby assume the character of allegiance to a system, a system, ironically, in which the articulated or said unsaying, without the benefit of any further unsaying, has been allowed to reify into a totalistic posture that then sheds its status as being one of Kierkegaard's points of view to becoming his one and only point of view.

Michael Sells reminds us that apophaticism's language of double propositions involves three essential claims.[92] The first claim is: "No statement about X can rest as a valid statement but must be corrected by a further statement, which itself must be corrected in a discourse without closure." An initial statement about X might well express partial truth in what is said; however, because of the difference between language and reality, a fuller truth can be expressed when what has been said initially has been unsaid in a second statement. The same can be claimed about a third statement that corrects the second but is then corrected by a fourth, and so on. The second claim is: "The meaningfulness of the apophatic moment of discourse is unstable, residing in the momentary tension between two propositions." Every attempt to unsay assumes the form of a said that requires another unsaying. The meaning of such language is created by the tensive interplay between the attempt at setting forth to say something that turns into a said and the resulting need then to say in such a way to take back the said. Apophasis is instrumental in allowing language to be opened to the fuller reality it is attempting to express. The third claim is: "The habits of language pull the writer and reader toward reifying the last proposition as a meaningful utterance. To prevent such reification, ever-new correcting propositions must be advanced." This third claim gives fuller elucidation to the meaning of "a

---

[92] Sells, *Mystical Languages of Unsaying*, 207.

discourse without closure" of the first claim. It can serve as a precaution not to be hoodwinked into allotting the status of finality to the last proposition presented. This claims that being the last word does not give that word the status of being the final word. It is merely the last statement to appear, but this does not exempt it from requiring another proposition or other propositions to unsay what it has said.

These three claims together clarify the truth about language, namely, that language lies, that language can be used to rectify language's lies, and that even then language's rectifications themselves also lie. While this is the case, there remains the fact that in its lying in this manner, language does manage to give expression to partial truth. Furthermore, it becomes apparent how apophatic language, with its built-in quality of striving to prevent linguistic closure, serves to critique totality and thus can function to safeguard anti-system affirmations wanting to be made.

With this reminder, the issue before us can be stated. In the treatments of apophaticism in Kierkegaard that we have reviewed, one senses as lying close at hand the temptation to elevate that apophatic viewpoint to the status of the predominating viewpoint of Kierkegaard's authorship. Pattison we saw declared the apophatic theme of the self's becoming nothing as the central theme of Kierkegaard's upbuilding discourses, but at no point did he argue for such self-annihilation or death as the prevailing theme of the entire literary output. Kangas, in his dissertation, had explicitly pronounced that he was *not* arguing "that Kierkegaard's theological and philosophical discourse is totally analyzable in terms of his relation to idealism and apophatic theology": he states that the reading of Kierkegaard he offers "makes no claim to exhaustiveness—neither with respect to Kierkegaard's relation to the tradition nor with respect to elements of Kierkegaard's thought itself. It is truly a 'point of view,' and, as such, non-competitive with respect to other points of view."[93] Kangas identifies his reading as "fragmentary," noting: "It strives for a measure of totality or systematicity with respect to its own problem and in relation to its own concepts, but does not make the further claim that this is the 'true' and 'only' Kierkegaard or the only concepts."[94] This early Kangas writing definitely unsays what is said. In the two Kangas books we examined there is less concern about making explicit the limitations of Kierkegaard's apophatic point of view, although in both

[93] Kangas, "The Draw of the Absolute," 10.

[94] Ibid., 13.

cases they avoid overstating the reach of apophaticism as being the last word characterizing the whole authorship. Finally, in the case of Kline's *Passion for Nothing*, while no absolutistic claims are made for apophaticism, constraint in this area does not seem to be a concern. The book argues for "Kierkegaard's Apophatic Theology," not Kierkegaard's apophatic accent or strand or theme, so in that sense it seems to be applying its argument to the whole of Kierkegaard's thinking. And yet, its consistent insistence on defying closure in favor of open-endedness militates against a totalizing reading of his provocative prose. His is a discourse without closure. This is apparent as well in Kline's interesting conclusion, which is a "Beginning Again." He speaks there of refusing to conclude the book, and instead of concluding it, Kline states that he "is going to reduplicate it," to "give it a new form, a reduplicated form," which I take to mean that he is going to actualize what it has to say in his life.[95] This is maybe the strongest evidence that he too has not succumbed to the temptation to elevate the apophatic to the status of the predominating viewpoint of Kierkegaard's authorship.

Today there is renewed interest in mysticism's representatives such as Dionysius the Areopagite, John Climacus, Maximus the Confessor, John Scottus Eriugena, Meister Eckhart, Nicholas of Cusa, and Johannes Tauler. These figures write of God in relation to the human and the creation in ways that break down customary dualisms and boundaries. Their apophatic deliberations are a resource for nourishing our thinking about God's incarnational presence in the universe and the intercarnational entanglements of creatures, each in and with the other. The fact that Kierkegaard was entangled with some of these figures of mysticism holds promise for fresh research to uncover influences of the intercarnational relationships. This study has concentrated less on the writings of Kierkegaard themselves and more on delving into entanglements of the world of secondary literature. The experiment here has focused on the intercarnational paradigm of death, and I think it has demonstrated the powerful place of apophatic thinking in Kierkegaard's authorship. In the valley of the shadow of death, thinking or dialectic, no less than desire and decision, are regenerated, as life before God brings comfort and a new-found capability not of the human's making. Such apophatic insights definitely need to be taken seriously, even if they should finally be regarded more as providing an important theological accent rather

---

[95] Kline, *Passion for Nothing*, 177–78.

than as constituting the prevailing view within Kierkegaard's thinking as a whole.

Kierkegaard's emphasis on the apophatic operations of the "deeper self" needs to be understood in its dialectical tension with his emphasis in the predominant portion of his authorship on the dialectic, desire, and decision at play in the projects of the "first self." The human, in relation to God, is in the world, and the entanglements of its intercarnational paradigmatic dimensions can be distinguished but not separated. Kierkegaard's systematic thinking disallowed an apophatic system.

Divine Revelation: Outlines of a Conceptual, Typological and Epistemic Account

Heiko Schulz

The following reflections are to be taken as part of a work in progress. As such, they are supposed to pave the way for and support any subsequent attempt of coming to terms with the intricacies of what particular theologians refer to by the name of (divine) revelation. Accordingly, my observations and remarks are tentative and far from definitive. I frankly confess that they do not even keep up with my own expectations about dealing with the matter at hand, much less, presumably, with the reader's. I also want to emphasize beforehand—indeed, happily admit—what even for the uninitiated reader will hardly go unnoticed, anyway: my account is heavily influenced by Kierkegaard. However, my paper is strictly speaking not *about* Kierkegaard, as I rest content with occasionally quoting and/or referring to some of his (or his pseudonymous authors') ideas without directly treating his own concept/s of revelation, not even roughly, much less in greater detail.[1] This notwithstanding, the main inspiration behind my argument is essentially Kierkegaardian, or so at least I dare to claim: for here again, as is often the case, my suspicion is that I learned what I (appear to) have learned primarily

[1] As to the latter cf., in particular: Lee C. Barrett, *Eros and Self-Emptying. The Intersections of Augustine and Kierkegaard* (Grand Rapids, Michigan: William B. Eerdmans Publishing, 2013), 266ff.; Torsten Bohlin, *Kierkegaards dogmatische Anschauung in ihrem geschichtlichen Zusammenhange* (Gütersloh: Der Rufer, 1927), ch. VII; Stanley Cavell, "Kierkegaard's *On Authority and Revelation*," in *Must we Mean what we Say?*, updated edition (Cambridge: Cambridge University Press, 2002), 151–166; Arnold Come, *Kierkegaard as Theologian: Recovering My Self* (Montreal & Kingston: McGill-Queen's University Press, 1997), 14–44 (esp. 15–24); Steven M. Emmanuel, *Kierkegaard and the Concept of Revelation* (Albany, New York: State University of New York Press, 1996); Sean Turchin, "Revelation," in *Kierkegaard's Concepts*, Tome V: *Objectivity to Sacrifice*, ed. by Steven M. Emmanuel, William McDonald and Jon Stewart (Farnham: Ashgate, 2015) (*Kierkegaard Research: Sources, Reception and Resources*, vol. 15), 239–244.

from him, although eventually it is, *horribile dictu*, perhaps not much that I have learned.

My paper roughly comprises three parts: It starts with a basic conceptual, or more precisely, phenomenological outline of revelation; a typological account, arguing for the need to distinguish between weaker and stronger (sc. Christian) types of what the term refers to is next; I conclude with a somewhat epistemologically flavored discussion of the relation between revelation and (in particular, theological) cognition. My overall argument will be organized around five core theses: (1) In its most fundamental form the term (divine) revelation refers to a *communicative act* on God's part, through which he can and intends to be identified *as God* by human beings, such that the latter discover in his communication an unlimited capability and unswerving will *to provide for them*—both physically and spiritually. (2) According to a fundamental dialectic the revealed is coextensive with the hidden: *as such*—just as, for instance, that which is found is coextensive with what was lost, as such. (3) As a special form of event, revelation is self-authenticating. (4) The idea of revelation in a stricter sense is to be found in Christianity only; in order to be meaningful this "stricter sense" hinges upon the idea that the latter, *qua* divine communication, must be conceived of as constituting the very conditions, on the part of its addressee/s, for possibly being understood, accepted and appropriated as such—and as salvific. (5) Theologically conceived a claim to divine revelation is a necessary condition for any—and *a fortiori*, any internally consistent—theological cognition to be possible; yet, if the prior claim (no. 4) obtains, then only Christianity, as opposed to both Judaism and Islam, has and could have established a theological cognition in the stricter sense.

I. THE REVEALED IS THE HIDDEN, AS SUCH

1. In what follows I will sketch a rough outline of a phenomenology of revelation: it is supposed first and foremost to highlight the dialectical aspects and implications of the phenomenon. As a point of departure I invoke two illuminating and in my opinion highly pertinent examples from Martin Buber's famous *Tales of the Hasidim*. The first one is titled "Hiding;" it is about Rabbi Pinhas of Koretz and goes like this:

> Rabbi Rafael of Bershad, the favorite disciple of Rabbi Pinhas, told: "On the first day of Hanukkah, I complained to my teacher that in adversity it is very difficult to retain perfect faith in the belief that God provides for every human being. It actually seems as if God were hiding his face from

such an unhappy being. What shall he do to strengthen his faith? The rabbi replied: "It *ceases* to be a hiding, if you *know* it is hiding."[2]

Although the term revelation is not explicitly mentioned in the Rabbi's short narrative, it is indirectly alluded to by its theme and title ("hiding"). For Rabbi Rafael "perfect faith" (presumably *qua* trust) is based upon, or at least intimately connected with a firm belief—the belief, namely, "that God provides for every human being." Faith, in other words, is basically trust in God's providential acting. Moreover, God *reveals* himself—as the loving and caring God that he is—precisely by being and remaining providentially present in and for his creation in general and human beings in particular. Thus conceived, the term "(divine) revelation" refers, in its most fundamental form, to (a) a *communicative act* on God's part, an act, through which he (b) can and intends to be identified *as God* by human beings, such that (c) the latter discover in his communication an unlimited capability and unswerving intention *to provide for them*—both physically and spiritually.[3]

Revelation, in other words, does not simply stand for just *any* communication on God's part;[4] it is, rather, coextensive with all and only those communicative acts, in which God reveals *himself* and as such; and yet, in turn revealing himself is coextensive with *acting*, in particular with acting providentially: God reveals himself by providing for his creation, so that, conversely, he appears and must appear to be hiding, whenever his creatures experience pain, suffering and evil. Accordingly, perceiving God is tantamount to perceiving (God in) his salvific acts and intentions—in fact experiencing *oneself*, the perceiving subject, as the former's very target. Invoking a Wittgensteinian idea, one might say that one cannot identify X as an instance of divine revelation without by the very same token recognizing and affirming oneself to be among its intended and actual addressees.

Now, if I am not mistaken, Rabbi Pinhas' answer to the question raised by Rabbi Rafael (how can faith be preserved and strengthened "in adversi-

---

[2] Martin Buber, *Tales of the Hasidim: The Early Masters*, trans. by Olga Marx (New York: Schocken Books, 1947), 122 (emphasis and quotation marks added).

[3] Similar accounts can be found in, for instance, *Revelation*, ed. by Ingolf U. Dalferth and Michael Rodgers (Tübingen: J. C. B. Mohr, 2014); Eilert Herms, *Offenbarung und Glaube. Zur Bildung des christlichen Lebens* (Tübingen: J. C. B. Mohr, 1992), ch. 8; Magnus Lerch, *Selbstmitteilung Gottes. Herausforderungen einer freiheitstheoretischen Offenbarungstheologie* (Regensburg: Friedrich Pustet, 2015); George Mavrodes, *Revelation in Religious Belief* (Philadelphia: Temple University Press, 1988).

[4] Unless one is willing to concede that *any* divine act of communication is, as such, salvific in nature.

ty?") clearly shows that at least in one respect the former is in fundamental agreement with his pupil: revelation entails, both conceptually and phenomenologically, powerful (divine) presence, perceived as such and as salvific by its witness and recipient. But then, given this mutual agreement the tacit irony, expressed in Rabbi Pinhas' answer, must lie elsewhere. It lies, if I am not mistaken, in the apparent misunderstanding, on Rabbi Rafael's part, with regard to what providential or powerful divine presence actually *means* or consists in—in particular, how it can be identified, recognized and experienced as such by its respective addressee and/or witness. Rabbi Rafael represents a first order-faith, as it were, whereas his teacher does the same on a second order-level. And here, according to Rabbi Pinhas, we must meet the challenge of encountering a deep ambiguity, if and whenever we are inclined to make a rash claim to revelation. For if God, instead of completely and unambiguously *hiding* in "adversity" (pain, suffering etc.) *reveals* himself in the latter—to the extent, namely, that it is *he* who hides in it—then one must likewise reckon with the disquieting possibility that he does not completely and unambiguously reveal himself in *happiness or good fortune*, but much rather hides or at best appears incognito in it. If, as Johannes Climacus puts in in the *Postscript*, "a person cannot know with certainty whether the misfortune is an evil..., then neither can he know with certainty whether the good fortune is a good."[5]

Now, such a dialectic of divine revelation should not all too easily be dismissed as abstract reasoning or mere theological speculation, for it can be supplemented and confirmed by everyday experience: whoever wants to hide or remain concealed is well advised to hide *that* he wants to be hidden, for revealing the intention of hiding is already a (first, albeit imperfect) form of revelation. As such it jeopardizes, in fact renders impossible *a limine* the realization of completely remaining hidden or undiscovered: in order to be hidden, one must be and remain hidden *as* being hidden, otherwise one cannot help but reveal oneself—if only as the *hidden*. Conversely, one cannot reveal something (much less oneself), without by the very same token revealing it (or oneself) *as* being revealed, and thus without, at least indirectly, revealing its (one's own) prior concealment and hiddenness—or, more precisely, its concealment and hiddenness as prior. Accordingly, if God wants to reveal himself, he must reveal himself as (the formerly) hidden, and if he wants to appear or reveal himself as hidden (theologically speaking, as in-

[5] *SKS* 7, 405n / *CUP1*, 446n.

scrutable, incomprehensible, or unfathomable), he must reveal himself—*as* unfathomable, distant, and in fact inaccessible except "in adversity."[6]

It is worth noting that this dialectic does not strictly rule out the possibility of a completely ironic God: a God, in other words, who hides in such a way as to even hide *that* he does and thus remains completely withdrawn from his creature's view. Complete hiddenness is obviously a perfectly consistent option—but how about the dialectically opposed one: a revelation, which is not restricted to merely identifying its subject as something or someone previously hidden, but which, instead, renders the latter *fully* transparent to its addressee? Put differently and in theological terms, what about the revelation of a God who reveals himself not only *sub contrario* (in adversity, as unfathomable, as *deus absconditus* etc.), but face to face, in blissful interpersonal transparency?[7] In my opinion this is no viable option, either conceptually or theologically, since hiding and revealing (here, oneself) are obviously asymmetrical in this respect. Whereas one may perfectly hide *as* hiding and as wanting to hide, one cannot reveal something or oneself without simultaneously revealing *that* one does. Revelation is categorical, one might say, whereas hiding is not. But if that holds true, and if, furthermore, God cannot but reveal himself as a powerful, salvific presence (see above), then it seems safe to conclude that the latter simply consists in (the discovery of) the *identity*—and divine *self*-identification—of the revealed and the hidden God: the former can and must be reduced to (the experience of) the latter, such that the revealed is and coincides with the hidden, *as such*. Accordingly, it makes no sense to ask and search for a face-to-face encounter with God beyond and *independent of* encountering him as the one who "provides in adversity," simply because the latter is to be *identified* with that face-to-face encounter—*nota bene*, as its sole pre-eschatically available or accessible form. As is well known, the Schechina "resides in exile," as a Jewish saying goes. In other words, it resides within its own dialectical incognito.

2. It should have become obvious by now, namely in light of the preceding paragraphs, that at least *one* reason for the asymmetry just described lies in the fact that under the confines of complete hiddenness we need not

[6] As for the dialectic of revelation and concealment within the confines of Protestantism, cf. Ingolf U. Dalferth, "Introduction: Understanding Revelation," in *Revelation*, ed. by Dalferth and Rodgers, 17–20.

[7] As, for instance St. Paul observes: "Now we see only reflections in a mirror, mere riddles, but then we shall be seeing face to face. Now, I can only know imperfectly, but then I shall know just as fully as I am myself known" (1 Cor 13:12).

(in fact we cannot) presuppose any addressee witnessing the latter, whereas in the case of someone revealing himself—namely in the sense of revealing his own prior hiddenness, or the prior hiddenness, as his own—one must imply the presence of a witness who as such is actually aware of and *experiences* (something as) a revelation. Moreover, if the latter is of the kind described, such that its source cannot be experienced without appearing as previously hidden and thus being "present in adversity" only, then the witness in question must be considered someone who is painfully aware of, in fact *missing and longing for* (salvific) revelation. Sure enough, such a view might appear counterintuitive at first, and Rabbi Rafael would not easily endorse it: Do we in fact have to admit that God *only* reveals himself in seeming absence *qua* "adversity," such that the awareness of his revelation as painfully missing is to be considered the latter's own *conditio sine qua non* and hence also part and parcel of the very concept of revelation? The answer is yes—at least considering what is suggested by a second paradigmatic narrative from Buber's *Tales of the Hasidim*. The piece, titled "Hide-and-Seek," is likewise attributed to one of the "early masters" (as Buber calls them), namely to Rabbi Barukh of Mezbizh:

> Rabbi Barukh's other grandson Yehiel was once playing hide-and-seek with another boy. He hid himself well and waited for his playmate to find him. When he had waited for a long time, he came out of his hiding-place, but the other was nowhere to be seen. Now Yehiel realized that he had not looked for him from the very beginning. This made him cry, and crying he ran to his grandfather and complained of his faithless friend. Then tears brimmed in Rabbi Barukh's eyes and he said: 'God says the same thing: "I hide, but no one wants to seek me.'[8]

Trivial as it may seem, one (in fact the main) reason, according to the story, why Yehiel proved unable to be found or discovered by his friend is that the latter refused to *search* for him, and this despite the fact that Yehiel himself waited patiently in his hiding-place, precisely *in order* to be found and to be found right there, in his *hiding*-place. Thus, Yehiel's alleged friend violated the rules of the game and thus also the fundamental bond, alliance, or mutual agreement, according to which one player hides, so (and in order) that the other might get the chance of finding him, whereas the latter keeps being loyal to his *alter ego* and to the common cause of playing (hide-and-seek) by faithfully starting and continuing to search for him. Accordingly,

[8] Martin Buber, *Tales of the Hasidim*, 97.

Yehiel not only remains hidden, because and as long as his friend fails to find him, but also and primarily because of his friend's refusal to search for him in the first place. *Per analogiam*, God also hides and in fact appears as almost fully hidden, precisely because, inasmuch and as long as he is being ignored—either completely or at least ignored *as* hiding and thus waiting to be discovered and revealed. God cannot reveal himself as long as he cannot hide, and he cannot hide, if and as long as nobody is willing to search for him—*as* the hidden one, waiting to be discovered and found. He is not hidden because of his refusal to let himself be found, but, rather, because of the refusal to seek him, on the part of those supposed to be his (human) partners in a spiritual game of hide-and-seek.[9] God is thus doomed to suffer from what more recently has been coined "death by neglect."[10]

3. Now, the dialectic presented so far suggests a certain prestabilized harmony, as it were, between divine hiddenness or concealment and revelation: the revealed god is nothing but and in fact can be reduced to (the awareness of) the hidden god—*as such* and as painfully absent behind a veil of human misery. Sure enough and as mentioned before, this dialectic may seem odd at first sight; yet it should not all too easily be dissmissed as mere speculation. For consider, as a related case in point, the dialectic of searching and finding. Here also the latter boils down, strictly speaking, to the former—namely *as such*: finding or discovering something is tantamount to recognizing it as that which had been missing and thus had been searched for all along. What has been found is identical with what has been searched for—*nota bene*, as such. The same dialectic applies elsewhere, too: the remembered is identical with the forgotten—discovered as such; fulfillment is identical with the promised—as such; forgiveness is identical with sin—appropriated as such; whatever happened is coextensive with what has been predicted—perceived as such, etc. Correspondingly, finding God entails, on a second order-level, finding *that* he is to be found (and to be found only) in being the one searched for, as such.

---

[9] Consider a parallel case: human beings (and animals in general) die from starvation, if and whenever they are hungry and there is *no food available* for or beyond a certain period of time; yet, they also die from starvation, if and whenever there is food available, but, alas, they are *not hungry*. Therefore, in order for physical survival to be possible, (at least) two conditions must be met: the facticity of hunger and the availability of food—both identified or recognized by the subject *as such* (and only by the latter).

[10] William McDonald, in conversation.

Theologically we can even go one step further: most religions would probably agree with Kierkegaard that "To Need God Is a Human Being's Highest Perfection,"[11] which is thus a non-contingent property, an essential presupposition and the ultimate meaning of genuinely human existence. Now, if—first—the fulfillment of this fundamental need depends, among other things, on the self-appropriating belief *that* this need is essential ("I am a human being, therefore *my* highest perfection is to be in need of God"); if, furthermore, such belief or insight is not to be had except for a God hiding under the veil of apparent non-existence and/or absence (due to cruelty, arbitrariness, indifference, powerlessness, etc.); finally, if this veil is deceptive, thus rendering its addressee susceptible to a fatal misconception of what is actually instrumental for his highest self-fulfillment, then we yield a double paradox in conclusion: (a) In order to reveal himself—for the sake of undistorted divine-human interaction and communion—*God* must hide himself and thus in effect jeopardize and risk missing his chief goal.[12] (b) *Human beings* cannot attain the very insight or belief, in which their highest perfection as human beings is expressed and realized, without at the same time being deceived about the true meaning and implications of that insight, at the risk of forfeiting the latter and thus also the perfection, which depends on it.

II. REVELATION IN THE STRICTER SENSE: CHRISTIANITY AND THE LOGIC OF EVENTS

1. So far I construed the concept of (divine) revelation (a) as a salvific communicative act on God's part, (b) the actualization of which is marked by an intrinsic dialectic of hiding and revealing, such that (c) a recognition, by its addressee, of the hidden *as* the revealing God (and vice versa) becomes possible—if and to the extent, namely, that (d) the addressee is able and willing to perceive and treat alleged signs of God's absence as, in reality, indispensible means to express and eventually satisfy his own need for him.

Now, it can hardly come as a surprise that there is nothing inherently *Christian* in the account so far, for the fundamental dialectic attributed by me to the concept of revelation appears to be an essential tenet and leading

[11] The title of an edifying discourse from 1844: cf. *SKS* 5, 291 / *EUD*, 297.

[12] Cf. John Sanders, *The God Who Risks: A Theology of Divine Providence* (Downers Grove: Intervarsity Press, 1998), for an account of divine providence based upon the idea of (an inevitable) risk on God's part.

premise of religious belief in general—at least within religions consciously invoking the idea of revelation.[13] At least in the case of Judaism, Christianity, and Islam we probably agree without any further ado that all three of them conceive of themselves as making—and in fact having to make—a claim to (an unsurpassable) divine revelation, both in terms of accounting for the genesis and the possible truth of their respective faiths. Now, in what follows I will try to show, first, that the idea of revelation in a stricter sense is *only* to be found in Christianity, as opposed to both Judaism and Islam. Second, and as a corollary, I will argue that in order to be meaningful this "stricter sense" hinges upon the idea that revelation, *qua* divine communication, must be conceived of as constituting the very conditions, on the part of its addressee/s, for possibly being received, understood, accepted, and appropriated as such—and as salvific in nature. In order to avoid misunderstandings, I would like to add beforehand that in pursuing this double argumentational goal I do not have any apologetic objectives in mind. Accordingly, I will completely ignore the question, whether what is *claimed* by Christianity as true (about God's revelation in Christ) is *actually* true—or at least rationally justified as an object of faith; instead, I will exclusively address the issue, whether what is claimed here as truly *Christian* is *in fact* truly Christian (plus, albeit indirectly, whether what is claimed to be truly Jewish and Islamic actually deserves to be called by that name).

2. Now, before being in a position to evaluate my first claim, we must make sense of the second, and in order to prepare for this latter task I suggest a little detour, for the sake of clarification, into the notion and logic of *events*. The simple reason is that in my opinion a certain property of events *simpliciter* will shed new light on and in fact will justify the need for a distinction between a concept of divine revelation in a looser or weaker and a stricter (viz. Christian) sense. Needless to say that the tacit assumption underlying and motivating this move is that revelation ought to be considered an *event*. This assumption should not seem overly surprising, much less outlandish or far-fetched, due to the fact that the concept of revelation has earlier been spelled out already in terms of God's (providential) acting. Actions, however, are widely (though not undisputedly) taken to be events, and

[13] And the case could probably be made that a claim to some kind of divine revelation is among the most widespread, perhaps even universal features of religion; cf. Ingolf U. Dalferth, "Introduction: Understanding Revelation," 1f.

rightly so in my opinion.[14] Now, the notion of event, which has garnered remarkable attention over the past years and decades both in philosophy and theology,[15] poses a considerable problem or riddle in its own right, and this in more than one respect. I will not engage and take sides in the rather heated debate, though, but instead restrict myself to highlighting just two particular traits of the phenomenon in question—traits, which allow for shedding some fresh light on the distinction between looser and stricter notions of revelation.

First and foremost, the term "event" belongs in the class of what I prefer to call "hermeneutical terms." We need and utilize these terms in order to make sense of other terms, concepts or ideas, but they themselves cannot (at least not completely and adequately) be made sense of in light of something else. The strangely "utopian" or ineffable quality in conjunction with the philosophically fundamental function of events *qua* hermeneutical terms has repeatedly been emphasized; moreover, it has been worked out meticulously and in various forms by philosophers like Alain Badiou and Martin Heidegger.[16]

It is not necessary in the present context to dwell upon a comparison of their respective views, though, because for the time being—and for the sake of the argument presented here—it fully suffices to point to yet another essential property of events, a property that is in fact closely connected with their hermeneutically foundational function: events are *self-authenticating*. Take, for instance, understanding a joke or falling in love. Both terms denote events—and as such they are self-authenticating. It does not make sense, in other words, to try and persuade Peter that what he is laughing at is actually not funny; likewise and positively speaking, falling in love suffices

---

[14] Cf., for instance, Roberto Casati and Achille C. Varzi, "Events," in *The Stanford Encyclopedia of Philosophy*, 2006 (http://plato.stanford.edu/archives/entries/events; last visited: July 7, 2014), 5f.

[15] Cf., among others, John Caputo, *The Weakness of God: A Theology of the Event* (Indianapolis: Indiana University Press, 2006); *Events*, ed. Roberto Casati and Achille C. Varzi (Dartmouth et al: Dartmouth Publishing Company, 1996); Ingolf U. Dalferth, "Ereignis und Transzendenz," *Zeitschrift für Theologie und Kirche*, vol. 110, 2013, 475–500; Jean L. Marion, "The Event or the Happening Phenomenon," in *Excess. Studies of Saturated Phenomena* (New York: Fordham University Press, 2002), 30–53; *Understanding Events: From Perception to Action*, ed. by Thomas F. Shipley and Jeffery M. Zacks (New York: Oxford University Press, 2008); Slavoj Zizek, *Event: A Philosophical Journey through a Concept* (Brookville and London: Melville House, 2014).

[16] Cf. Alain Badiou, *Das Sein und das Ereignis*, trans. by Gernot Kamecke (Berlin: diaphanes, 2008); Martin Heidegger, *Das Ereignis* (Frankfurt: Klostermann, 2009).

for infallibly recognizing what happened as just that, falling in love.[17] Both events are as such not only necessary, but also sufficient for identifying or determining categorically *what* they are: (a) an event of (b) understanding a joke (or, alternatively, falling in love). Events are self-containing, as it were, such that an event is a term which is "immanent to itself," [18] as Badiou puts it.

Now, for the sake of illustration, consider the extinction of the dinosaurs 65 million years ago. What happened here cannot be deemed an event in and of itself, but only and insofar as there is somebody *witnessing* to it *as* an event: there is no event without witness/es. However, this witnessing itself does not and cannot come about by virtue of a mere *fiat* of the will on the part of the subject *qua* recipient or witness; rather, its possibility and genesis depend upon something (admittedly, something referentially opaque) that we can only attribute to the event itself and as such. Without any doubt there are countless things involved, when it comes to describing some event X as "the extinction of the dinosaurs 65 million years ago"—a "field" of innumerable facts, aspects and quasi-atomistic elements, which are, in some sense or other, formative for what Badiou calls the "site événementiel" ([evental field][19]) of the respective event. And yet, it is obviously not up to us, the recipients or witnesses, to account for the extent, the elements or the boundaries of such a "site" or field, but rather the event itself, which renders the former recognizable (a) *as* an event, and this (b) by the name of *X* (for instance, "the extinction of the dinosaurs"). But if that is the case then events are "entities,"[20] which are in and of themselves constitutive for establishing the ontological and epistemic conditions under which they come about, and can be recognized and be addressed by their proper name. For, indeed, there is no event without a *name* ("9/11," "the extinction of the dinosaurs" etc.) and probably also without a corresponding narrative—and *therefore* there is no event without witnesses, either.

---

[17] At least, if what is at stake here *is* actually a case of falling in love; for otherwise we may very well be able to err or to deceive ourselves about the actual mental state we are in; sure enough, *veritas est index sui et falsi* (Spinoza), but he who misses the mark also fails to recognize *that* he does so.

[18] Badiou, *Das Sein und das Ereignis*, 208 (my translation).

[19] Ibid., 200.

[20] And in light of my previous claim that "event" is or functions as an hermeneutical term, this *façon de parler* might already be inappropriate.

Now, this puzzling self-containing quality of events[21] is exactly what makes them relevant for understanding *revelation*—as such and in its various types. For if the latter is to be considered a kind of event, and if all events are self-authenticating, then also revelation is self-authenticating. For here, too, the object of understanding turns out to be constitutive for the latter's own possibility. As was previously shown we cannot determine or force an event to come about—or, more precisely, we cannot determine something to be perceived, regardless of whether by others or by ourselves, as an event. On the contrary, the event *qua* event suggests itself; it "gives itself to us," so to speak, though in such a way as to simultaneously authenticate itself. But this is exactly what we expect from divine revelation: God as the divine revealer does not only communicate something or himself, but in doing so he simultaneously creates and establishes the very conditions, on the part of his addressee, for possibly and actually receiving and understanding his message.

3. Keeping all this in mind we are prepared now for addressing the final and decisive question: why assume that at least in religious matters we are well advised to distinguish between *weaker and stronger* or looser and stricter notions of revelation—and this in favor of exclusively reserving the latter category for the *Christian* understanding? My tentative answer is that speaking of divine revelation in a stricter sense suggests itself as meaningful, perhaps even as indispensible only, yet also whenever and inasmuch as the respective addressees of God's revelatory message are not merely to be considered *actually*, but rather *necessarily* incapable of and excluded from receiving, understanding and appropriating this message. But this is precisely claimed or implied by the Christian doctrine of *sin*, and if I am not mis-

[21] Which is by no means sufficient, much less exhaustive for an adequate account of the term; any such account would at least have to pay special attention to what Zizek, referring to an event *simpliciter*, describes as "*the effect that seems to exceed its causes*" (Zizek, *Event*, 5). One of his examples is the event of falling in love: "I do not fall in love for precise reasons (her lips, her smile…)—it is because I already love her that her lips etc. attract me. This is why love…is evental. It is a manifestation of a circular structure in which the evental effect retroactively determines its causes or reasons" (Ibid., 4). In Polanyian terms we might say that the focal whole ('she is lovable') is genetically and logically prior and as such also constitutive for possibly becoming aware of certain subsidiary clues (her lips, her smile…), which then, and "retroactively,' function as tacitly persuasive reasons for finding her lovable. Cf. Michael Polanyi, *The Tacit Dimension* (Chicago: Chicago University Press, 2009 [1966]). Moreover, the work of Esther Meek, which heavily draws on Polanyi, suggests, among other things, that Zizek's example is all but accidental, since in her opinion there is a deep mutual dependence between (the events of) loving and (tacitly) knowing: cf. Esther L. Meek, *Loving to Know: Introducing Covenant Epistemology* (Eugene, Oregon: Cascade Books, 2011), especially chs. 4 and 14.

taken, exclusively here. Ethically considered, this doctrine is essentially paradoxical: the task of doing away with sin is established as unconditional, precisely by (implying) the impossibility of its own fulfillment; conversely, the task ceases to exist as mandatory and as necessitating its addressee in the very same instant, in which it lends itself to (and appears as possibly) being fulfilled by the former.

Kierkegaard's pseudonymous spokesman Johannes Climacus expresses the far-reaching *presuppositions* of this doctrine in his *Philosophical Fragments* from 1844. Here the whole argument turns upon Gal 4:4 as its sole—and *nota bene*, merely hypothetically posited—premise: when "the completion of the time came, God sent his son, born of a woman, born a subject of the Law, to redeem the subjects of the Law, so that we could receive adoption as sons." Climacus argues that it makes sense to conceive of the incarnation as the (eternal) "completion of time" only, if it was meant to be part and parcel of a divine revelatory message (sc. of salvation and the kingdom of God for all those honestly seeking forgiveness), the successful communication of which requires first to create, in its potential addressees, the condition for properly receiving and appropriating it. For thus far these addressees appear as irreversibly separated and excluded from it; moreover, they must be held accountable for the exclusion, namely, via sin. Successfully communicating the divine message (in which the former judgment functions as an integral part) requires, in other words, the establishment of the conditions for generating faith in the sinner. Hence, summing up, we may quote Climacus who observes that according to its most fundamental premise

> Christianity is the only historical phenomenon that despite the historical—indeed precisely by means of the historical [sc. Jesus]—has wanted to be the single individual's point of departure for his eternal consciousness [sc. faith], has wanted to interest him otherwise than merely historically, has wanted to base his happiness on his relation to something historical.[22]

It is worth noting that Climacus is far from claiming to be able to adjudicate whether the fundamental Christian doctrine of incarnation *qua* manifestation of the eternal in time is in fact *true* or not. All he wants to call attention to and pinpoint is (the truth about) what in his opinion must be deemed *truly Christian*. Hence the question/s raised at the beginning of his book (on the latter's title-page) remain largely unanswered—at least to the extent that what is expected here is a straightforward doctrinal assertion:

[22] *SKS* 4, 305 / *PF*, 109.

"Can a historical point of departure be given for an eternal consciousness; how can such a point of departure be of more than historical interest; can an eternal happiness be built on historical knowledge?"[23]

Yet, if I am not mistaken, all this is largely absent from any idea of revelation as it is utilized and maintained in Judaism, and here, in particular, in Buber's Hassidic narratives. For even though, for instance, Rabbi Bershad is told and led to accept, by virtue of a revelatory insight, that what he perceived as "adversity" is in fact God's way of telling him that he is present and omnipotently provides for everyone precisely *within* his apparent absence, there is no hint whatsoever in the respective narrative that the *reason* for his apparent absence is to be located in a principal und subjectively insurmountable obstacle: sin. To the best of my knowledge, things are similar in Islam. From this it follows that my previous insinuation, according to which a stricter, more radical sense of revelation can and has to be claimed for Christianity, stands uncontested, at least for the time being.

III. REVELATION AND THEOLOGY: SOME CONCLUDING REMARKS

1. Now, before moving to the final step of my analysis, which seeks to determine the function of revelation in and for theology, a brief methodologic remark on the relation between theology proper, religious studies and philosophy of religion seems advisable for propaedeutic reasons.[24] In my view, *theology*—in any case, Christian, in particular *systematic theology*—is nothing but a specific, namely systematic and thus intrinsically normative type of *religious studies*. As such, it not only describes and analyzes historically, typologically, and cultural-hermeneutically, which *claims* are being or have been made as to an authentic expression of the Christian religion or faith; for this is the genuine task of religious history or, within the confines of Christian theology, of church history or historical theology. Systematic theology rather seeks, with a decidedly normative purpose in mind, to determine, if, to what extent and under which restrictions these claims have *rightfully* been made in the history of Christian thought. The methodologically guiding principle, upon which such normative enterprise builds can best be expressed by a

[23] *SKS* 4, 213 / *PF*, 1.

[24] See in greater detail Heiko Schulz, "Legt (nur) der Glaube den Glauben aus? Evangelische Theologie als christliche Religionswissenschaft," in *Evangelische Theologie. Eine Selbstverständigung in enzyklopädischer Absicht*, ed. by Heiko Schulz (Leipzig: Evangelische Verlagsanstalt, 2016), 202–236.

felicitous formulation (reflecting in turn a famous saying by Dietrich Bonhoeffer) by Bernhard Dressler: *etsi Deus* [in case of Christianity: *etsi Christus*] *daretur* [as if God / Christ were given].[25]

Finally, *philosophy of religion* builds upon both religious studies and systematic theology. It represents a critically motivated form of religious studies, namely, insofar as it assesses major claims of Christianity (or any other religion) in terms of the latter's *truth* and/or *rationality* conditions. It does so, however, in the light of its own prior conception of what Christianity and/or religion "*truly* are" or are "in *truth*." Thus conceived, philosophy of religion finds itself on top of a pyramid of disciplines dealing with religion: every philosopher of religion is, at least to some extent, a systematic theologian *and* a religious scholar; every systematic theologian has to be considered at least a religious scholar; *some*, but not all religious scholars are systematic theologians,[26] whereas some systematic theologians are also philosophers of (the Christian) religion. *One* substantial implication of this model is that the systematic theologian—*nota bene*, *as such*—does not and cannot have the slightest concern for the actual *truth* and/or rationality of Christian faith; instead, all that he or she, properly understood, can and has to focus upon is the question whether and to what extent some purportedly Christian claims *truly* deserve that label. The external question of truth—as such a major tenet of religious philosophy—is here suspended, for the time being, in favor of an internal, purely coherence-theoretical form of the very same question.[27]

---

[25] Cf. Bernhard Dressler, "Religion geht zur Schule. Fachlichkeit und Interdisziplinarität religiöser Bildung," *Zeitschrift für Praktische Theologie*, vol. 56, 2004, 3–17, 17. Needless to add that rightly understood no one could hit upon the idea of wanting to prevent the religious scholar from pursuing normative interests in the sense described; however, precisely by pursuing these interests he would (have to claim to) become a Systematic theologian—either with regard to Christianity or Judaism or any other form of positive religion, which she devotes her interest to. It is of course always assumed here that the religion in question is (rightly) taken to make *truth claims* in a dogmatic or quasi-dogmatic sense. Any religious scholar driven by the quest for (internal) normativity would therefore have to be considered capable, at least in principle, of writing a Christian dogmatic, a dogmatic, which would at least not *a priori* have to be deemed different from that of a (here, Christian) theologian.

[26] And of course they are, as systematic theologians, to be considered capable of and justified in tackling Islam or Hinduism, thus pursuing the question, if and to what extent all (or at least some of) that, which claims to be a "true" and therefore theologically appropriate expression of Islam or Hinduism, has a right to that claim. Such an option is excluded only, if a religion does not develop or express itself by way of a theology proper, as is perhaps the case with Judaism (see below).

[27] Please note that by insisting on the strictly internal character of theological inquiry I do not mean to suggest that the latter is (a) possible and (b) intelligible only for a *believer* in the

Hence, there are two different types of truth-conditions to be met and distinguished with regard to Christianity (or any other religion, for that matter), which should not be confused: (a) conditions, the fulfillment of which reveals Christianity to be *true* (= philosophical truth-conditions); (b) conditions, the fulfillment of which reveals what Christianity *truly* is (= theological truth-conditions). It goes without saying that no one will or at least should deny that a systematic theologian, in the sense described, is in principle capable of and fully justified in pursuing a genuine interest in philosophy of religion, much less contest his right to embark upon that very project or perspective (hopefully in a competent manner). Yet, he is not *obliged* to do this. By contrast, his or her colleagues in philosophy of religion are *nolens volens* compelled to lay claim to theological competence, for no one can meaningfully address the *truth* claims of a given religion without having arrived—or at least, without having to *pretend* to have arrived—at an adequate conception of what that religion *truly* is.

2. The reason why I bring up these methodological or encyclopedic issues—if only briefly and in conclusion—is quite simple: if a theology proper is to be possible at all, then its genuine task of spelling out its own internal truth conditions in the sense described must lend itself to being construed as inaccessible to any external approach. In other words, it must prove incapable of being reduced to the realm of either religious studies *simpliciter* or philosophy of religion. Yet, the only irreducibility proof available in the case at hand is (the appeal to) divine *revelation*. Hence, no theology proper is possible except by internally claiming divine revelation as a necessary condition of its own possibility.[28] Now, if my previous argument is sound, according to which a concept and doctrine of revelation in any stricter sense is to be found in Christianity only, then only Christianity, as opposed to both Judaism and Islam, has and could possibly have established a theology, including the notion of theological cognition, in any stricter sense. Claiming

---

respective religion under scrutiny. Required only, on the part of the theologian, is the latter's willingness and ability to *accept* its major doctrines in the service of trying to spell out their content and interconnectedness in terms of a coherent whole.

[28] Cf. Steiner's similar point: George Steiner, "The Scandal of Revelation," in *Faith and Narrative*, ed. by Keith Yandell (Oxford: Oxford University Press, 2001), 68–85 (especially 84f.); other philosophically and/or theologically promising, at least challenging approaches to the epistemic issue/s regarding revelation include Nicholas Wolterstorff, *Divine Discourse: Philosophical Reflections on the Claim that God Speaks* (Cambridge: Cambridge University Press, 1996), especially ch. 15; Mats Wahlberg, *Revelation as Testimony: A Philosophical-Theological Study* (Grand Rapids, Michigan: William B. Eerdmans Publishing Company, 2014).

the facticity of divine revelation—in fact, its necessity, due to the fatal epistemic and ethical implications of sin—is then part and parcel of the "truly Christian." Accordingly, dogmatics precedes fundamental theology, at least within the confines of Christianity.[29]

In order to avoid misunderstandings I hasten to add that I am far from maintaining the *truth* of the Christian claim to revelation. In other words, my paper does not intend to assess this claim from the vantage-point of philosophy of religion—much less in comparison to related claims in Judaism and Islam. And although I am of the opinion that such assessment is possible, indeed—and in favor of Christianity—I have completely and deliberately ignored the issue in the present context, since it would deserve and require a fully separate treatment. My primary goal with this paper has been much more modest, and its results, if plausible, will pave the way for the stricter philosophical issues at best. This notwithstanding, the upshot of my analysis is perhaps not useless or completely insignificant, for if the previous account can at least roughly pass for convincing, then it might help explain an otherwise somewhat mysterious fact: to the best of my knowledge neither Islam nor Judaism have shown great interest so far in developing a theology proper in the sense described; instead, they have, at the expense of the latter, taken much greater pains in establishing robust traditions in law and exegesis on the one hand (as in the case of Islam), Talmudic teaching and commentary on the other (as in Judaism). Whether such theological abstinence may be deemed advantageous or not—both from an internal and external vantage-point—is not my task here to decide. Honestly speaking, I am glad it is not.

[29] Please note: the fact *that* this is the case is to (and can only) be maintained from the standpoint of the latter.

Index